The labour market Ate my babies

BARBARA POCOCK

The labour market Ate my babies

Work, children and a sustainable future

THE FEDERATION PRESS
2006

Published in Sydney by:
    The Federation Press
    PO Box 45, Annandale, NSW, 2038
    71 John St, Leichhardt, NSW, 2040
    Ph (02) 9552 2200 Fax (02) 9552 1681
    E-mail: info@federationpress.com.au
    Website: http://www.federationpress.com.au

National Library of Australia
Cataloguing-in-Publication entry

    Pocock, Barbara.
    The labour market ate my babies: work, children and a sustainable future

    Includes index.
    ISBN 1 86287 604 5 (*from January 2007*: 978 1 86287 604 0).

    1. Labor market – Social aspects – Australia. 2. Work and family –
    Australia. 3. Youth – Australia – Attitudes. I. Title.

331.120994

Typeset by The Federation Press, Leichhardt, NSW.
    Printed by Ligare Pty Ltd, Sydney, NSW.

Preface

Over the three years since the publication of *The Work/Life Collision*, I have had the opportunity to talk with people doing all kinds of work and care in Australia, including young people, workers in a wide range of jobs, parents, carers, employers and those involved in the management of both large and small organisations, and in our parliaments, governments, unions and community organisations. While diverse perspectives exist about the nature of the challenges we face, and the solutions that might work, it is clear that many Australians share a concern about how we are living, organising our households and communities, and how we are working and consuming.

We are a rich country. Yet a great number of individuals are puzzled at the busy intersections of work, community and household life, and their implications for how we live, care for each other, and for the generations that follow.

This book focuses on young people. It examines their views about their parents' jobs, as well as their perspectives about the organisation of their own work, time, money and households – now and in the future. It aims to cast light on how we are organising work and living at present – and, most importantly, how it might be better configured in the future for the benefit of individuals and society.

It is therefore a book that is about, and most appropriately dedicated to, young people – in the hope that they can continue to improve how we work, live and care. We can always do better.

I have benefited from conversations and help from many individuals, friends and colleagues through this book's gestation. I want to thank them all. My greatest debt is to the young people who participated in focus groups: I thank them for generously offering their perspectives, for listening to and arguing with each other, and for making the collection of their thoughts so enjoyable.

I particularly thank Jane Clarke who conducted these focus groups with me, and did much of the work organising them. Her observations have greatly enriched the book. I thank Clive Hamilton and The Australia Institute for generously supporting the conduct of these focus groups.

Dr Richard Denniss and Dr Susan Oakley talked with me about these ideas with good humour and encouragement and both commented on the manuscript, for which I am very grateful.

I departed from my long-time colleagues at the University of Adelaide on my way through the book, and I owe them a great deal, especially Ken Bridge, Rosslyn Prosser, Susan Oakley, Chilla Bulbeck, Kathie Muir, Sonya Mezinec, Thalia Palmer, Margie Ripper and Marg Allen.

In January 2006 I moved to the University of South Australia and the Centre for Work and Life where I am now lucky enough to enjoy the stimulating company of Research Fellows Dr Helen Masterman-Smith, Dr Pip Williams and Jude Elton as well as the efforts of the Centre's Administrator, Kath Lockett and its post-graduate students. I thank each of them for their valuable support.

I would also like to thank the Australian Bureau of Statistics and its staff as they continue to perform a service of incalculable value to those trying to make sense of work and social life in Australia.

In 2005, in England, Claire Stentiford, and Sue Ledwith and her colleagues at Ruskin College Oxford, were generous hosts and friends, as was AV Jose at the ILO in Geneva. Both Ruskin College and the International Institute of Labour Studies at the ILO hosted my research visits and I thank them for their support.

The Australian Research Council funds my Queen Elizabeth Fellowship (2003-2007) investigating the changing work/life patterns and preferences of Australians and this continues to underwrite my work. The University of Adelaide and now the University of South Australia have also contributed to this Fellowship. Together these institutions have allowed me to focus on a fairly narrow research terrain and stay with it, and I am very grateful to the taxpayers of Australia for making this possible. Everyone trying to think through complex issues should have such space, and I know how lucky I have been at a moment when scholars are increasingly starved for untrammelled time.

As ever, I owe my extended family, friends and neighbours a great debt for their friendship and company. I especially thank John, Jake and Indi Wishart.

Barbara Pocock
Adelaide
September 2006

About the Author

Professor Barbara Pocock is the Director of the Centre for Work and Life at the Hawke Research Institute in the University of South Australia.

Barbara has been researching work in Australia for over two decades. Her first degree was in economics and her PhD was in gender studies. She has worked in many jobs – in universities, advising politicians, on farms, in unions, for governments and as a mother of two. She is widely published. Her books include *The Work/Life Collision* (2003) also published by Federation Press. She has a life-long interest in work and inequality.

Contents

Abbreviations

ACTU	Australian Council of Trade Unions
ABC	Australian Broadcasting Commission
ABS	Australian Bureau of Statistics
AIFS	Australian Institute of Family Studies
AIHW	Australian Institute for Health and Welfare
ASSA	Australian Survey of Social Attitudes
DEWR	Department of Employment and Workplace Relations
DEWRSB	Department of Employment, Workplace Relations and Small Business
HILDA	Household, Income and Labour Dynamics in Australia Survey
ILO	International Labour Organisation
LSAC	Longitudinal Study of Australian Children
NIFTeY	National Investment for the Early Years

CHAPTER 1

Introduction and overview

This book analyses work and its effects on Australians. In so many ways, having a job is a good thing. It is the best antidote to poverty, it is a source of self-esteem, friendship and social engagement. Work feeds us – physically, socially and emotionally – and being without work is a disaster for many who cannot find it. But work, and its changing conditions, affects us in ways beyond a pay packet and a sense of belonging. It is these larger effects of work in a society increasingly built around the fetish of paid work that this book examines. It especially focuses upon young people and some of their views about the world of work and its effects. Taking the pivotal market of labour as its primary terrain, I ask how paid work and the commodification of our lives and our time affects social reproduction and especially children and young people. I examine the ways that future generations of workers and citizens will weigh up the labour market and organise their lives.

The importance of young people's perspectives is important for several reasons. First, we know all too little about the next generation of workers and carers. What they think matters a great deal to future outcomes at work and at home. Secondly, current market, work and care settings have important implications for children and young people in their years of dependence upon adults. The connections between these spheres, and their implications for young people in particular, are all too rarely analysed. The evidence about the importance of early childhood experiences to long-term life outcomes is growing: it is convincing. We cannot afford to get things wrong in our treatment of children and young people in their early years.

The past 50 years have seen a remarkable change in the way we live. The increasing role of markets in our lives is among the most notable. The most demanding and rewarding of these markets is the labour market, where human activity – our creativity and sweat – is bought and sold. Most of us participate in this market for much of our lives, either buying or selling labour of one form or another. A great deal of our consumption involves the purchase of embodied labour: that is, the effort of fellow-humans that is incorporated in the food, clothing, care and other goods that we buy. Our consumption, as well as our own work, is the stuff of the labour market.

More and more young Australians participate in this most significant of all markets – selling their labour from as young as 14 (and much younger in many other countries) and hungrily consuming much that the market then offers them. These new generations of future workers face new work demands and a reshaped labour market. They are already affected by changes in the work patterns of their parents, and plan their own work and household futures – sometimes in reaction to their own youthful experiences. The ways in which they 'make a living' over their life-course will in some ways be the same and, in other ways, radically different from those of their forebears.

Some of last century's most significant political battles have been fought over the terms of the labour market and its regulation. These battles are ongoing and they are underway internationally. They are of vital significance to the way we live, care and work. Beyond politics, labour markets and consumption increasingly constitute our selves: the way we bring up our children, what happens in our households, the way we live, take pleasure, reproduce, consolidate our identities and 'spend' our time.

These days we bring the market analogy to bear on so many areas of how we think. It is common to find market analogies at work in our thinking about our environment, our children, our relationships and throughout our value systems. The currency of 'cost/benefit' analysis is widespread. We buy and sell things that previous generations would have considered impossible to purchase: all forms of human 'services' – body organs, children, care, cleanliness, spirituality, sex, psychological well-being, laughter and other emotions, art and cultural expression, education, health and, some hope, even happiness. Few things in our world are not on offer from someone as a commodity.

The powerful engine of the market affects almost all aspects of our lives. It shapes our labour. And it is increasingly at work in our social sphere, affecting whom we socialise with, how we socialise, how we parent and care for others, and how we conduct our household life and relationships more broadly. The market increasingly enters our social and intimate life because there is money to be made there, and satiation bought – or more accurately – *sought*. More and more, this is because we are giving so much of our time to the labour market, so that we must in turn pay for the things we can no longer make or create ourselves. In addition, new needs are under constant construction, so that in rich countries like Australia many citizens pursue a rising plane of consumption: bigger homes, more white goods, bigger cars. The specialisation of production is a cornerstone of the market and, as advocated by Adam Smith (1776), is the source of enormous economic efficiency. However, the expansive commodification of our time and needs has unexpected effects. It creates important social and economic externalities, and these are generally unmeasured and unmarked. But they are far from immaterial. And many affect young people as well as adults.

A critical element in this discussion is the activity of care. We are a very dependent species and the increasing specialisation of labour means that most of us can do only a narrow range of things. Fewer and fewer of us can fix our own car, make our own clothes, grow our own food. All of us depend on the care provided by others at various times in our lives – most commonly as children, in our old age, and when we are sick. Humans in industrialised countries now spend many years in dependency of one form or another – whether depending on the market for most goods and services, or directly on the care of others or the state in childhood, sickness, disability, or old age. Sometimes this care enters the market, becoming simultaneously both paid labour and consumption. At other times it is the unpaid care provided by a wife or husband, parent, child or friend – sometimes reciprocated, and sometimes not. The activity of care is often undertaken alongside our paid labour. At other times, it consumes more of our time and paid work is set aside.

This book explores some aspects of the labour market and the commodities that we buy and sell in our work, household and social lives. It explores how much our lives have entered the market and become commodified, and why. It considers the price of this marketisation, especially through paid work and particularly from the point of view of children and youth.

Discussion of 'commodification' has been central to analysis of labour, and to social welfare regimes, though different definitions have been applied. A founding principle of the International Labour Organisation (ILO) is that 'labour is not a commodity'. While neoclassical economic theory treats labour as a commodity and happily embraces the market commodification of human effort, this denies a fundamental truth about workers: that they must reproduce themselves or the labour market cannot work. Such reproduction is a social function, which is undertaken by both individuals (when parents have a child) and society (when social fabric sustains households).

Esping-Anderson (1990) has used the concepts of 'commodification' and 'decommodification' to distinguish social support regimes according to the extent that they allow citizens to exist without having to sell their labour. He discusses different national forms and levels of such support in 'three worlds of welfare capitalism'. In his analysis, 'decommodification' is most pronounced in social democracies like the Nordic countries where people can exist independently of market work through, for example, the support of universal social welfare systems. Where a livelihood is provided by means of social supports outside waged labour, 'decommodification' permits citizenship independent of waged labour: to rear children, for example.

Using a definition of commodification that refers to the extent to which we engage in paid labour, it is clear that around the industrialised world we are seeing an increase in labour commodification – and its *re*commodification as a disembodied factor of production. Our time is increasingly bought and sold. Much of this sale is now on an hourly basis, as a 'pure' commodity as if it were not connected to a human body, and human households, reproduction and social life; as if it were coal or paper or some other disembodied factor of production. For example, the drift to casualisation in the Australian labour market is – in its worst manifestations, where it is not a true choice – a return to an old, primitive labour market, one where human labour is just another input. These changes have implications for '*making a living*', in the fullest sense of that phrase.

The 'recommodification of labour' occurs in an environment with three important characteristics. First, we are living in a time of 'intensified minimal private familism' as the traditional family and household morphs and in many places struggles to play its role in sustaining and reproducing. The declining birth rate is one of its bellwethers across the industrialised world. Secondly, it occurs in an environment of underdeveloped and thinning 'public familism' where public supports like fair, comprehensive labour standards for all, a strong voluntary sector, public education and health supports, early childhood education and childcare services are overloaded, becoming more costly, or simply unavailable. I discuss this framework in Chapter 2.

Into these fissures steps the hungry market. It readily provides substitutes for both private and public supports – at a price. This book examines the price. It attempts to bring into public view some of the hidden externalities of the labour market. As Madeline Bunting says in her analysis of Britain's long hours culture and its costs, markets 'externalise the social costs' of the way in which they work and in doing so they 'generate a crisis of human sustainability' (2004, p xxi).

William Beveridge said markets make a good servant but a bad master. This is especially true of both the labour market and the market for care. While both of these can be sites of successful market activity, when they go wrong the human costs are high. What is more, their systems of accounting are perverse and inadequate when they fail to count the human effects of arrangements that are negative – whether in damaging babies and children, widening inequality, weakening communities or loading up women with impossible workloads cloaked by private guilt.

Voracious markets externalising social costs

The image at the core of this book is of the voracious market and its most important wing: the labour market. The market is not bad in itself. Markets are powerful sorters. They enable the expression of preferences, through money. Price signals reshape behaviour: a large rise in petrol prices remakes how we travel, what car we buy and – in time – car production. A big jump in the cost of garbage disposal stimulates conservation and recycling. Environmentalists know that repricing water and dirty sources of power are powerful levers to change consumption and production.

But in many ways the market is bad if left to its own devices or poorly managed. It will eat us if it can. It will not reproduce us properly and – without help – it will load up its costs on the silent and those external to the work and commodity frontiers. Most of these are women. Many are children and young or aged people who cannot speak of its effects upon them. Left untrammelled, it fuels inequality.

There have been many eloquent books about the market and its power and limitations: Fred Hirsch's *Social Limits to Growth* (1977) and Robert Kuttner's *Everything for Sale* (1997) spring to mind. But this book is not about what is wrong with markets in a general sense. It specifically analyses *labour* markets and their effects – upon young people, adults, households, fertility and care.

Of course, labour markets result in many positive outcomes. They do not eat our kids: but their current settings affect how many children we have, the circumstances in which they are born and grow up, the experiences of their mothers and fathers as well as the people who will in turn depend on them. A hungry labour market and its hungry twin, the commodified product and service market, eat into our social reproduction in ways that are consumptive, hidden and deserve more thought and action. These *offset* their many positive benefits. Against a background of shrinking private and public sources of support, the effects of this hungry market are both deep and wide. And things do not necessarily have to go this way: we could do better through better market settings and better market surrounds.

I argue that the hungry market is affecting young Australians in two particular ways of growing significance. The first of these is through their parents' work, specifically their growing attachment to paid work, changes in that work and in households, and – in the absence of strong public supports – their reliance upon market help to rear children and care for others who depend on them (including the aged, infirm, disabled and sick). In particular, the commodification of care of young people through the private childcare market has proceeded with great speed in the past five years in Australia. This provision is highly concentrated among a few very profitable firms that are among the largest publicly-listed childcare services in the world. New markets have been built around it: highly profitable ones that feed off public funds to create rapidly increasing and sizeable shareholder returns. We have cause to pay very close attention to the quality of care in Australia and the potential effects of poor quality childcare, both on the development of young people and in creating new circuits of inequality.

The second way in which the market is affecting young people is through the accelerated and early onset of commodification and consumption in their youth. The consumption of many young Australians is fuelled by the rapid growth in advertising that is intently and purposefully focused upon them. It also seems that they are increasingly reliant upon a sense of self – built through work and buying. These habits of work, consumption and self-actualisation are generating 'an early onset work/spend cycle' which seems likely to drive further falls in fertility and an increasing attachment to 'living' through work and spending, with important implications for health and well-being. These are the externalities of the market. They affect the sustainability of societies. Far from deliberate choices, they are active products of the logic of a hungry market, in the presence of a fraying and uneven public and private fabric.

Making the market strange: analysis and policy

There was a time when markets did not run everything. When a calculation did not accompany so many decisions – to stop work, have a baby, arrange care for your mother. In that time, before

we internalised the market and the frame of cost/benefit calculation quite so enthusiastically, many babies died, many old
people were poorly cared for, labour consumed many bodies.
That world was far from perfect.

Today we live in a country with per capita Gross Domestic
Product (GDP) of over $26,000, and rising. While GDP is far
from an adequate marker of well-being, there is no doubt that
markets have delivered us great benefits and that GDP reflects
some of that improvement. However, that improvement has
been far from even, with growing income inequality in many
economies, including Australia. Increasing *average* levels of
income do not make questions of inequality irrelevant, as recent
research about the impact of inequalities on societies finds
(Wilkinson 2005). Analysis of a broad range of indicators in
developing countries leads Richard Wilkinson to conclude that
'the quality of social relations is better in more equal societies
where income differences between rich and poor are smaller'
(2005, p 33). In more equal societies, 'affiliative' behaviours are
much more common than dominating and ranking behaviours.
More unequal societies tend to have 'higher rates of violent
crime and homicide, and ... people living in them feel more
hostility, are less likely to be involved in community life, and
are much less likely to trust each other' (2005, p 24). Inequality
is thus socially corrosive. Alongside this, where social ranking
matters more than social cohesion, and that ranking is achieved
through consumption, the implications for environmental sustainability are significant.

To take just one example of the relevance of inequality to a
discussion about the effects of work on children, if patterns of
labour market participation are driving greater dependence on
marketised care, and that market for care sets in train a
widening spiral of inequality based on better care for those with
higher income and wealth, then new circuits of inequality are
being stimulated by the labour market and its context. And
these circuits are being created ever earlier in the life-cycle,
with great possibilities of amplification over the life-cycle. It is
one thing to be able to buy a child a better high school education; quite another when wider cognitive abilities are created

between very young children based on parental income and capacity to provide quality care.

We have become uncritical of markets and their implications for inequality, and careless of the thinning private and public supports *through which markets are sustained and made possible*. Better settings and policies can significantly improve outcomes for all, and especially for those least able to exercise political power: babies, youth, the aged, the infirm, sick, disabled and the poor. A rich civilised society can do much better. This book concentrates on analysing the current intersections of work, consumption and public good. In the process, it attempts to make the labour market strange – to try to see its corrosive as well as its positive effects with greater clarity.

What makes the labour market hungry? An overview of the argument

The components of the hungry labour market, and its youthful circuits as argued through the book, are set out in the Figure 1.1 (next page).

The hungry market affects our larger lives in many ways. Figure 1.1 sets out seven, which are analysed through the ensuing chapters. The links between consumption and changing patterns of paid work in Australia are complex and powerful – and they are being given new strength through changes at work. The point of view of young people sharpens our awareness of some of their hidden costs and externalities. For example, more paid work potentially drives more parent-replacing consumption of services and more guilt-salving expenditure. At the same time, changing cultures of parenting, intensified advertising to adults and children and new youth cultures drive new levels of consumption. This book links paid work to children's perceptions, and examines the nature and speed of a tight yet expansive work/spend cycle. While other studies have explored how parental work affects young people, this study takes the analysis further by linking it to consumption and sustenance, and by considering how changing patterns of youth and adult work affect our society.

Figure 1.1. The hungry market: a map of the book

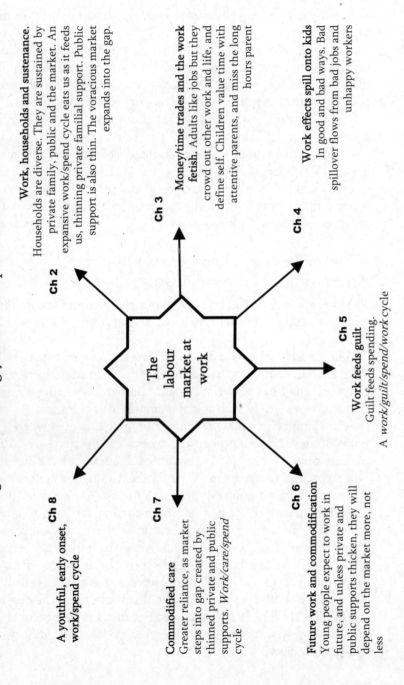

Ch 2

Work, households and sustenance.
Households are diverse. They are sustained by private family, public and the market. An expansive work/spend cycle eats us as it feeds us, thinning private familial support. Public support is also thin. The voracious market expands into the gap.

Ch 3

Money/time trades and the work fetish. Adults like jobs but they crowd out other work and life, and define self. Children value time with attentive parents, and miss the long hours parent

Ch 4

Work effects spill onto kids
In good and bad ways. Bad spillover flows from bad jobs and unhappy workers

Ch 5

Work feeds guilt
Guilt feeds spending.
A *work/guilt/spend/work* cycle

Ch 6

Future work and commodification
Young people expect to work in future, and unless private and public supports thicken, they will depend on the market more, not less

Ch 7

Commodified care
Greater reliance, as market steps into gap created by thinned private and public supports. *Work/care/spend* cycle

Ch 8

A youthful, early onset, work/spend cycle

The labour market at work

Private, public and market sustenance (Chapter 2)

Chapter 2 considers the intersection of work, consumption and care in Australia, and the boundaries of commodification around them. It outlines the sources of sustenance and care that underpin us all, including private, public and market sources. It argues that the minimal and thin private family and the overburdened and under-developed public 'family', in combination with a voracious market, are reshaping our sources of sustenance, and those available to children and young people. This framework is helpful in considering the tasks ahead: I argue for support for an enlarged and healthy 'private familism' (by which I mean, the ways that the private household sustains us), an expansive 'public familism' and a constrained and carefully-managed market. We return to these in the final chapter of the book.

The labour market: It feeds us and it eats us (Chapter 3)

Chapter 3 examines labour, the biggest market, and how more and more adults live within its thrall for more and more of our lives. The work 'fetish' brings us pleasures and pain. It narrows us as well as broadens us. It feeds us, even as it eats us. It defines more and more women, just as it has men for many decades. While many enjoy their jobs, their terms are changing, and not always for the better. This chapter explores several ways in which the labour market affects our capacity and means of sustaining ourselves. While it increases our incomes, and thus our capacity to purchase market-based sources of pleasure and support, it also increasingly is the place where we 'make' ourselves to the exclusion of other activities, including private care of ourselves and others.

Time versus *money and thinning 'private familism': How children see it*

Chapter 3 also considers children's views. Through children's eyes it weighs up the time/work trade-offs made by parents. It seems that many young people want more time with their parents rather than extra money through more parental work. Many say that one parent does not necessarily substitute for another. They might have a mother at home outside school hours, but she does not necessarily substitute easily for an absent father who might be working long hours. Many children with a parent who works long or unsocial hours are keen to avoid falling into the same pattern when they become parents themselves. The chapter sets these views in the context of other studies that find negative effects of unsocial hours of work on children. It seems that the growing demands of paid work for parental time are thinning out parental care and elements of public support, opening the door to greater reliance upon purchased goods and services, giving new momentum to the work/spend cycle.

Job spillover: Children's views of the pleasures and pain of work (Chapter 4)

Paid work can have strong 'spillover' effects on children. Chapter 4 explores both the positive and negative aspects of this spillover from the perspective of children. Many working parents probably underestimate the ways in which their jobs *positively* affect their children. On the other hand, many children can easily name negative aspects of their parents' jobs. These vary by occupation and industry, and especially by the hours that parents work. Many children do not like it when their parents work long hours, and they observe negative effects of those hours both for their parents and themselves. This suggests that the key question for parents is not whether they go to work or not, but *the state in which they come home*. 'Bad' jobs affect households badly. They contaminate family relations in a number of ways. While the 'work and family' debate is dominated by the issue of whether mothers should work, a more important question for young people is how jobs affect their mothers *and* fathers. Negative spillovers are especially associated with a bad fit between what parents *want* at work (in terms of occupation, hours or security, for example) and what they *get*. Unmet parental preferences (for example, when a parent must work when they do not want to or for longer than they desire) are often associated with negative spillover in the eyes of young people.

Work, parental guilt and the market (Chapter 5)

One important consequence of the squeeze on time is the households' turn to the market. This turn is especially led by mothers and carers who feel, most directly, the double demands of jobs and care. In an effort to keep a foothold in the labour market they buy more from others: care, clothes, food, counselling, coaching, education services of all kinds, and so on. The list is endless and it grows each year with strong competitive pressure, especially felt by parents, to keep up with the new standards of intensive parenting that are promoted through public discourse about proper parenting. Chapter 5 considers the nature of intensive parenting in Australia today, and its intersection with the marketing of care, love and the 'precious, perfect child'. Parental 'performance' can be assisted by a ready market. Intensive parenting is an important element in the intensification of private family life, which generates pressures especially on mothers, as well as giving momentum to the household work/spend cycle.

From the perspective of young people, parental guilt is obvious and widespread. In many households, guilt is seen as especially afflicting parents who work long or unsocial hours or spend extended periods away from their children. This guilt meets several common responses, including the substitution of 'stuff' for time. Most young people are not on the lookout for material compensation; they prefer more time. 'Contrition through spending' appears to work better for the market than for young people. What is more, the 'cure' enlarges the disease, and a pernicious 'work/guilt/spend/work' cycle is obvious to some young people.

Future plans: Work, households and domestic labour (Chapter 6)

Chapter 6 considers the future plans that young Australians have for work and care. The majority of young people – women and men – expect to have jobs *and* a family. Implicit in their youthful plans is a high level of labour force participation – one that might go a significant way to meeting prospective labour market shortages that are predicted to arise from an aging population. But very substantial institutional changes will be necessary if workplaces and labour markets are to accommodate these preferences and give these future parents and workers the kind of flexibilities they seek.

Most young people expect to live in dual-earner couple households, and to share care of their children with their partner. These preferences will drive a continued decline in the traditional male-breadwinner households. Instead, more and more households with children will be dual-earner households. Given that work and family pressures are most intense in these households, we can expect intensification of these pressures as a larger proportion of households are affected. There are no signs of easy mitigation of the poor fit between work and family in the Australian pipeline.

And what of unpaid work? There are those who think that a natural reallocation of domestic work to men is in train as young men volunteer to take up a fairer share and as their potential and actual partners insist upon it. However, Chapter 6 finds signs that this is no easy reassignment. Inequality in housework is likely to be long lived. This means that the market in domestic services, pre-prepared food and childcare can be expected to continue to expand strongly and that gender troubles around domestic work will persist. The turn to the market to make up for the loss of women's labour at home is likely to continue, increasing the commodification of household sustenance and – in turn – fuelling increased paid work.

Kids as commodities and the runaway market for childcare (Chapter 7)

In Chapter 7 we turn to the issue of childcare. Young people's experiences of childcare are of interest to childcare debates. It seems that many children have positive memories of their care. Chapter 7 considers some of these memories and perspectives. It outlines the nature of care expectations and plans of some young Australians, and considers their implications for future care. It is likely that young people's plans for extended family care and shared care with partners will be sorely tested by reality – both in terms of workplace flexibilities like leave, and the availability of grandparents. This will probably drive continuing growth in demand for formal, commodified childcare, making questions of quality, accessibility and cost more and more significant.

Australia's 'system' of childcare is already strained. In a few short years demand for formal non-parental care has grown quickly, outstripping supply as more and more parents, especially women, turn to the market for help with care. At the same time, for-profit provision through private corporations has expanded rapidly, creating super-profits for shareholders, but leaving open questions about the standards of care. At present both public and private commodified care rely on very large hidden and involuntary wage subsidies by underpaid staff who work, at least in part, for love of the job and endure high staff turnover, low returns to training and poor conditions. While a large literature exists about childcare and many controversies arise, it is evident that good quality care is essential to positive outcomes for children, and it seems that future parents will rely on it more, not less.

Consumption and the future work/spend cycle: Early onset and new momentum (Chapter 8)

A growing number of young Australians are working for money at younger ages. Some are earning to pay for study and to make a contribution to essential living costs in their households. Others are working to fund their consumption of things that they say are not essential: fashion, labelled clothing, jewellery or games. Chapter 8 analyses the nature of this consumption, its links to the youth labour market and jobs, and the ways in which young people construct their social connections and status through 'stuff'. The early onset of a youthful work/spend cycle is obvious, with important implications for long-term patterns of living, working and consuming. A new and faster treadmill is under construction, bolstered by a growing dependence upon identity through work and stuff. What are its implications for reproduction, care and social fabric – not to mention for an aging population?

Young people live within a powerful force field of competitive consumption. Many young people are very conscious of and clearly influenced by advertising and the market's encouragement of a close association between 'being cool' and 'having stuff'. This youthful competitive consumption drives paid work patterns in two obvious ways: through pressure on parents to buy 'stuff' and through young people's own paid work to generate spending money. There is no doubt that working parents feel the pressure of this acquisitive race; nagging is a common tactic and advertisers actively encourage 'pester power'. Time-pressed working parents find it difficult to resist.

The future: Expanding public and private household supports and moderating markets (Chapter 9)

The concluding chapter discusses the consequences of a voracious market as well as some ways in which the work and community location of young people can be improved to facilitate better outcomes for individuals and the larger Australian community.

To summarise, there are powerful links between changing work patterns, consumption and social reproduction. These create externalities for sustainability and social cohesion. We increasingly *eat into* our capacity to reproduce and sustain society well. One effect is the falling birth rate, at least in part a consequence of changing sources of identity-through-work, and the strain of caring in the face of shrinking private household

support, inadequate public support and hungry labour and consumption markets. Increased youth participation in paid work
enables increased competitive consumption among young people.
Alongside this, increased parental work drives greater commodification of care and parental spending through guilt-induced
consumption. Work/spend cycles are *socially* constructed and
contagious. This is especially obvious in relation to young people
who make a clear link between social status and consumption
and see an indelible connection between making your way
socially, and distinguishing yourself through consumption.
Powerful cycles of 'work/spend' among young Australians represent an early induction to work/spend habits that perhaps
contrast with earlier generations' frugality and thrift. High consumption habits are energetically propelled and inculcated by
both aggressive advertising targeted at youth, and a product
market that is rapidly responsive to a thirst for coolness through
'consumption of newness'.

What are the consequences of the powerful momentum of
consumption, commodification and materialism? Table 1.1 sets
out some potential consequences of the hungry market for the
fabric of community, households and families. These include
effects on inequality, gender equity and pressure on public and
private resources.

For young women and men, the institutions that shape their
labour market and care transitions remain critical to outcomes.
A supportive regime of public support, which includes parental
leave, integrated quality part-time work and quality accessible
childcare, is of primary significance. Without supports that facilitate work/care transitions, responsibility for children will
jeopardise labour market status, and people will be forced to
'choose' between limited options. They may also experience
high levels of private worry and family instability, care that
creates risks for children, and growing gender and social
inequality, as Table 1.1 (next page) sets out.

The preferences of both young men and young women will
sorely test existing workplace and labour market institutions and
practices. The realisation of plans for shared maternal and paternal care, or even intermittent maternal care backed by active

fathers, is dependent upon workplaces and labour laws that permit and protect part-time work, give flexibilities at work and provide paid and unpaid leave – for both fathers and mothers. The gap between current provisions and those young Australians may need and prefer is wide. Without such provisions, choice and preferences will be rhetorical rather than real.

Table 1.1. Consequences arising from the hungry labour and commodity markets

Issue	Effects
1. Commodification and materialism	Accelerating and expansive materialism fed by a labour fetish
2. Well-being and health of adults	Changes at work (especially expanding hours, contracting rights and increasing insecurity), spillover, risk – all have potential health impacts
3. Well-being and health of children	Poor quality care in early childhood has long term health, development and cognitive effects (McCain and Mustard 2002, Shonkoff and Phillips 2000). Children look for time with unstressed parents.
4. Inequality	Socio-economic inequality in societies undermines well-being and social health (Wilkinson 2005)
5. Overloads private household capacity	More is asked of those still standing in the private family, to fill the shortfall created by time and effort given to paid work
6. Deepening inequality for women	Filling the gaps left by thinned private familism falls to women, fuels gender inequity, and is unfair to mothers and carers
7. Low birth rate	Growing attachment to paid work/spend, and inadequate public and private support probably means fewer and later children
8. Overloads public capacity	More is asked of the public sector to fill the gaps created by the time and effort given to paid work

Who speaks? The data

This book relies on analysis of data from a variety of sources, including a range of labour market and other data collected by the Australian Bureau of Statistics (ABS), and survey data from other sources including the Australian Survey of Social Attitudes (ASSA), the Longitudinal Study of Australian Children (LSAC), and the Household, Income and Labour Dynamics in Australia (HILDA) survey.

Chapters 3 to 8 include discussion of the perspectives of young people. These rely on a set of 21 focus groups conducted in late 2003 among 93 young Australians. The methods used in the collection of this data, and the characteristics of focus groups, are set out in the Appendix. These young people were in two age cohorts: one set of ten focus groups among 10-12 year olds from Year 6 at primary schools and another set of 11 focus groups among 16-18 year olds from Year 11 in high schools.

The focus groups were located in the country (four groups), in low-income urban areas in Sydney and Adelaide (eight groups) and in higher-income areas in Sydney and Adelaide (nine groups).

Children's perspectives are relevant to both public policy and individual and household decision making. While no sensible labour market policy should be based exclusively on what young people think, it is useful to bring their preferences and perspectives to labour market debates and policy questions, given that these often reflect implicit assumptions about how children are affected by labour market phenomena, or take no account of them at all. How young people plan to organise their own work and households are issues that are little researched in Australia. The fit of their youthful plans with the institutional, cultural and political possibilities they meet will shape the quality of young people's adult lives. They are not immaterial to older citizens and the larger issues of social reproduction and social cohesion.

CHAPTER 2

Understanding households, work and social reproduction

In order to live, Australian citizens and households do more and more of two things: work for money and borrow. In the past century, what we might call the frontier of commodification – the basket of goods and services that we now buy rather than make ourselves (like clothes, food, entertainment, social life) – has expanded, driving the pursuit of money. Our market dependency has increased. At the same time some sources of family, community and state sustenance have contracted. What are we to make of these changes and how do they place coming generations as they set out to make their way as citizens, workers and carers? How will they be sustained?

Sustenance is more than something the able, healthy and adult give to the disabled, unhealthy, childlike or aged. From CEO to newborn, we are all dependent on others to a greater or lesser degree over our lives. No person is an island. While Margaret Thatcher denied the social world, in her old age she depended upon it and the care of others, as she had in fact throughout her life – and in many ways more than most, as a public politician who was fed, driven, cleaned and maintained by the public purse. Some of this social world was secured by her through the market, but much of it was provided by the state and other sources of public infrastructure.

Making sense of work, care, households and markets, and considering the future of young Australians within that context, requires us to get some key categories clear and to consider how they fit together. This chapter defines some terms and sets out a framework for thinking about households, families, work, markets and the public good, and the ways in which people are sustained. I start by discussing the family and the household, and then move on to consider how the private family is located within a larger political economy. That political economy is changing, and young people and future generations will face new challenges. I introduce the ideas of 'private familism' (or private household support) and 'public familism' (or public support for individuals and households) and consider their relationship with the market. I then discuss the changing nature of these sources of sustenance and the platform they provide, as background to consideration of the situation of young people. But first it is useful to consider what we mean by 'family'.

Defining the family and the household

Many Australians do not live in a traditional nuclear family. What is more, we all move through many family transitions: typically from a family household of origin, to a sole or group household while in post-school education, to a couple household, then a couple household with children, retired couple and then sole household. Even this relatively simple trajectory involves six transitions in household type. Many people also experience periods of living alone, sole parenthood and blended families. These increase transitions to eight or more for many individuals. It seems likely that the average number of transitions will increase rather than decline for generations ahead.

Each of these transitions has implications for housing, work, education, health, fertility, spending, family bonds, transport and community fabric. Many of these transitions are exciting. Others can be hazardous and risky. Household transition is a *certainty* of life for most young Australians, and many older ones as well. Looking ahead, this background of household change and dynamism makes the definition of family more complex.

Leaving aside the question of change over time, even at a single point in time Australians live in increasingly diverse household forms, many without children. Of more than 7,367,000 households in Australia at the time of the 2001 census, a quarter were sole-person households (ABS Cat No 4102.0 2005). More and more of us will live alone for stretches of our lives.

The ABS defines 'families' as households where the residents usually live together and residents are related by blood or marriage (whether registered or de facto), adoption, step or fostering relationships. Excluding sole-person households from a count of 'families', as this definition does, mistakes the nature of family. Despite the thinning of the nuclear family and extended kin networks, most people who live in sole-person households are located within some kind of kin network. They may be networks that are dense or sparse, emotionally close or distant, geographically near or far, but they are not very different in some ways to multiple-person households, and most of those who live like this still consider that they have, and live in, 'families'.

That said, the majority of us live in households of more than one person. But change is the only certainty here. Multiple-person families are diverse: couples with and without children, sole-parent, step and blended families.

In the 2001 census, 71 per cent of households in Australia were multiple-person family households, as defined by the ABS. Of these families, 41 per cent had children under 15 years old. Among these families with children, just over a fifth were sole-parent families (mostly headed by women), while the rest – around 80 per cent – were couple families with children.

A small but growing number of couple families are step-families (6 per cent in 2001) or blended families (4 per cent). Thus the nuclear family remains the majority household and family form, but it is far from exclusive, and recent trends are away from it. In the 15 years between 1986 and 2001, the number of families made up of couples with children rose by 3 per cent, while the number of one-parent families rose by 53 per cent, and the number of couple families *without* children increased by 33 per cent, so that the nuclear family with children dropped from a share of 54 per cent of all families in 1986 to 47 per cent in 2001 (ABS Cat No 4102.0 2003).

While the number of divorces granted in Australia has fallen slightly since 2001, the number is still high by historical levels and the expectation of divorce is increasing with around a third of those born today expected to divorce. The number of divorces granted in 2001 was the highest in 20 years, and around 10 per cent higher than ten years before and 22 per cent higher than

20 years before (ABS Cat No 3307.0 2004). These divorce trends suggest that household transformations are unlikely to proceed at a lesser rate in the near future.

'Households' or 'families'?

Whether Australians live with partners or relatives, and regardless of whether they have children of their own, most are embedded in extended families and they are not without caring responsibilities over their life-cycle – however those responsibilities are met. We are all born of parents, many of us have siblings, and most make friends and have neighbours.

The 2003 Australian Survey of Social Attitudes (Wilson et al 2005) suggests that the definition of 'family' in the minds of Australians is broad. It is built around the presence of children more than a marriage certificate or two parents (Wilson et al 2005, p 13-20). Most in the survey felt that a single-parent household is a family, and almost two-thirds also agreed that a couple without children constitutes a family. A large minority (42 per cent) see same-sex couples with children as a family, and just over a third felt that same-sex relationships should be recognised (41 per cent disagreed). More young people and women were positive about same-sex relationships and non-traditional family forms. Clearly, the accepted notions of a family have broadened significantly in recent decades.

A realistic discussion of families should recognise this and take a definition of family that is broad and inclusive of couple, sole-parent, step and blended, non-nuclear and same-sex families. Given the actual diversity in family shape and the fluidity of family over the life-cycle, it seems more helpful to talk of *households* than families when considering how we live. The set of households is larger than the set of more narrowly defined families (in all their diversity), and both are located within a larger social fabric. While families and households are vital components of community, there are obviously other sources of sustaining social connection and relationships.

Families are a central source of identity for most Australians. In the 2003 Australian Survey of Social Attitudes, three-quarters of respondents nominated their family or marital status as among their top three ways of describing who they are (52 per cent listed it as their first choice). However, work is the second most common source of identity. Fifty-five per cent of survey respondents listed 'occupation' among their top three ways of describing themselves (16 per cent listed it as their first choice). The family is clearly a basic unit of Australian social life and private identity. That private household social life occurs within a community and is complemented by identity through occupation and work.

The bounds of community have shifted in Australia and the workplace has taken a place alongside – and in some cases supplanting – the local home-based community. Many make increasing connections through jobs. However, jobs are transitory and most people want to live lives that are bigger and more stable than occupations. For most, social fabric remains larger than the workplace. For many young people it includes relationships that are maintained virtually and are unhinged from home. In a labour market that demands geographical mobility, friends and community can be dispersed.

Figure 2.1 illustrates this discussion of families, households and community, suggesting that diverse family types are nested within households that are in turn nested with a larger geographic and increasingly virtual and mobile community at work and home. Future generations are likely to see more diversity in these household forms and the community in which they are located, not less.

The changing political economy context of the household

Lives are made and households constructed within a complex political and emotional economy. We are sustained – or not – by a range of supports over our life-cycle, and these sources of sustenance are shaped by their surrounding political economy. This economy changes over time, and from place to place. Its trajectory is different in Britain, the US and Australia. It is useful to consider the forces that shape that political economy and the

Figure 2.1. Families, households and communities: Nested sub-sets

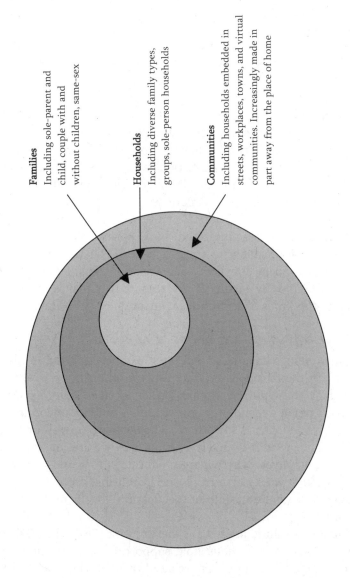

Families
Including sole-parent and child, couple with and without children, same-sex

Households
Including diverse family types, groups, sole-person households

Communities
Including households embedded in streets, workplaces, towns, and virtual communities. Increasingly made in part away from the place of home

kinds of political economy within which future generations will make their way.

The household, and the community within which it is located, are affected by the nature and settings of the market (including the labour market), the role of government and other institutions, the politics of gender, the regulatory framework, cultural norms and the state of the economy. These shape households. For example, the increase in the age at which young Australians first leave home or have their first child reflects current labour market, education, welfare and housing settings in Australia, along with the gendered cultures in which they are embedded and which they recreate.

Particular social, political, cultural and economic settings favour certain household (and work) forms. As Jan Dizard and Howard Gadlin put it in their review of the US family and its evolution: 'Society makes some relationships more likely or more durable, by virtue of the resources it makes available as well as the kinds of aspirations it encourages' (1990, p 23).

Sources of sustenance: Forms of 'familism'

Human beings have large and often extensive periods of dependency in their lives when they rely on others, most predictably as babies and children, then often in old age. Many experience other times of dependency: for example – and not uncommonly – when we are caring for others, when we are unwell or injured and cannot fend for ourselves, and when we are making transitions in our lives: whether from education to work, from job to job, around work, maternity and parenting, from old skill or occupation to new skill or occupation, or from location to location.

There are three main ways that societies deal with periods of dependency: private household support, state or public support and commodified support purchased through the market. These forms of support relate to Esping-Anderson's discussion of 'decommodification' and the different regimes of support that allow independence from market work. Most modern societies can be located within a three-dimensional spectrum according to the levels of sustenance their citizens draw from private households, public support and the market.

Dizard and Gadlin use the term 'familism' to describe the sources of sustenance that people rely upon in life, and I build on this concept in considering sources of sustenance available now, and into the future. There are different sources of this sustaining familism, beginning with the sustenance that most people find in their private household.

Private household support

Dizard and Gadlin (1990) define 'private familism' as 'a reciprocal sense of commitment, sharing, cooperation, and intimacy that is taken as defining the bonds between family members'. They suggest that these bonds are, in their most ideal form, 'material and emotional bonds of dependency and obligation' which make 'the home a base to which you can always return when your independent endeavours fail or prove unsatisfactory' (1990, p 7).

Over the 20th century, the fabric of 'private familism' in America has thinned out and become minimal, creating an argument for more expansive public support. The gradual evolution of the US nuclear family has changed the boundaries of private 'familism', narrowing them from a 'thick' set of extended family relations (held together by duty) to a thinner set of nuclear relations (held together by the idea of romantic and parental love). In this nuclear, thinner, self-contained family, extended kin relationships have become 'more peripheral and the husband-wife bond more intense, along with their attachment to children' (Dizard and Gadlin 1990, p 12).

In Britain, before the industrial revolution, extended families were often the base around which 'a living' was defined, whether by inheritance among the rich or by living within the protection of a paternal lord, and – as the industrial revolution unfolded – by employment as a family unit (father, mother, children and perhaps other family members). The industrial revolution saw the contraction of private household support from a notion of extended kin and the community and relations between lord, serf and surrounds, to the blood, nuclear family.

By about the 1850s, the ideal notion and practice of a modern family began to cohere and, as Dizard and Gadlin put it, the greater intensity of nuclear family ties was accompanied by 'the desiccation of [extended] kinship as a vital force in society' (1990, p 22).

The evolving post-war private family: It works, it consumes

The emergence of the nuclear family as the dominant family form of the 20th century in countries like the US, Britain and Australia underpinned the emergence of individual, independent workers, paid and organised as such, broken away from extended 'thick' familial relationships. It also provided the basis for consumption. The nuclear family was both *a source of labour* and *a consuming unit.* In the US, the family car and house were the cornerstones of an expansive consumption. They embed, in technical terms, the breadwinner model and the nuclear family: Dad drives, works, and produces; Mum reads the map, cleans, cares and reproduces. The family home and family car are designed for this family. The evolution of the household shows how, at any moment in time, particular public policy, technical design, social norms and economic factors make certain living forms not only possible but dominant. They *seem right* in that context. However, this context and the institutions within it evolve over time.

'Public familism' and its historical trajectory

Dizard and Gadlin also introduce the idea of 'public familism': that is, the supports and fabric of the public sphere that also sustain people. Primary among these is the state and the supports it provides (like education, health, all kinds of infrastructure and public care like childcare). However, the fabric of public support is not confined only to the public state sector. It also includes other forms of public support like labour standards that create a living (or non-living) wage and income security (or insecurity) and contributions from other sources including public philanthropy, voluntary work, community supports, and church and charitable institutions. Among these planks of public support, labour standards are a very important component, as they shape the *possibilities and strength* of 'private familism', as we see throughout this book.

Dizard and Gadlin's account of the evolving political economy of the US family brings to the fore the notions of work and consumption. The accumulation phase of capitalism in the 18th and 19th century was highly dependent upon the frugal, saving family unit that (initially through low wages) facilitated an expanding, accumulating capitalism. In the 20th century this gave way to a capitalism that – while it continued to accumulate – was highly dependent upon household consumption. This consumption is particularly associated with certain family and household forms that are increasingly cut loose from extended kin and located within shrinking private household support. This private familism was self-contained, nuclear and had it its centre waged man, caring woman, house, car and suburban life.

In the post-war period this minimal family form was supported by an expanding 'public familism' through an expanding welfare state. It was also joined by a third source of sustenance: the market. This market is a two-way street, however, both sustaining and draining personal effort. The 20th century saw a rapid expansion in forms of market goods and services as consumer capitalism fed off rising wage-earners' incomes and households with expanding consumption norms.

In Dizard and Gadlin's account of the US, the emergence of wage-earning/consumption capitalism relied on five important factors: first, the expansion of public support through a welfare state that offset the vagaries of living on waged labour (through unemployment benefits and pensions, for example); secondly, rising standards of living through wage increases and a new Fordist social contract between employers and workers and their unions; thirdly, a massive injection of advertising to stimulate the appetites of workers and their families and turn them away from protestant thrift to ready consumption; fourthly, a rapid expansion in consumer credit; and finally the weaning of families away from kin-dependency (hand-me-down clothing, shared meals and food and the exchange of familial labour and

skills) to market-dependency and the purchase of many commodities and services through the market.

Thus a dual system of commodified labour and commodified
sustenance through market consumption was born – the classic
work/spend cycle – with each side of this market settlement
(labouring citizens and buying citizens) essential to its functioning (see Figure 2.2). This commodification occurs on two
interconnected and mutually reinforcing sides of a cycle: more
of our *time* is commodified as paid *labour* and more *money* is
exchanged for a very large, and growing, proportion of life *supports and activities.* In the classic work/spend cycle, commodified labour and consumption fuel each other apace. In some
places this amounts to an increasing frenzy of over-work and
over-consumption. The work/spend cycle symbolises the simul-
taneous *money* and *time* economies that shape our lives.

Figure 2.2. The classic work/spend cycle

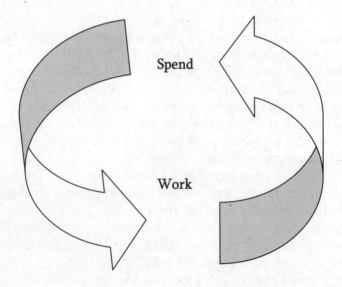

Thus the post-war shift in the US family form to dual earners has fuelled expanding consumption, against the background of rising material expectations, cheap debt, aggressive advertising and fragile, intermittent or shrinking public support. Cultural and personal norms have also shifted so that people increasingly seek the opportunity to 'be themselves' in democratic relationships, whether within or outside a nuclear family.

This new 'familial' political economy has important consequences for households. When the extended family is large, strong and pervasive, it is capable of providing a raft of support when a new baby arrives or an aging parent becomes sick. When the nuclear family is dominant, and is geographically isolated from extended family, located in a sea of suburban self-containment, and dependent on two earners to 'make a living', then it may be incapable of providing adequate support when a new baby arrives or an aging parent becomes sick. This is the 'minimal' family in Dizard and Gadlin's conception.

These authors are making their observations in the US in the late 1980s, imposing a rough schema on a complex history. Their generalisations, however, assist understanding of contemporary patterns and have real resonance in other industrialised countries like Australia.

They describe a shrinking and inadequate 'private familism'. They are not romantic about private families: such families were (and are) far from easy or reliable sources of support for many women, men and children. In many places they foster and create gendered inequities, constraining women's freedom in particular. Such 'familism' is far from the ideal of an 'enchanted' family. Family life as it is actually lived is diverse, fluid and changing. However, today such private family life is a source of less sustenance for many than some forms of extended kin family were in earlier times. And, as Dizard and Gadlin argue, the current dominant private family form is at times inadequate to carry the weight that society – individuals, governments, employers, children, the sick and infirm and especially men – places upon it.

While it was never perfect, this private familism provides inadequate sustenance to individuals over their life-cycle, in a situation of high rates of divorce, intensive pressures on couples to sustain self-contained companionate relationships, and where the economy of household life relies on two incomes, as well as 'back-up' income from students, young adults, and retired individuals. For those who work long hours or with more intensity, or who must be geographically mobile to chase work, such private household support is especially worn thin. This increasingly fragile and atomistic household is, as Julie Froud, Sukhdev Johal and Karel Williams have said of the UK, increasingly incapable of 'mediating the consequences' of a new political economy (2002, p 84). New sources of sustenance are called for, especially more expansive public supports.

In this world, families cannot, alone, function as stable 'havens in a heartless world' to use Christopher Lasch's phrase (1977). What is more, turning to the larger economy, commodity capitalism is dependent upon this minimal family – feeding as it does the labour market on the one side and fuelling voracious consumption on the other. Pressure within the minimalist family has ambivalent implications for the economy beyond the private sphere of households and well-being. Low birth rates, the prospect of a tightening labour supply and a contraction in the size of consuming 'units' have important implications for both sides of the classic work/spend cycle that sustains commodity capitalism. New sources of labour are called for, along with new sources of consumption. Women's entry into paid labour (with its consequences for private household support) and accelerated consumption (including through and by children) each feed this cycle, simultaneously giving it new momentum while draining private sustenance. What this double-headed hungry market means for its human inhabitants, especially children and youth, is a question at the heart of this book.

Public, private and market sustenance in Australia

While the Australian political economy trajectory is different in some important ways from the US and British paths, it has its own obvious work/spend cycle, and its own changing configuration of private, public and market sustenance.

Like the rest of the industrialised world, Australians live in a world that is highly commodified: that is, we exchange money for an increasing range of needs and activities, which have entered the market as opposed to being secured through reciprocal non-monetary exchange outside the market, whether through inter-family or other modes of exchange.

Others have written about what rising levels of consumption means for Australia's social and ecological health (Hamilton and Denniss 2005). This book explores what work in particular means for our selves, reproduction of ourselves and the reproduction of society: in short, what work means for social reproduction. We work harder and we increasingly live on bought food, wear bought clothes, grow little of our own produce, and purchase significant parts of our recreation, fitness, entertainment, social life, transport, holidays, education, care, health, household and psychological maintenance and cultural experiences. There are arguments about whether we are more dependent on others than in past times. Even in the most romanticised rural community of non-monetary reciprocal support there were high levels of dependency, but a dependency that was outside the commercial market. Today's high levels of dependency are highly commodified. Whatever the historical comparison – and it is beyond us here – there can be no argument that Australians live increasingly dependent lives in a web of extraordinary specialisation and technical complexity. Just try to fix your car, toaster or washing machine. Many young people have a shrinking capacity to look after themselves and are gradually increasing their dependence upon the market for various reasons, as discussed below.

Using the categories of public sustenance and private household sustenance we can begin to build up a useful framework for understanding the location of family and household in Australia's current political economy and the prospects for young people and future generations within it. How will they be sustained?

I adopt a definition of sustenance that means *the relations and practices that sustain us*. This differs from Dizard and Gadlin's definition of familism as the traditional, reciprocal, relations and intimacy of private familism. In thinking about the fabric that sustains us over the life-cycle, I rely on broader sources of support that include private, public and market sources of sustenance. These are defined in Table 2.1.

Market sustenance

Market sustenance includes all kinds of goods and services that are purchased for money. These exchanges are more often cold and instrumental than warm and reciprocal. This is not always the case, however, as some market exchanges involve emotions and can be accompanied by contrived, simulated or actual warmth or friendship.

Of course the market is not and never can be a *family*. I am not suggesting that forms of sustenance from the market are the same as those available from other sources. But the market increasingly supplies many forms of sustenance (with or without emotional warmth as a side-dish). In the face of thinned and inadequate household sustenance, market sustenance expands to fill the gap. Many 'products' of traditional private household support can now be bought under commodity capitalism: food, meals, cleaning, shopping, home management, Christmas catering, gardening and all types of 'hire a wife/husband' services, present buying, companionship; social connections, a wife, sex, sporting companions, drivers and care of all forms – of children, the aged, the infirm, the sick.

While there are many profound criticisms of markets and their embedding of inequality, their imperfections, and their externalities, there is no doubt that they are powerful providers of household sustenance.

Whether we are very rich or very poor, a disabled child or a prime minister, a plumber or a mother, we are all sustained by the three forms of support over our lifetimes set out in Table 2.1.

How are these potential sources of our sustenance configured at present in Australia?

Table 2.1. Sources of sustenance and their characteristics

Sources of Sustenance: Forms of Familism

PRIVATE HOUSEHOLD SUSTENANCE

Sources	Support found within the boundaries of the private household (including but not limited to families)
Means of exchange	Mostly uncommodified (ie no monetary exchange)
Nature of goods	Includes housing, food, clothing, education, health care, shared income, care
Relationship	Often warm, often reciprocal, set within bonds that can be loving or demanding, between kin or close friends

PUBLIC SUSTENANCE

Sources	Support provided by state, employers, charity, civic and community organisation or regulation
Means of exchange	Can be commodified (where state gives money, for example) or uncommodified when laws or direct services are provided
Nature of goods	Includes pensions, labour regulation (minimum wage, leave and other workplace regulation)
	Goods supplied include: food, clothing, housing, money, education, health care, care
Relationship	Can be cold or warm. Usually non-reciprocal (but not always in case of charity, civic and community organisations)

MARKET SUSTENANCE

Sources	Goods and services purchased in the market
Means of exchange	Money
Nature of goods	Goods supplied include: food, clothing, housing, money, education, health care, care
Relationship	Market exchange, non-reciprocal, mostly cold, sometimes warm

Intensive private household sustenance

Private household sustenance in Australia has suffered a contraction of capacity in similar terms to that described in the US by Dizard and Gadlin (1990) and in Britain by Froud and others (2002). In this situation – when families are smaller, leaner, time-poor, dual-earning, highly consumption dependent – several things are possible. Those who sustain private familism can paddle harder: they can intensify their labour and care at home to make up for the missing extended support that a more expansive private household might have provided.

This work of creating an expansive private capacity in the face of the new 'minimal family' largely falls to women. Dominant cultural expectations of women and the feminisation of care, cooking and housework assure this with awesome predictability. Failure to deliver the ideal of an expansive private capacity provokes private guilt for personal, private failure. Given that the effort of intensified, 'paddling harder' private sustenance falls largely to women, this guilt especially afflicts women.

An intensive, feminised, private sustenance can be found in many households across Australia on many days of the week. It can be read on the face of the harried worker as she grabs her briefcase and runs from the office to childcare, or negotiates with siblings about whose turn it is to have Dad this weekend, or attempts to talk a supervisor into scheduling her leave in school holidays or agreeing to part-time work.

Private sustenance is a vital source of support in many households. However, it is easily romanticised. There is no prospect of a return to the 'enchanted' family of a romanticised past, sustained by a thick familism through the efforts of mothers in particular. While there are loud rhetorical calls by some for this ideal, enchanted family – the private haven – it cannot return to what it was imagined to be. Many do not strive to return to the bread-winner household with its 'male/worker female/carer' allocations, especially given that these now mean, in most households, a reality of 'male/worker female/carer *and* worker'.

However, clamour for the traditional nuclear family with its assumptions of hierarchies, orderliness and gendered roles rises in pitch in some quarters even as this family-form contracts. As this family appears more fragile, its champions become ever more voluble in its defence. However, lived reality contradicts the clamour as more and more Australians accept diverse family types and understand that separation and divorce can affect any household. Many do not strive to have children or to live in a couple. Others work hard to maintain such a family, but find they cannot even with the best will in the world.

Pious hope for a return to the enchanted family is misplaced in the face of the growing evidence that many people who set out to raise children in a nuclear family do not end up there – for a great diversity of reasons. But beyond this, the growing reality is that even the nuclear family, for those who sustain it, cannot – alone – sustain life in the presence of thinned public support and a voracious market. Pious hope is a weak social force and a hopeless carer. The enchanted family it seeks to reinstate is as prey to declining fertility, stressed parents and children, instability, voracious markets and demanding jobs, as most other household forms. This pious defence struggles to meet the profound evidence of experience: families are fragile, long-term relationships are hard to secure, and violence, inequality, repression and bad outcomes for adults and children occur in families, alongside good outcomes.

Feminist and other critiques of the family have made the notion of the family problematic for good reason. They have not, however, made it irrelevant. Despite the powerful critique of the traditional family, very few (including most feminists) manage to construct households that are very different. The family – broadly defined – has a powerful hold on most Australians, even those who have written its most vigorous critiques. And it should not be left to be discursively manipulated by those who are increasingly panicked into bolstering its traditional form in the face of its actual, practical, morphing versatility. In this context, the key question amid the diversity of families and households and their fortunes over time is what forms of public support and which market settings will build thick private household capacity and sustain healthy households and communities in the future?

The expanding boundary of market sustenance

The boundaries of market sustenance have been expanding in recent years, with an increasing role for the market in the provision of all kinds of goods and services. The preference for market-provision, which is the mark of the neo-liberal state, has been readily expressed by the Howard Government as it has shifted services to the private market, supported contracting-out, and privatised many previously public supports.

And the market has readily responded to its opportunities. In 2001 Arlie Hoshchild used an Internet advertisement for the wife-like services of 'a beautiful, smart, hostess, good masseuse – $400/week' to trace how the commodity frontier has moved 'into the world of our private desires' (2003, p 41). There are some important needs that lie beyond the boundary of the commodified market: true love, true friendship, non-instrumental sex, parental and child love among them. Of course what we mean by 'true' love and friendship, and its market availability, is open to debate: simulated love is for sale on the market in a number of forms. It is embedded in the advertising of many products. And 'emotion' labour is for sale in many parts of the product market. It now forms a direct component of many services: we want a teacher who really cares, a flight attendant who conveys calmness, a doctor who really 'knows' us and a hospice carer who lovingly attends to a dying friend. Consumers hope they are buying intensive care, warmth and emotional empathy when they hire a nanny or take a baby to childcare. Emotional labour is now much studied, and as pay rates go, it is relatively cheap. Clearly the market has proved extraordinarily adaptive in rising to meet the gap created by a private household support that is in places, worn thin, failing and hungry for substitutes.

What's wrong with market sustenance?

However, market sustenance has its limits. Five main problems exist. First, it is cold, narrow and instrumental. Money still does not buy love and there are important gaps in what the market can reliably supply.

Market sustenance has a second deeper problem. It fuels inequality. Finding sustenance through it takes money – and more money can buy better care, education and other forms of support. These confer advantages upon purchasers and create social mobility over generations, thus fuelling an ever-widening spiral of inequality.

Thirdly, market sustenance does not adequately protect in moments of transition. Making money in exchange for time and effort has some predictability to it. However, loss of health and the vagaries of the labour market make it an unreliable support. What is more, rates of return for labour vary widely, and far from completely rationally or fairly. So the market makes a poor primary means to reliable, fair, family-like support for many who have limited buying power. The inequities and unreliability that lie at the heart of market access make it a poor provider.

Fourthly, market sustenance relies on an ever expanding commodification of time through paid labour. This further shrinks the minimal family and requires more intensive efforts of the women who undertake its work.

Finally, market sustenance increasingly reaches into the heartlands of personal care, like childcare, where quality is hard to monitor and assure and where the price of poor quality is high but hard to measure, or visited upon the young and poor who cannot speak for themselves. We turn to this in Chapter 8 in our discussion of childcare.

Markets need mediating

Since the onset of industrial capitalism, the need to mediate the market has been recognised and such mediation has underpinned the expansion of the welfare state and the creation of labour (and other market) standards and workers' rights. These safety nets of civilised societies make market capitalism work, ward off starvation and rebellion and ensure some decommodification of human beings – that is, opportunity for workers to live at least for limited periods, without having to sell their labour.

The boundaries and standards of welfare safety nets and labour standards are always in flux. How should single mothers be supported? Who pays for retirement? What kind of health and education system should we have, and who should pay for it? Should there be a minimum wage, at what level, and underpinned by what regime of unemployment benefits? The welfare state and its platform of public familism are very variable. However, in general terms in many industrialised countries such platforms tended to rise and widen in the post-World War II years up until the mid-1980s, and have tended to fall and contract since.

The state of public sustenance in Australia

Given the important limitations and hazards associated with market sustenance, it is essential that it is accompanied by expansive public supports. This includes supports that underpin childhood, old age, unemployment, immigration, sickness, disability, education and health care. These public sources of sustenance allow us to learn vocational and professional skills, permit a working mother to recover from birth and assist employed parents to both work and care for their young children, disabled child or aged parents. They provide health care, housing, education and infrastructure that facilitates both market and private household support.

Neither market sustenance or private, intensified, minimal familism can do the job – either alone or in combination. They need their essential third partner: public support, which works by underwriting and complementing the supports of private and market familism. What is more, most forms of market sustenance could not exist without the public supports of law, some forms of health care, emergency services of all kinds, much education provision, infrastructure like roads and communications and public governance itself.

Australia's traditional liberal welfare state has historically offered relatively moderate levels of public support, compared to social democratic welfare states in Europe, for example, in relation to maternity and parental leave benefits and the provision of childcare. Other categories of assistance are better than those that exist in the US at least, for example labour law, employment benefits and support for single parents.

However, recent changes on these fronts under the Howard Government have seen a contraction in some significant sources of Australia's public supports in the form of welfare provisions, with more restricted access to public support for single mothers, the unemployed and those with disabilities. Beyond this, they have seen a failure to respond adequately to the crisis of thinning private household supports. The contraction in public supports has been especially pronounced in terms of minimum labour standards and support for sole parents. In other respects it has expanded, especially through family payments to some households.

In terms of public familism established through labour market regulation, Australia has traditionally placed a sizeable portion of the weight of public sustenance on comprehensive labour regulation, through the provision of a living minimum wage and basic general employment conditions like sick and holiday leave, pay premiums for working unsocial or long hours, long-service leave, meal breaks and so on. Such public supports protect the individual's capacity to both work and reproduce themselves and contribute to social reproduction more broadly.

The decline in general labour standards since 1991, their lack of enforcement and widening gaps in coverage have affected a significant proportion of Australian workers. Changes in the industrial regime – including a contraction in the living wage and non-wage conditions, in access to paid holiday and sick leave, reduced job and income security and lengthening hours of work – have shrunk public sources of familism with a shift like that illustrated by Figure 2.3.

The fourth-term agenda of the Howard Government (2004-2007) promises even greater gaps especially in relation to welfare and industrial reforms. These exclusions, weaknesses and failures to enforce have very potent consequences especially when they occur in a situation of shrinking minimalist private household sustenance and contracting public familism. The sources of sustenance are inadequate to the demands placed upon them. The market cannot meet them: indeed, the market exacerbates them. Employers are not eager to expand and underwrite workplace supports. Public sources of sustenance including that secured through the workplace is reduced and worn thin, while the

Figure 2.3. A schematic illustration of the changing balance of sources of sustenance in Australia

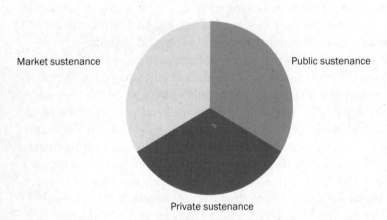

Sources of Sustenance

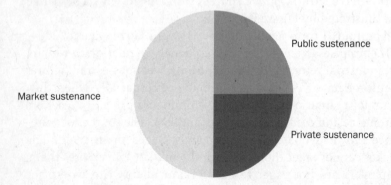

Changes in Sources of Sustenance

private family is increasingly minimalist as its fabric – like extended family, thick community and mother/ carer at home – diminishes, and the family-based work/spend cycle takes ever deeper root.

The consequence is that the quality and breadth of personal sustenance is worn thin. In this situation, the labour market and its larger market context, undermines our social reproduction. Metaphorically, it eats our kids. The lack of sustenance – on the three fronts of family, public and market – means we cannot sustain ourselves well. The price we pay is uneven but it is widely felt. It affects the birth rate, the conditions of life of those who live in dependence on those who earn, children and the infirm and aged. But its reach goes beyond 'the dependent': it affects the quality of community life, social cohesion and the true national standard of living.

What is more, as the average age of the population rises, with declining birth rates, a large dependency burden arises for youthful workers. They must either pay larger taxes, or services must decline. Thus more minimal forms of sustenance – whether sourced from the private family, public sector or the market – drives lower living standards and widening inequalities. Better public support – through quality systems of care, education, health, workplace supports and labour practices like paid leave, for example – can provide long-term solutions. They will be more gender equitable. They can counter the fragility of private household support and give more security in the face of the random uncertainties and luck that turns many families into hazards rather than havens. And effective public familism can provide consistent and quality support for those making transitions, sustaining individuals over their life course. It can counter inequality and provide support for all, not just those with money.

Gender and sustenance

Not all sources of sustenance have the same effects on different groups of people. I have argued that market forms of support generate a spiral of widening inequality between the rich and poor. Similarly, not all sources of sustenance deliver the same outcomes for women and men. Private household support is built upon long-lived and robust gendered divisions of labour, with women cast as the unpaid carers with limited financial independence. As they increasingly join men in paid work, this overload of domestic work for women has shifted all too little. Private household sustenance renders many women unequal given their economic dependence or lesser power within the private household, their overload of paid and unpaid work, and the ways in which their paid work participation and retirement sustenance is shaped and constrained by their domestic responsibilities, given the current regime of welfare, workplace and labour practices in Australia.

Potentially, public and market sources of sustenance *can* particularly assist women and redress gender inequality. However, neither form of sustenance necessarily delivers this. Markets can provide childcare and other commodified care – at a price. The trouble with the market as a road to gender equity, however, is that it can deliver for well-off women while leaving the less well-off behind. So as a road to equality for women, it is unfair and partial. Public supports (like publicly-provided childcare and aged care, support for women and men to take leave from paid work to care, and arrangements that facilitate the combination of work and care) can be powerful supports for women. Depending upon how they are organised, they potentially provide a much wider general road to gender equality.

Young people and sustainable futures?

This chapter has mapped how households are changing. In the future, young Australians will live in very diverse household types, and these will change many times over a lifetime. The traditional nuclear family – the majority family form at present – will exist alongside many other household types, and most people will move through this form among others. Such diversity is now widely accepted.

In terms of sustenance, the household and private family are, and will remain, primary sites of support. But the political economy trajectory of the family has seen it thin in recent decades, as extended kin networks have given away to a leaner, nuclear household whose supports are often disrupted by mobility and household change. The labour market and its demands, especially the growth in dual-earners, intensive, and growing hours of work, as well as the increasing commodification of our lives, have eaten into the sustaining capacity of private households. Too much is asked of it. It is leaner, more minimal and consumed by the shift of effort to the paid labour market.

Public supports in Australia have not filled the gap. Indeed contractions in public services, their shift over the boundary of commodification into the market, or their inadequate provision in the first place (for example, public childcare, paid leave for working carers) have increased demands on private household support which has intensified pressure on women in particular and turned many towards the market to seek relief. This feeds a voracious work/spend cycle as well as a widening spiral of inequality. Market sustenance can provide some help but it is Janus-faced: while with one face it sustains, on the other it eats us with its hungry appetite for the sale of labour through paid work, its creation of new 'needs' through advertising, and by harnessing the construction of the self to consumption, especially among young people. This has consequences for the quality of life, our capacity to reproduce ourselves and social cohesion. The hungry market cannot supply many basic needs, or do so fairly. It corrodes and eats us, even as it sometimes feeds us.

This is the world that young Australians now grow up in, and step out into. We begin our assessment of its implications for young people by examining the growing place of paid work in our lives and households.

CHAPTER 3

Work, children
and time versus money

The market in which we sell our time and effort, the labour
market, is one of the largest markets in most countries and
certainly the one with widest human effect. This chapter considers the ways in which we are increasingly defined *as people*
by this market and how its reach into our lives and households
is growing over a widening span of our life-course. It outlines
some evidence about adult views of work and jobs. I then
consider how work affects some of those who depend on us:
children and young people. While many adults find their jobs
satisfying, young people do not always share the enthusiasm,
and weigh up time/work trade-offs in different ways, reaching
challenging conclusions. This discussion encourages a greater
focus on the ways that jobs affect both adults and children and
the importance of ensuring a good fit between how adults *want*
to work and how they *must* work, including in relation to tasks,
hours, intensity and travel. The discussion encourages us to pay
less attention to mothers and the effects of their labour on
children, and much more attention to fathers.

The growing reach of 'labour'

The proportion of the Australian population who are in paid
employment is now at its highest since data were first collected.
It has risen fairly steadily since the end of World War II. In
April 2006 the workforce participation rate was 64.4 per cent
(ABS Cat No 6202.0, 2006). Over the past quarter century,
declining rates of workforce participation by men have been
offset by women's growing attachment to work.

The labour fetish

Paid work has taken on a sacred centrality in social, political, economic and personal life in many countries over the past century and a half. More and more of us sell our time and effort for money. However, the meaning of paid work has moved beyond this simple, if vital, exchange. Work takes up more of our time, it constructs our identity, and much our non-work status is shaped by the nature and demands of our work. 'Work' and a job (or its absence) shape status.

Guy Standing (2002) has characterised the centrality of work in the 19th and 20th centuries as a fetish. We worship at work's inanimate shrine and invest it with magical powers. Without deliberate decision, it has moved to a central position in many lives – indeed the whole *course* of lives, beginning early in the teenage years and only ending in the last decade of life for many. It is central to the organisation of life for the majority of citizens aged between 15 and 60 years old. Indeed work's reach beyond these age groups is growing in many countries, as participation rates rise for youth and seniors and we are encouraged to work for longer to sustain economic growth through both production and consumption in a work/spend cycle.

The exhortation to *work more* is rarely subjected to a critical assessment of its impact on our larger lives, selves and society. If we *work more* in paid jobs, must we then *work less* at caring? Will we have fewer children and have less time for them? Will their care be degraded? If we work more, will we be happier and our well-being greater? How does a society built on 'job holding', in Hannah Arendt's (1958) phrase, treat those who don't have a job? And how does uncritical participation in a 'work/spend' cycle affect the quality of our lives, and our ability to socially reproduce ourselves? The reach of paid work goes beyond its formal consumption of our living hours. It is naturalised as a defining basis of identity, of access to citizenship and to many social supports, and – most significantly – as an organising axis for social standing.

Home is a weak competitor against demanding and enjoyable work in many settings, despite the emphasis that the majority place on 'home'. As Arlie Hochschild has put it, weak family culture is often out-competed by 'the emotional draw of a work culture' (Hochschild 2003, p 145). In her analysis, the attractions and pulls of paid work are such that 'work becomes home and home becomes work'. Family life and community are thinned as they face a 'competing urgency system and a rival conception of time' (2003, p 146). She points to the contradiction that many families live: between the family that they *are*, and the 'hypothetical family, the family they would be if only they had time' (2003, p 146). This dissonance requires emotional work to deal with guilt, competing needs and time poverty. The powerful culture of the workplace overshadows larger life, with particular consequences for women who are increasingly joining men in 'the religion of capitalism, its grip on honor and sense of worth, its subtraction from – or absorption of – family and community life.' (Hochschild 2003, p 148).

Having a job is the route to citizenship for many Australians. It makes you. While some reject this notion as a crass reduction of human existence to earning, the truth is that jobs are often the first thing we talk about when describing ourselves, and being without work, 'between jobs' or caring for someone at home runs a long way behind in the social status stakes. Alongside the pleasures of work, the decline of the extended family as a basis of social support and the growing commodification of our lives create a strong economic impulse for work for longer periods of our lives.

'Everything is work or else it is nothing'

Work and its elevation to fetish has had many critics. Writers like Ulrich Beck mock the centrality of work to the modernist sense of self:

> Everything is work, or else it is nothing ... a chasm of irresponsibility seems to open up with the end of paid work ... having lost their faith in God, [people] believe instead in the godlike powers of work to provide everything sacred to them: prosperity, social position, personality, meaning in life, democracy, political cohesion. Just name any value of modernity, and I will show that it assumes the very thing about which it is silent: participation in paid work. (2002, p 63).

Criticising the corroding effects of 'status anxiety', Alain De Botton observes that 'work is the chief determinant of the amount of respect and care' we are granted (2004, p 108). In Australia, Clive Hamilton (2003) has lamented the centrality of waged labour to identity at a time when he sees liberation from it as possible in a 'post-scarcity' environment. These writers want to retrieve a larger notion of *socially useful work* from the narrow, economistic confines of paid labour, and include in the definition of work artistic, contemplative, cultural, political and citizenship activities as well as care and all forms of socially reproductive labour. They regret the centrality of wage-earning labour – a narrowly-defined form of commodified toil. They are critical of how the focus on waged labour has driven a preoccupation with the economic and upon money income as the source of happiness, self and a good future. They describe how work constructs identity.

The labour fetish of the 19th and 20th centuries has left several legacies. A narrow focus on paid labour and employment has led us away from defining work more broadly and seeing the ways in which *care work* underpins and makes possible employment. A preoccupation with paid labour also conceals the ways in which care work is unevenly allocated by gender.

20th century 'labouring man' and the feminisation of labour

In the case of Australia, the 20th century was – using Guy Standing's terminology – 'the century of labouring man'. Work dominated many aspects of personal, political and household life for men. In addition, the fortunes of many Australian women were shaped by the workplace fortunes of their male partners as well as their own paid work, so that the imprint of male labour had a reach well beyond the men who directly laboured, to their wives, children and extended families. The breadwinner household was a family affair, and for much of the 20th century this was both a labouring household and a blue-collar household.

The 20th century fetishisation of paid labour was always more a male affair. All the established national and international definitions of employment exclude the primary spheres where many women laboured – informal work, care and reproduction. The sidelining of the breadwinner's partner – working and caring woman – has long been remarked, along with the preoccupation with measuring and valourising only the forms of labour that enter the market and are commodified.

Since the 1970s, however, male participation in paid work has steadily declined and is expected to continue to do so. But the decline in male participation over the past three decades has not seen an overall detachment from the world of work among Australians because women have more than made up for it. Overall participation rates continue to trend steadily upwards hovering at 64.4 per cent in April 2006.

Australian women have joined labouring men in their labour fetish in unprecedented numbers. While the rate of increase for women is predicted to slow down in coming years, there is no doubt that future generations of women will have a greater labour market attachment than their foremothers.

Given this historic shift, the 21st century is plausibly labelled the century of labouring man *and woman*. Figure 3.1 shows the steady convergence of male and female labour participation rates over the past quarter century. It is possible to imagine a time when they meet – in around 2025 if we continue the pattern of the past quarter century.

Employment among mothers and fathers

Participation in paid work is not without its significant modifiers, especially in relation to the arrival of children. This affects the labour market participation of mothers drastically while leaving men's relatively undisturbed. The Australian Institute of Family Studies' (AIFS) long-term study of parents and children (the Longitudinal Study of Australian Children (LSAC)) gives us some insight into parents' work patterns (and the prospect of learning more in the years ahead). The 2004 wave of LSAC collected the views of parents of over 10,080 Australian children, evenly divided between infants three to 19 months old and children four to five years old (AIFS 2005).

Figure 3.1. Participation rates by sex, Australia, 1978-2006

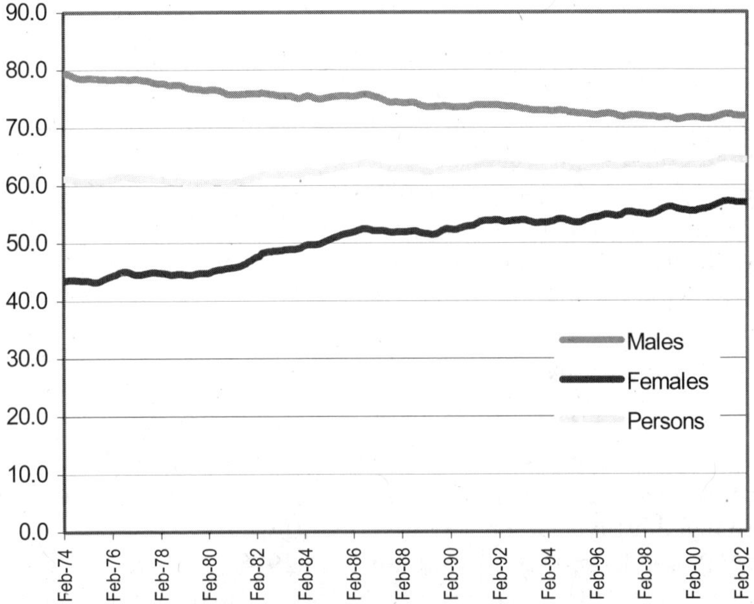

Source: ABS Cat No 6202.0.55.001 Labour Force, Australia, Spreadsheets. Table 01. Labour force status by sex, trend

In the study, the overall rate of employment among mothers of infants was 39 per cent. For fathers it was 92 per cent. Among mothers of four to five year olds the rate of employment was 54 per cent. Employment among fathers of pre-schoolers was similar to that among fathers of infants (93 per cent).

The proportion of mothers who go back to work soon after having a child has risen steeply in recent decades. Thirty years ago around 17 per cent of women were back in the labour market before their youngest child was one year old. In 2001 it had doubled to 36 per cent (Pocock 2003, p 74). The LSAC survey tells us that in 2004, 22 per cent of mothers of four to five year olds who lived in couple households had gone back to work before their children were six months old. Among mothers of the younger cohort of infants, 25 per cent were back at work by the time their children were six months old. In this survey,

40 per cent of mothers were back at work by the time their baby was a year old – and the trend continues upwards (AIFS 2005, p 11).

This means that work increasingly affects mothers as more and more of them hold jobs while also having children. This juggling experience begins for many Australian mothers when their children are very young: for two in five, before their baby is one. The reshaping of work and motherhood, and their early combination, also changes the experiences of the men who live with women who are simultaneously mothers and workers – as well as their children.

Mothers work hard to compensate for absence through work

Although women's time in paid work has increased steadily, some studies suggest that parental time spent with children has changed little between the 1920s and the 1970s, or between the 1960s and late 1990s (Bryant and Zick 1996a,b; Bianchi 2000). It seems that parents – especially mothers – try to compensate for their time at work by making sure that they share key activities with their children. US studies suggest that during the early years of childhood mothers with jobs spend less time with children, but the difference is surprisingly small, with working mothers spending about 80 per cent (or more) of the time spent by non-working mothers (Zick and Bryant 1996; Bryant and Zick 1996b). What is more, the gap in time spent in *active participation* is even narrower (Hofferth 2001).

Similarly, Australian studies suggest that while mothers without jobs spend more time with their children than employed mothers, the time spent *in direct interaction* with children is not very different (Nock and Kingston 1988). A 1997 study of Australian parents with children under five years old found that mothers using non-parental care protect the time that they give to children's activities that are associated with cognitive and social development ('developmental care') while reducing the time that they spend on either physical, or 'passive', low-intensity care (that is, care done while doing other things) especially when they have a job (Bittman, Craig and Folbre 2003). These writers confirm that there is a small trade-off between time in paid work and time in activities with children (2003, p 148). Much more of this effort is made by mothers than fathers, although men's participation in care of children is increasing very gradually based on time-use analysis. In 1997, Australian mothers of children under five years spent on average 447 minutes a day on childcare, compared to 168 by fathers.

These studies suggest that mothers work hard to compensate for their absence at work, prioritising time with children especially time for things that develop children's capacities. However, they do have less time for physical care and 'hang around time'. Alongside changes in caring responsibilities for workers who are parents, a series of ongoing changes at work continue to complicate the experience of work and its effects on workers and their households.

Work has changed: Inequality, long and unsocial hours and insecurity

Paid work is not diminishing as a source of identity in Australian life. However, we are witnessing a significant shift in the gendered nature of that identity. Men are less, and women more, the source of it. Mothers are increasingly affected by the combination of job and care.

Further, more and more women enter work independently of men, and prior to relationship and household formation. These young women have an occupational and industry identity of their own, increasingly backed by qualifications and some attachment to career. Recent years have seen extraordinary growth in the qualifications of young Australian women. In the 20 years to 2001, women's overall participation in higher education increased by 126 per cent, compared to a 46 per cent growth among men. In 1981 women made up 45.5 per cent of higher education students and by 2001 this increased to 56.4 per cent (Preston and Burgess 2003, pp 501-2). Such investment has increased women's attachment to work and to their identity through their jobs, especially among professional women who on average experience a decade or more of paid work before having children or forming households (Reed, Allen, Castleman and Coultard 2003). They are much more attached to their identity at work, and through work, than their mothers. And that attachment increasingly collides with their later identification as mothers and carers. Of course, many begin work with an education-related debt unknown to their mothers.

The labour fetish, and its role in the construction of identity, which strengthened for men over the 20th century, has significantly strengthened for women in the past 30 years.

At the same time, paid employment itself has changed in Australia. Several trends are notable. First, there have been significant changes in the industry and occupational distribution of employment with growth in service sector and knowledge intensive employment. Second, the past three decades have seen widening inequality among wage earners. Inequality has increased among both women and men since the late 1980s in Australia, and especially among men (Watson et al, 2003; Saunders 2005).

Third, there is much greater variation around 'normal' hours, and greater insecurity at work. Fewer employees now work around 40 hours a week. At the long hours end of the spectrum, an increasing number of Australians regularly work overtime. In November 2003, 37.3 per cent of employees did so, up from 33.6 per cent in August 1997 (ABS Cat No 6342.0 2003, 1997). Overtime is more often worked by parents of young children than it is by employees generally: in November 2003, 39.1 per cent of parents with children less than 12 years old worked overtime regularly, compared to 36.6 per cent of employees without young children (ABS Cat No 6342.0, 2003). The proportion of Australians working excessive hours (more than 50 a week) increased from 15 per cent in 1979 to 20 per cent in 2000, giving us one of the highest such proportions in the developed world, and showing an increasing trend that is now rare among industrialised countries which are much more likely to be reducing such long hours (Lee 2004, p 42).

Unsocial working hours have also increased in Australia. In 2000, 64 per cent of workers worked at night (between 7 pm and 7 am) or on the weekend, compared to 56 per cent in 1986 (ABS Cat No 4102.0 2002, p 132).

The time effects of work also extend to the time spent commuting to and from work. This has increased in recent years, as has the number of Australians who commute. This adds to the effect and reach of paid work in Australia. Nine million workers now commute to work each week, most of them by car. Many face increasing traffic density. Between 1945 and 1999 distances travelled by passenger cars increased fifteen-fold (Cosgrove 2000, p 1). The average commuting time for Australian workers was three hours and 37 minutes in 2002 (Flood and Barbato 2005, HILDA data). Much longer average commutes are undertaken by workers who work longer hours, compounding the effects of their jobs. Long commutes are themselves associated with higher stress, less time with family and community, for sport and for oneself (Flood and Barbato 2005).

On average, commutes are longer in Sydney in particular, and men's are longer than women's. Flood and Barbato find that 'one in five men (21 per cent) who work full-time and have children under 15 spend more time travelling to and from work than they do with their children ... On average this group commutes for seven hours and 43 minutes a week compared to three hours and 54 minutes per week spent playing with their children' (2005, p 29). As we see below, children notice the effects of time spent travelling on the moods and availability of their parents, especially their fathers.

At the other end of the hours spectrum, there has been rapid growth in part-time work, so that 29 per cent of all employees and 45 per cent of women worked part-time in April 2006. Most of these part-time workers, and a growing number of full-timers, are employed on casual terms. Over a quarter of Australians now work casually, making us an international standout among developed countries in terms of the proportion of the workforce in precarious forms of employment.

Some of these characteristics, like long or unsocial hours or less secure employment, are know to be associated with problems for adults. Much less is known about their effects on children. International studies of non-standard hours find that evening and night work create stress for parents, and that shift work is associated with marital problems and divorce (Strazdins et al, 2004). Night work has been shown to be especially harmful for marital stability in households with children (Presser 2000).

Increasingly, the risks related to work have shifted to the shoulders of workers. Where previously employers often shouldered the risk of short-term economic downturns and maintained employment through economic and production cycles, now an insecure or hourly contract (or the absence of any contract at all) shifts temporal control to employers and economic risks to employees. The growth of independent contractors (including some who are defined as such although they are in effect employees) shifts the risks of injury, income and time management to the 'contractor' in a return to insecure pre-industrial employment forms. While some employees accept the risks of contract and casual work, employee's views vary depending especially upon the presence of a back-up income in their households, and on their personal relationships with their employers and supervisors. Where workers have little real say over their hours or days of work, and lack a genuine reciprocal negotiating relationship with their boss – as many do – they often do not like their casual terms (Pocock, Prosser and Bridge 2004).

These ongoing steady changes in Australia have seen a shift in risk, widening earnings inequality and growth in service sector, white collar, part-time, casual and long hours jobs. All this has occurred in the context of greater household contributions to paid work.

Work will change more:
New workplace relations law

Looking to the future, it seems likely that these trajectories of change will strengthen in effect and pace in coming years. The Howard Government's radical changes to industrial relations law in 2006 are likely to have significant effects over time. Several features of the national law, amended in early 2006, are distinctive. They give greater power to employers – in terms of dismissal, bargaining, industrial action and other measures. They encourage a further shift away from collective bargaining towards individual contracts, and they lower the minimum standard that individual contracts must meet. The previous 'no disadvantage test' required that agreements at least matched the totality of award pay and conditions including various penalty rates, overtime provisions and allowances. Under the new law, this is no longer the case and agreements must meet only a few basic provisions including minimum ordinary pay rates and a few leave provisions.

Other changes are likely to result in smaller wage increases for low-paid workers than might have occurred under the Australian Industrial Relations Commission, and the latter's powers have been greatly circumscribed.

These changes are likely to see wider inequality in wages as those with skills and higher levels of power in the labour market leave behind lower skilled workers, new entrants and those with limited bargaining power. In terms of job security, weaker dismissal rights and weaker protections in relation to casual and contract work may see further increases in precarious forms of employment. On working time, the new law is likely to reduce compensation for work at unsocial times or overtime, fostering growth in work of these forms, and giving employers greater control over working time. Early indications are that this is so with most new Australian Workplace Agreements registered in the three months after the enactment of 'WorkChoices' surrendering award conditions like leave loadings and penalty rates (Norrington 2006).

Work and time: What working families need

One of the Prime Minister's rationales for the 2006 changes in federal industrial law was their potential to create greater opportunities to balance work and family. However, such opportunities depend on real say for employees in negotiating, for example, the total hours of work and their configuration over the year, week and day. A sizeable and growing body of international research makes clear some of the key things that working families with dependents need as they attempt to reconcile working life with family life. They require a living wage, with some predictability and security and the opportunity to live free of financial stress. In addition, security of employment is vital to family formation. Beyond this, many of the issues affecting families are related to employee say over, and control of, working time. Such say and control is quite different from employer say over, and control of, working time. Sometimes workplace outcomes can meet both sides of these needs in the classic win/win: for example, part-time work that meets employer requirements while allowing parents to work in school hours. However, in many cases, employer and employee flexibility requirements are not the same. In this context, enabling rights, facilitative rights and minimum legal standards are vital supports to employee say and control.

Key working time issues for working carers include adequate, predictable and common family time, flexible working conditions that allow workers to deal with unexpected or predictable family needs including the opportunity to change working time (for example, to part-time work), avoiding excessive working hours and adequate paid and unpaid leave to deal with personal and family sickness, birth, early parenting, death and other times of intensive family care or incident. Beyond this, quality, accessible, affordable childcare is also vital to underpin the paid work of many parents as discussed in Chapter 7.

Unfortunately, the industrial relations changes of early 2006 introduced by the federal Howard Government move in the opposite direction on these issues. They have *removed* rights for mothers returning to work to request to work part-time, to share more unpaid leave with their partners, or to take up to two years unpaid leave on having a baby. These new 'rights to request' resulted from the Family Leave Test Case decided by the Australian Industrial Relations Commission in 2005. The expected growth in individual contracts, if it continues the pattern of existing Australian Workplace Agreements, is likely to see poorer outcomes in terms of paid leave, and other work and family provisions. The evidence about such agreements suggests that they have been actively used by employers to increase their control of employee working time: over half of Australian Workplace Agreements in 2002 and 2003 did not have penalty rates, 41 per cent lacked annual leave loadings, 18 per cent did not provide shift penalties and 41 per cent did not provide other forms of allowance (DEWR 2004, p 91). Such agreements were required – at least in theory – to match in overall terms the pay and conditions in awards, so that hourly rates, for example, were sometimes higher to compensate for the loss of other payments and conditions. Under the new arrangements from early 2006, agreements are not required to compensate for such lost conditions, so that overall employers will gain more control over time, and no longer have to provide agreements that compensate for working unsocial hours or overtime rates.

In this environment, working life is set to change further and the early evidence is that it has – for the worse.

What do adults think of their work?

Clearly, the nature of work has changed in Australia and, with significant changes in the regulatory environment, more changes are in prospect. At the same time, work plays a growing role in the definition of the private self, in social connection and in terms of the time that it takes from households. Women are increasingly affected and involved in paid work and, as for men, its place in the definition of self has increased.

Many Australians find their work satisfying. In 1995, 63 per cent of employees in workplaces with 20 or more employees were satisfied with their jobs overall (Morehead et al, 1997, p 287). Results of the more recent Household Income and Labour Dynamics Survey (HILDA) confirm these positive assessments, with many employees finding satisfaction through their jobs. Many parents believe that their children are better off because of parental work.

In talking about work, employees often talk about the pleasures of their jobs and the positive connections they make through work. As discussed in Chapter 2, the Australian Survey of Social Attitudes shows that while almost three-quarters of Australians list their family or marital status as a significant way of describing themselves, occupation is the next most common source of identity with 55 per cent nominating it as one of the top three ways of describing themselves (Evans and Gray 2005). Beyond identity, many find that work gives them a sense of competence: 70 per cent of parents of young children in the 2003 LSAC survey agreed that working made them feel more competent.

The 2001 HILDA survey asked respondents to indicate their level of agreement (on a scale of 1-7, with 7 indicating strong agreement) with the statement 'I would enjoy having a job even if I didn't need the money'. The results suggest that many Australians value the non-monetary aspects of their jobs.

Table 3.1 shows that almost 60 per cent of men and women agreed that they would enjoy having a job even if they didn't need the money. Only a quarter disagreed, and 17 per cent were indifferent to the proposition (that is, neither agreed nor disagreed). There is little difference between men and women.

Almost twice as many were in *strong agreement* than were in *strong disagreement*. 18.7 per cent strongly agreed, while 10.1 per cent strongly disagreed with the statement. Casual workers were more negative than permanent workers. Workers in their middle years (35-64) were more likely to be positive than either younger or older people. Factors like control over when you work, lower stress, and learning new skills – among others – were associated with more positive levels of agreement.

Table 3.1. 'I would enjoy having a job even if I didn't need the money' (per cent of total)

	Male	Female	Persons
Disagree	25.5	25.2	25.4
Indifferent	16.3	17.3	16.8
Agree	58.2	57.4	57.8
	100	100	100

Source: HILDA Wave 1, 2001. The data, which are weighted, excludes those who did not have a useable answer. In the table 'disagreed' refers to those who marked 1-3, indifferent refers to those who marked the midpoint (4) and 'agree' refers to those who marked 5-7.

More professional and managerial workers hold positive views about work, over two-thirds agreeing that they would enjoy having a job even if they didn't need the money. However, the pleasures of work are not confined to white-collar workers in more senior positions. Over half of cleaners and labourers and elementary clerical, sales and service workers agree that they would enjoy having a job even if they didn't need the money. Just over a quarter would not. Clearly, paid work confers significant sources of enjoyment beyond the pay packet, even in jobs that are relatively low-paid, low-skilled and probably offer less personal autonomy.

Table 3.2. 'I would enjoy having a job even if I didn't need the money' (per cent of all in occupation)

Occupation	Managers, Administrators	Professionals	Elementary clerical sales & service workers	Labourers & related workers
Disagree	17	17.4	26.3	27
Indifferent	15.4	16	18.3	15.4
Agree	67.6	66.5	55.3	57.6
	100	99.9	100	100

Source: HILDA Wave 1, 2001. The data, which are weighted, excludes those who did not have a useable answer. In the table 'disagreed' refers to those who marked 1-3, indifferent refers to those who marked the midpoint (4) and 'agree' refers to those who marked 5-7.

The majority of Australian adults gain satisfaction from their jobs and consider work as central to their lives, putting considerable household time into work, whether living in dual earning households, as sole-earner couple households, or living alone, with or without children. Most parents find a greater sense of competence through their jobs.

Do young people share their parents' pleasures and rewards from work – or do they see things differently? And how are they affected by changes like increasing hours of work? We now turn to their views.

Children, work and time

While there is a great deal of research about adults' views of their jobs, there is much less about *children's* views of adults' work. The few studies that exist suggest that children are 'sophisticated observers' of work and its effects on family life and on themselves (McKee et al, 2003).

In the late 1990s Ellen Galinsky undertook a comprehensive look at the views of US children about their parents' work and job/time trade-offs. She compared their views with those of their parents. Galinsky argues that the 'work/family' debate has been misframed with too much focus on whether working mothers in particular are 'bad' for children, and not enough focus on how *work affects parents and, through them, children*. She concludes from US studies that:

> [H]aving a working mother *is never once predictive* of how children assess their mothers' parenting skills on a series of twelve items that are strongly linked to children's healthy development, school readiness, and school success. Other characteristics of their mothers' and their fathers' lives are very important (1999, p xiv, emphasis in original).

Juliet Schor concurs about the evidence of maternal employment effects: 'after years of study, there is decisive evidence that children suffer no ill effects from maternal employment' (Schor 2004, p 14). Key issues for children in the US, however, relate to the time that work takes as well as its conditions. Many US children would like more time, not more money from their parents. A 2003 survey of US children aged nine to 14 revealed that less than a third spent a lot of time with their parents, and many want more (Schor 2004). Sixty-nine per cent of children in this 2003 study said they would like to spend more time with their parents. They were especially looking for more time to have fun with parents:

> [I]f granted one wish that would change their parents' job, 63 per cent said it would be a job that gave them 'more time to do fun things together'. Only 13 per cent wished their parents made more money. (Schor 2004, p 209).

In her study Galinsky found that older children, more than younger children, longed for more parental time, especially 'hang around time' and particularly with their fathers. She argues that the *nature* of parents' jobs is very important to children. Thus the real question about parental work arising from past research, in the US at least, is not whether parents work but *how their work affects them and how attentive or focused they are able to be towards their children when they are with them.*

This result is confirmed in a Swedish study of parental work which found that work affects parents' 'state and physical condition' (Nasman 2003, p 51). This 'colouring' spills over to family life 'overriding the idea of work and family as separate social spheres' (Nasman 2003, p 51). This spillover was higher where parents worked irregular or long hours and for single mothers. It manifested itself most obviously through parental fatigue, although it was not confined to this side-effect: 'Parents are tired but also fretful, irritated, angry, grumpy, surly, sad, dizzy, inattentive, preoccupied and in pain' (Nasman 2003, p 52).

In a Scottish study in the oil and gas industry where many fathers were required to spend long periods away from home, McKee et al (2003) found that children were profoundly aware of their parents' work and its effects. These children noticed the effects of their fathers' long hours and absences as well as the exhaustion of their mothers. They were negatively affected by household mobility and 'disrupted friendship networks, lack of a sense of belonging, and lack of rootedness and distance from kin' (McKee et al, 2003, p 43). According to the authors, these children could 'competently assess how work made their parents feel' (McKee et al 2003, p 39) and many wanted to avoid the stress and tension arising from external control of working patterns in their own future adult lives.

A few years ago, Lewis, Tudball and Hand (2001) undertook interviews with a group of Australian parents and children from 47 families in Melbourne drawn together using a snow-balling technique. The majority of children in this study felt that their parents worked 'about the right amount of time' and – like Galinsky – they suggest that 'it is not whether and how much parents work, but how they work and how they parent, that matters' (2001, p 23). Most of the children talked about the impact that work has on the time that parents spend with them (2001, p 23) and 'the responses were divided roughly evenly between those saying that they wished their parents spent more time with them and those who said their parents currently spent enough time with them' (2001, p 24).

Many parents in this study wanted to have more time with their children and 'some parents had changed jobs to reduce pressure, although they lost work status and income' (2001, p 24). Some children in the study were delighted when their parents' hours became more 'reasonable' (for example, when they gave up shift work). This Australian study supports some of Galinsky's US results, especially the significance to parents and children of time spent together, and the value children attach to having their parents available to attend school and other events. These studies tell us something about children's perspectives about parental work, but there are few of them and they provide only limited information about children in diverse situations.

A recent Canadian study suggests that unsocial hours have measurable effects on child welfare, with children whose parents work non-standard times more likely to have 'emotional or behavioural difficulties, indicative of child stress' compared to children of parents who work standard hours (Strazdins et al, 2004, p 1517). This effect is independent of socio-economic status and childcare and is stronger in younger families as well as more disadvantaged households.

The next section considers other evidence about Australian children's views of parental work/time trades, collected through focus groups in 2003.

Young people's views about parental work

As described in Chapter 1 and the Appendix, these focus groups involved 93 young Australians who were fairly evenly divided between ten to 12 year olds (Year 6 in primary school), and 16 to 18 year olds (Year 11 in high school) in high and low-income areas in two cities, Sydney and Adelaide, as well as in a rural area.

Participants were organised through schools named as follows:

- Comfort Primary and Comfort High – higher-income schools in Adelaide;
- Leafy Primary and Leafy High – higher-income schools in Sydney;
- Strive Primary and Strive High – lower-income schools in western Sydney;
- Struggle Primary and Struggle High – lower-income northern and western Adelaide, respectively;
- Country – a combined primary and high school in a rural area.

Time versus money: Young people's preferences

We asked young people to discuss the trades of time and money in their households beginning with the question 'If you could choose to have more time with your parents on the one hand, or more money because they worked more, which would you choose?'

A fifth found it difficult to choose and nominated both. Of the 65 who expressed a choice, however, less than a third chose more money while more than two-thirds chose more time. The preference for more time over money varied by income, location and the nature of parental work. As might be expected, the preference for more time was more pronounced in higher-income areas, and in Adelaide where the cost of living is lower. Similar proportions of males and females expressed a preference for more time (over 40 per cent of each). However, more males preferred 'more money' than females, who were more likely to say they liked things as they were. These results are summarised in Table 3.3.

Of course, these results are indicative of the views of the 93 young people in our focus groups rather than reliable indicators for the larger population. However, they suggest a preference for more time in the minds of many young people, even those whose households are located in less financially comfortable areas. The preference for more time over more money was consistent among both younger and older children: only a fifth of those in Year 6 and Year 11 preferred more money to more time, while more than double this proportion preferred more time. However,

Table 3.3. Young people's preferences
for more parental time or more money (per cent)

	More time	More money	Both	As is	Don't know	Total
Country	92	8	0	0	0	100
Lower-income	38	25	22	16	0	100
Higher-income	44	23	21	4	8	100
ALL	48	20	19	8	4	100

N=93

younger children were more likely to have difficulty choosing and more of them nominated 'both'.

The preference for time over money was stronger in the country where almost all young people showed a preference for more time with their parents, even though each of these had a mother at home at least outside school hours. They were mostly sympathetic to their parents and their work but looked for more time with their fathers in particular. Like young people in the city, they understood the need for money.

Where children feel they currently enjoy enough time with parents, they often choose more money. As Andre from Leafy Primary put it: 'I'd probably choose more money because I can see my parents basically whenever I want. My Mum [an architect] doesn't do that much work and my Dad [an artist] is at home'. Charlie at Leafy High wanted more time with his father ('I don't really see my Dad'), as well as more money because his father's employment in the entertainment industry is unpredictable. His 'both' answer reflects his view that he sees enough of one parent (like most, his mother) and not enough of his father.

A full-time job does not necessarily mean a lack of time. Ellie, for example, lives with her mother who works full-time. She sees how much pleasure her mother's job gives her, and they manage to spend plenty of time together. She observes that her mother 'really enjoys her job ... but I still see her, and my Mum and I are pretty close and we still can spend heaps of time together. So it's good. She really likes it ... She says it's really satisfying' (Ellie, 16, Leafy High).

Young people are pragmatic about parents' need to earn

Young Australians are pragmatic about the necessity for paid parental work. They value their parents' jobs and income, and the stability and security that they bring to the household especially in some lower-income areas. For example, at Struggle Primary both Eddie and Harry are keenly aware of the importance of earnings, not least because it means they can buy things they want:

> I would like them to work a lot because my Mum needs money to live and pay the rent and bills cause she's got a lot of bills to pay. Cause I've got Foxtel and I've got other stuff (Harry, 11, Struggle Primary).

> When my Dad wasn't working, I liked him at home because I liked to play with him and that. But now he's not really any fun any more ... because he's always at work. So I've got no one to play with so it's no fun at home. But sometimes it's a good thing because when he works he gets the money and we need the money. Yeah. (Eddie, 12, Struggle Primary).

Eddie's father works six days a week for a furniture removal company. Eddie misses him a great deal, and is concerned about the effect of his Dad's job on his health. He feels bad about his Dad's illness 'because I can't play with him and, yeah, he can't buy me stuff without the money'.

Many young people express feelings of ambivalence. They can see the need for parental work, as well as the social benefits parents enjoy, but they also look for family time – 'proper family time' as Hayley calls it – to do things like solve problems together:

> I like my Dad to work because all his friends work at the same place, but I don't like it because sometimes we can't have proper family time, and I like having family time because sometimes if we have problems, they help solve them (Hayley, 12, Strive Primary).

A work/spend cycle is clearly evident to many young people: 'They earn more money so they can buy you more things, but I don't get to see them as much if they're working more' as one girl at Struggle High puts it.

In many cases, specific family circumstances construct preferences. A young man at Struggle High places great value on time with his parents both of whom are very sick and not working, even though 'we absolutely need the money'.

Amid the diversity of individual situations, several patterns are evident. The first of these relates to income levels, the second to location and the cost of living, and the third to hours of parental work.

Stronger preference for money where incomes are lower

Predictably, 'more time' was the dominant preference in higher-income areas. Those in lower-income areas were concerned about financial pressure and the need to have money to pay bills and were willing to trade time for monetary relief from these problems. However, even in lower-income areas, over a third of young people chose more time over more money, and only a quarter unambiguously chose more money. More of them wanted to keep things 'as is' than in higher-income areas.

In Adelaide households that are financially comfortable, and in country households, more young people preferred additional time with their parents over more money. In households feeling financial pressure money matters more. Nonetheless, a fair number of young people even in poorer areas want more time with their parents. They mention specific money pressures like meeting loan repayments and bills. Some cannot choose between more time or more money, especially where money is tight: 'I can't really pick because we need the money, but I also need my parents ... so I don't think I could choose' (Audrey, Strive High). Audrey's Dad is retired, and her mother works part-time. She mentions earnings 'stability' several times and is keenly aware of the financial pressures experienced by her parents. She wants that stress relieved:

> I'd prefer more money ... so my parents wouldn't have to rely on the banks for a huge loan, like take 20 years to pay it off, you know. I'd prefer to have more money so they can be stable and also pay off their debts at the same time. It wouldn't matter to me if I didn't see

them, if my time with them lessened because they were working more. It wouldn't matter to me. (Audrey, 16, Strive High).

Young people in lower-income areas show a high level of understanding about how their parents' work patterns fund necessities. They understand their parents' situations, especially if they are older: 'I'd prefer a bit more money because we've got a lot of loans to pay off and we're really tight for money recently, so I'd prefer a bit more money, not too much that I don't see them at all, but just a bit more' (Melinda, 16, Strive High).

At the same time, several young people spoke of the demands that work made on their parents. One wanted her parents to work less so that they were less tired: 'because then they get to rest more, so they don't have to work as hard as usual'. These children see their parents working *hard,* and they feel that this is for *them.* They see money as essential to alleviate pressure on parents.

High cost cities: Money matters more

A sizeable difference in time and money preferences exists between those who live in a higher-cost city like Sydney, whether in low- or higher-income areas, and those who live in Adelaide or the country. Sydney children were much more likely to prefer more money.

At 17 years old, Mike at Sydney's Leafy High lives with his father, a plumber, who is separated from his mother. His consciousness of the financial cost of rearing children has led to his decision not to have any: 'If you didn't have kids you could keep it all [money] to yourself. Just be rich'.

Not all older boys are happy to see their parents very little. Thanh, 17, living in a single-income household in a lower-income area of Sydney would like more time with his mother but he understands the economic necessities that drive her work pattern: 'I want more time with her, but I know there will be problems that will occur if I choose that ... if my Mum doesn't work we don't get money'.

Even among those living in higher-income areas in Sydney the preference for money is stronger than in lower-cost Adelaide.

However, it is far from universal, and not without qualification. Hannah, 16, in a relatively low-income household on the North Shore prefers more money 'because if we didn't have the money, even if we had more time together, it might not be so good because obviously money is so important. It will affect us all. It will just be really hard'. She also reflects that this would mean less time with her parents who would have to work harder and 'money can't really bring happiness you know'. Others distinguished between what you want and what you need.

'The right money *and* the right life'

Many in Sydney see the money *versus* time question as one of balance, but a balance underpinned by money, as well as by changes in working and earning patterns over the course of life. The expectation of change, adaptation and transition marks the views of many young people as they look ahead to their own working lives. Vanessa at Leafy High is not as oriented to money as her classmate Mike. She aims to take it in turns with her partner to work and to care for children 'so that they are raised properly with the right money and the right life. You need a balance'.

A demanding job drives preference for more time

The third difference with respect to money and time preferences occurs around job demands, especially parental jobs with long or unsocial hours. We did not ask direct questions about the impact of, or views about, working hours; instead we asked about the 'upsides/good' and the 'downsides/bad' of mothers' and then fathers' jobs. Forty-three of the group of 93 young people had at least one parent who, in their perception, worked long or unsocial hours. This is not surprising given the growing proportion of Australians working longer and non-standard hours (Lee 2004, ABS Cat No 4102.0 2002).

Only a couple of children who live with a parent working long or unsocial hours felt that these did not affect them, and in one case, this was because they were, as they put it, 'used to it'. Todd, 11, at Comfort Primary, would choose more time with his

Mum who leaves for work at 7 am and arrives home at 6.30 pm 'because I don't see her very much. I see her at nights. I like Mum working, but sometimes it gets pretty lonely'.

The absence of one parent, who for example, works long hours, drives a preference for more parental time that is parent-specific, with the parent at home not necessarily making up for the one who is absent.

For example, Bob, 11 at Comfort Primary, whose Dad sometimes works long hours while his Mum is part-time, wants to spend more time with his parents 'especially my Dad because he hasn't spent a lot of time at home'.

Many young men of 16 to 18 years, it seems, do not give up looking for more time with their fathers. Others speak of feeling distant from their fathers because of the limited time they have with them. In the country, both Kyle and Kevin miss their fathers:

> I reckon my Mum [who works part-time] is pretty much fine the way she is. Just leave her like that. But I suppose a little more time with my Dad would be good, seeing as I usually get to see him for about five minutes in the morning after I get up and he usually gets home around the time I'm doing homework so I only get to see him around tea time, and onwards at night. So not too much going on there (Kyle, 16, Country High).

> I probably would want more time. Not so much my mother, cause she's around a fair bit. I see her all the time. My old man, he works a fair bit. I see him mainly at teatime, and after that he's on the phone, and I'm doing my homework. I don't really talk to him that much (Kevin, 17, Country High).

Kevin, whose father works long hours, would like more time playing backyard cricket with his Dad, more 'hang around time': 'I wouldn't mind if I just sat in the next room, but it would be better if he wasn't doing as much work'.

A number of young people whose parents worked long or unsocial hours defined their own futures *against* their parents'. They plan to make sure they spend enough time with their own children, or want to avoid demanding jobs and are determined to have weekends off. They refer to the kind of 'work/eat/sleep' cycle that long hours workers sometimes perceive for themselves (Pocock et al 2001):

> Dad earns money and gets out, but he hardly spends any time with you. He comes home, eats tea and watches TV. We'd like *time* ... He feels bad because he can't spend time with the family. (Kelsey, 12, Struggle Primary).

Bonnie's Dad is a truck driver and she notices that he doesn't like long trips that mean he is away for days at a time:

> He's just not there, and you start to miss him after a while ... Sometimes he has to miss things and he doesn't like that. He's done it since I was a little baby and he's missed all kinds of things when I was a baby and things like that. He's missed out on lots of things and he doesn't like it, he doesn't like going in the truck all the time (Bonnie, 11, Country Primary).

When it comes to choosing between time and money, she does not hesitate: 'more time, even if that means you mightn't get everything that you wanted'.

Time versus money:
Family type and the 'hyper-breadwinner'

It might be expected that young people who live in traditional breadwinner households with a mother at home would have a lesser preference for more time than where both parents work. Similarly, we might expect young people living with a sole, working parent to have a higher preference for more time, although this is likely to be shaped by income. Surprisingly, the pattern of preferences is not very different between children living in different kinds of households. Around half of those living in dual-earner couple households, single-earner couple households or in sole-parent-earner households preferred more time, while many fewer – about a fifth – in each would choose more money through more parental work.

This is because many children in traditional, breadwinner households miss their breadwinner parent and look for more time with them. They may spend 'enough' time with the other parent, but this does not prevent them from looking for time with the absent, working parent, especially one with a demanding job. In some of these households it seems that, a form of 'hyper-breadwinning' is evident. The breadwinner is often absent for long periods as he (they are mostly fathers) takes on the task of earning enough to maintain the household. For many this means doing overtime, working unsocial hours, or travelling long distances to work intensively, for example, at a mine. As Ali at Leafy Primary in Sydney describes his Dad's situation as a taxi driver:

> I think it's not good because I don't see him in the morning at all. He has to leave really early before I wake up and he comes home really late so it's annoying cause I never really see him. I never really get to interact with him. So it's kind of lost time with him (Ali, 11, Leafy Primary).

The good thing about his father's job is that he 'gets lots of money'.

Time and household relationships

Time patterns in households affect relationships in many different ways. For example, while all of the young people in the country had a mother at home or working school hours only (none full-time), several were very conscious of long hours and their impact on household relationships and saw the need to balance money with time. Adam, son of a carpenter and an aged care worker, comments on the strain that long hours can cause, while at the same time recognising that it might make sense to work intensively at some stages of the life course:

> It's good to get money coming in and probably it's good to work as hard as you can when you're younger so when you're older you can retire with some money. But there should probably be a limit to so much before your relationships with other people start to strain because you are never there (Adam, 16, Country High).

A 'good parent' needs time

For many children, *time* is a key first requirement of a 'good Dad' and a good relationship with parents. Time is also seen as valuable in relation to mothers but as many children see more of their mothers, lack of time is more often an issue with fathers. Many young men defined a 'good Dad' as someone who spends time with them:

> Actually taking the time to go down and watch you do sport ... and maybe kick the footy or play cricket with you, just helping you out ... Watch the footy together. He tells me about what's happening [on the field]. He's more experienced than me. I think that's pretty good (Kevin, 17, Country High).

> I guess Mums aren't really as important to guys as Dad's are. [You] don't talk to your Mums about some things I suppose. But I don't really talk to my Dad about all that much stuff as he's not usually there, so I talk to my Mum heaps about it ... If he was around more I'd talk to him more (Kyle, 17, Country High).

Kevin and Kyle see the value of 'hanging' with their parents, which leads to talking:

> Interviewer: Is it talking with your folks or is it 'hanging' with them?

> Hanging sort of leads into talking (Kevin, 17, Country High).

> If you hang around your folks, you'll probably end up talking to them about things ... If you don't hang around them they might not see you're worried about something (Kyle, 17, Country High).

This also resonates in the cities. Smithy, 17, who lives with his mother and step-father, misses his biological father a great deal. He speaks with delight about his father's new-found artistic success, but looks for more time with him:

> I guess its hard because I don't see him very often cause he's always travelling, he's always in a recording studio ... and what not, and I would like to see him more, like to see him every week like I'm meant to, but sometimes it will be a month, two months, in between seeing him with only a couple of phone calls here and there. He's in some random place. I just miss not having my Dad *there*. It's just not the same (Smithy, 17, Leafy High).

Kelsey, 12, at Struggle Primary describes a 'good Dad' as someone who 'spends time with you'. Her friend Kelly agrees: 'someone who mucks around with you'.

What do young people want parental time for?

Reinforcing Galinsky's US findings, young people are looking for unstructured time with parents. The most common activity young people say they want their parents around for is 'just being together' to 'do nothing/do anything'. For example, Anna from a non-English speaking background feels that she learns a lot from hanging around her parents:

> Finding your roots and stuff ... Like where you come from, how your background is, keeping the tradition going, all that. It's a good thing (Anna, 16, Strive High).

Some children value time when the whole family is together, others time spent with a specific parent. Typical of other 11 year olds, Bob wants to hang around with his Dad more: 'Just kicking the footy or soccer ball around with him'. Thomas too would choose more time with his Dad 'to kick the footy ... help us with the veggie garden'.

Primary school students like the time their mothers spend with them. They like 'hanging time', weekends, and time before and after school. Many children value a clean house, and young men in particular mention cooking and plenty of food in the house as a benefit arising from a mother at home:

> Well the housework is always done and stuff, which is good. And she cooks tea, which is good. I don't know if there are any down-sides for her. I suppose she doesn't get much help around the house. We help her for a minute, and then, that's it. Yeah, she's doing it all (Robert, 17, Country High).

Young people, from both primary and high school, spoke of the importance of their parents being there for special events such as sports, public performances, when they are receiving an award, or for special family events like birthdays:

> Important things, like starting a new school, or moving or when something really bad or really good happens. And you want to tell them and you want them to be proud of you (Tanya, 16, Strive High).

This confirms the findings of Galinsky (1999) and Lewis et al, (2001). Children like to share their successes, and they also want time with their parents when they have problems. Many remember with sadness key events that their parents have missed and do not find that 'make up' strategies later really compensate: they wanted their parents to witness their achievements and activities. The young man whose father has missed his birthday for three years in a row seems unlikely to forget it. At Leafy Primary, Charlie, 12, thinks it is important to have his Mum around on speech day: 'Hopefully Mum is there. She's been working on every speech day ... [I've felt] disappointed cause it's been like two years in a row now. But she'll be able to make it to this one because she won't be at work'.

Conclusion

Work is increasingly important to the identity of adults and to private household sustenance. Many adults – indeed the majority – enjoy having a job and find it satisfying. Their pleasure goes well beyond the pay packet – to social connections, a sense of worth and contribution, and the use of skills and experience.

However, while paid work feeds a sense of adult work and fuels household consumption, it is not without costs in the eyes of many children. Long and unsocial hours of work are especially negative in the perceptions of children, confirming the available evidence from larger studies about unsocial hours and their measurable effects on the well-being of children.

Young people are pragmatic and they can see the rewards of paid parental work. They understand the time/care trades that their parents are engaged in, and many think that the balance is about right in their households. Others would prefer more time with their parents over more money and these are the majority in our small qualitative study.

Against what we might expect, this stronger preference for time over money is consistent whether one or both parents work, or whether living with a sole parent who works.

However, three other sources of differences in preferences are evident. First, as we might expect, the 'time over work' preference is stronger in households in higher-income areas where money is less of a problem. Secondly, the higher cost of living in Sydney is associated with a more pronounced preference for money over time, compared to lower cost centres like Adelaide and the country. Thirdly, children living with a parent who works long or unsocial hours show a stronger preference for more time over more money. Finally, it seems that children do not view money/time trades from a 'whole of household' perspective. Instead, they think of their parents as distinct, so that having a mother at home a great deal – while appreciated by many – does not necessarily make up for a parent who is not there much less (most commonly, a father). It is striking how many 16 to 18 year old men say they would like more unstressed, unstructured time with their fathers. In some cases their disappointment is palpable and openly shared with peers in discussion. Some describe feeling distant from their fathers as a result.

This confirms what other researchers have found: that over-attentiveness to mothers' work crowds out attention to that other parent, the father. It seems that growing hours of work, and their unsocial timing, affect many working fathers, and through them the perceptions and preferences of their children. In this way, changes at work eat into household relationships and children's self-perceptions of their welfare. The expansion of unsocial and long hours gives new momentum to this effect, and the radical changes to Australia's federal industrial relations system in 2006 give it a further impulse.

Many young people like unstructured 'hanging time' with their parents. They are not looking for just *any* time with parents: they want time with an *unstressed* parent. Going beyond the question of how much time we spend at work or in care, this raises the issue of how specific jobs affect those who care, and the question of job spillover. The next chapter turns to these questions.

CHAPTER 4

Job spillover: How parents' jobs affect young people

Most parents of infants and preschoolers agree that their jobs make them feel more competent, according to the 2003 LSAC survey. Almost half also believe that these positive effects spill-over on to their children. Thirty-seven per cent felt that the effect was neither positive nor negative, and only 14 per cent felt that it was negative (AIFS 2005, p 12). However, the same survey shows that many parents of infants and pre-schoolers would like to work less. Around a third of mothers of infants (3-18 months old) in the survey would like to work less than they do, even allowing for the impact this would have on their income. The level is higher among fathers at 37 per cent. What is more, working parents often feel rushed. This feeling is more common among working parents than among those who do not work: 47 per cent of parents in the LSAC survey said that they felt rushed always or often, compared to 36 per cent of parents who were not in the labour market (AIFS 2005, p 12). As we see from the views of young people in this chapter, parents are right to be concerned about how work affects children, especially where parental work aspirations are unfulfilled. When parents feel rushed, chances are that children are aware of this, and concerned about it – both for their parents as well as for the spillover onto themselves.

Young people often understand why their parents put a great deal of time into paid work. Beyond *time*, however, children are also affected by the *nature* of work that adults do. They experience spillover into the home from the jobs that their parents do. This chapter explores *how* parental work affects young people, going beyond analysis of the trade of work for time discussed in the previous chapter, to consider *how* work, the nature of the labour market, and the changing character of paid work, affect children.

Obviously, not all jobs are the same. And not all children's views are the same, even about jobs that might appear similar. The effects of work on children are diverse and context-specific. Nonetheless, some similarities are striking and they are generally in accord with other research, leading to a conclusion that job spillover from the labour market into children's lives is significant. Much of it is positive, with children well aware of the pleasure that many adults get out of paid work. However, for others it is negative, especially where parents are exhausted by their work or dislike it. Long or unsocial hours in particular have significant consequences, and children – who are accomplished 'mood monitors' – have adopted various strategies to deal with bad-tempered parents.

The basic notion of 'spillover' is that one sphere of life, such as work, creates secondary effects that spill into another sphere, such as home, or onto a person such as a partner or child (Pleck 1977). Spillover takes several forms: it can be positive or negative, and it can flow from work to family, and from family to work. Some suggest that positive 'work to family' spillover is more common among women, and negative 'work to family' spillover more common among men (Pleck 1977; Barnett and Marshall 1992).

To work or not to work is *not* the question

A great deal of public attention in Australia has focused on *whether* parents should work, especially whether mothers should work. For many young people, this is the wrong question. They understand that their parents need to work and they do not see parents' work as intrinsically bad or good. For example, Kelly from Struggle Primary says that when both her parents started working she thought 'Why? But now I like it'. Like many of her friends she can see a positive side: '[Now Mum has] heaps of friends. They are really nice and funny. They bought me things'. Positive spillover is obvious to her.

The important question for many young people is not whether parents go to work but *the state in which they come home*. Children and young people comment about the *nature* and *effects* of their parents' jobs rather than about *whether* they work or not. Many can see positive outcomes for their parents from their paid jobs, outcomes that flow on to children in the way of material comfort and, beyond this, to a happier parent and a happier household. This is consistent for different age groups and various household types.

Young people are very alert about *how* work affects parents. These work-to-home spillovers are not confined only to paid work: parents working at home in unpaid household work are also affected by their jobs and not all of these effects are positive. Job spillover is not related to paid work alone. Once again, however, it is not the job itself that causes noticeable spillover but the way it measures up against parents' preferences. Children notice mothers who do not have paid jobs and seem *happy* doing domestic work. Others perceive maternal depression, tiredness, physical injuries, social isolation or a heavy domestic load for their mothers.

Thus paid work results in clear spillovers on to children. The daughter of two full-time working parents who said 'My parents try not to bring the work life home' was unusual among participants in our focus groups. She appreciated their containment: 'I don't really need their stress as well as mine' (Jade, 16, Comfort High). Many young people agree with her. The labour market and the world of paid work have significant effects upon the worlds of young people; they are intersecting spheres. And young people take action in response to this intersection, often withdrawing from a parent who is 'spilling' work into home, or contesting the spillage: 'I say, well *I've* had a hard day at school!'.

Most young people in this study can easily tell what kind of day their parents have had when they come home. To use Nasman's expression (2003), jobs 'colour' parental moods, and influence a parent's 'state and physical condition'. However, these effects go beyond mere mood 'colouring'. They are directly transmitted to others in the household, including children, who not only *observe* their parent's 'colour' but are themselves 'coloured' by it. As studies in other countries have found, young people in Australia sense tired, stressed, injured, worried, grumpy or sad parents (McKee et al, 2003) and are alert to *negative* spillovers; it is these they notice and respond to, often withdrawing from their parent to cope. However, they also perceive many positive spillovers from parents' jobs with dividends for both parents and their children.

Positive work spillover

Young people see many benefits from their parents' jobs beyond the income that they earn. They see their parents enjoying using their skills, making a contribution, enjoying their workplace friendships and social contacts. They like the things parents bring home from work – old computers, food, golf balls, pens. They speak positively when their parents' work is flexible, when parents' work school hours, and when children are sometimes able to participate in their parents' work.

There are some gendered differences: young men are more likely to notice positive physical outcomes ('stuff' from work), the chance to ride vehicles associated with their parents' jobs, and skills transfer ('he teaches me stuff, he brings stuff home for me to take apart'). A number of boys particularly like the fact that their father's job means they can ride motor vehicles. Young women are more inclined to mention the social benefits their mothers experience as a result of their work.

Many young people see that their parents have fun at work. Delta at Strive High sees that her Dad loves his information technology job, that he is 'good at it', and that his seasonal overtime during university enrolment brings them valued extra income. Peter's father also works in information technology and loves his job. Peter enjoys many positive consequences as a result; he can 'get more stuff' when his father is happy. He compares his father to his mother:

> I just tease my Dad about his job cause it just looks like such a bludgy job and he gets paid, I think, fairly well and he works from home most days ... He just cruises ... plays his games on the computer then eventually he'll have a phone call that might mean he'll talk for three hours or something, some conference. And he travels all over, well not so much any more cause he got deep vein

> thrombosis, but he has a job that he's enjoying and he just *loves* his job and that's always good. So he isn't like my Mum, always kind of 'I'm sick of working, sick of that'. He's always basically in a good mood which I think is good ... Because when he's in a good mood you can get things out of them that normally you couldn't when they're in a bad mood ... such as money, going out places (Peter, 16, Leafy High).

These positive perceptions are not confined to white-collar or professional employment. Children of both blue and white-collar workers and professional and less-skilled jobs perceive many positive benefits from work for their parents. Tanya at Strive High feels that her Dad's job delivering parcels is good for his health 'because he has diabetes. So he has to get a lot of exercise and it's just good health cause he walks a lot'.

Jobs also sometimes introduce excitement into children's lives. Nathan's father is away from home for two weeks, then home for two weeks, working on a remote mining facility. Nathan, 12, thinks this is 'not too bad sometimes. It's exciting when he comes back'. Others feel that their mothers enjoy making friends, having laughs and social connections through their jobs: they readily recognise the many pleasures that parents take from their paid work. This is evident to children in diverse households, in both high and low-income areas, and among high school and primary school aged children. They offer many positive reflections about parents' jobs:

> She has heaps of friends [at work]. They are really nice and friendly (Kelly, 11, Struggle Primary).

> It just makes her happy because she gets to meet new people, and she comes home with funny stories (Nicky, 12, Comfort Primary).

Several young people of non-English speaking background spoke of the confidence their mothers gained from their jobs. As Vanessa (17) says of her mother 'she has grown a lot through having her own business. She's just got a lot more friends'.

These positive views affect young people's own plans. Chloe, 17, who lives with her mother, a physiotherapist, in leafy Sydney sees many positive benefits from her mother's job: a sense of pleasure, purpose and ongoing learning. She values the fact that her mother is flexible and available when Chloe needs her and 'It makes me think about what I want to do in my future to get those same sort of [rewards]'.

Several children could see that their parents benefited from getting out of the house – both mothers and fathers, and in both higher and lower-income areas. Eddie (12) from Struggle Primary thinks his father and mother enjoy a break from him, while also enjoying other aspects of their work: '[Dad] gets to have a break from us kids and he also gets to muck around with his mates ... And Mum can get away from us kids and relax with her friends'.

Some children mention stress and enjoyment simultaneously. As Melinda, 16, put it: 'She gets stressed ... but she likes it ... she's made really good friends since she's been there'. Clearly, effects can be mixed. As Hannah, daughter of a minister, says:

> Dad really enjoys what he does, that's why he does it ... He's very passionate about it ... The bad side though is it's full on, it's every aspect of his life. I don't think he gets time off and for me, for him, it's really hard because it's really demanding hours and everyone wants him and needs his advice. We constantly have meetings in our house and that's hard on the family I guess. Financially it's not that great but that's not why he does it (Hannah, 16, Leafy High).

Negative work spillover

Young people are very alert to negative aspects of parents' jobs. These include physical injury, emotional or mental distress, bad moods, stress, tiredness, sadness, uncertainty and fear. Tania, 11, whose father is a farmer, describes spillover explicitly: 'Well sometimes he gets angry at the cows when they don't move. And it sort of spills over a bit [at people]'.

Such spillover is common to both higher and lower-income areas. However, it often takes different forms. Young people in lower-income areas talk more about the *physical* impact of their fathers' and mothers' jobs on their parents' bodies. For example, ten-year-old Harry says that his step-Dad's 'body hurts' from work. While it is not clear how his mother's illness relates to work, the impact on Harry is obvious:

> It's hard for me to let my friends inside to play … It's really hard because my Mum works really hard, but she's got no battery when she's sick (Harry, 10, Struggle Primary).

In the same lower income area in northern Adelaide, Eddie's Dad moves furniture and drives a truck. Eddie (12) notices the physical impact. 'He gets lots of cuts and bruises'. Kelsey (12) also at Struggle Primary, makes similar observations about the physical effects of her Dad's job as a mechanic: 'he had a six wheel ute fall on him and he had a metal bar hit him in the temple. I couldn't give him a hug because it hurt him'.

Kelsey sees many positives, beyond money, from her mother's job but her mother has an injured shoulder from her work in the chicken factory and that means she cannot work with her friends. This upsets Kelsey: 'She used to go with her work friends to the pub on Fridays. She was happy'. Her mother's duties have changed so that she is no longer with her friends, and her job is on the line:

> She has heaps of friends. They are really nice and funny. They bought me things … Mum gets up at a quarter to four each morning to go to work and comes home on a break to take us to school and then goes back to work and then picks us up from school. We used to get free chickens … It's bad seeing her upset. They may have to sack her because of her injury. They don't have a use for her (Kelsey, 12, Struggle Primary).

In Sydney, at Strive Primary, Lee notices that her Vietnamese father who works in a car wash often has a sore back. At Strive High, Anna notices that her mother comes home from her customer service job 'sometimes stressed out. She doesn't know what to do, how to handle the situation'. In the same group, Delta's mother has a repetition strain injury arising from her sewing job ('She's worked pretty hard for a long time'), while Anna worries about the physical effects of her father's labouring job, and she feels sorry for him, in part because his demanding job often requires a long commuting journey:

> I feel sorry for my Dad because he spends months [labouring]. Seems like his whole life is busy … If he works in the area where we live, he's home early, but when he works at Bondi, he's home

about 7 pm ... He doesn't exactly *complain* about it, but ... I feel sorry for him myself. (Anna, 16, Strive High).

Also at Strive High, Melinda's mother 'gets really bitey'. Melinda 'leaves her alone most of the time, but also tries to support her'. A number of children tried to relieve their parents of strain from work:

> When she comes home she has to do all the cooking and my Dad's not home yet so she has to do most of the housework. She gets really tired and I always have to massage her and my hands get really tired as well (Lee, 11, Strive Primary).

Lanh's parents in western Sydney both work in a restaurant and he notices that they are often very tired: they work a 13-hour day. His mother and father are 'stressed, tired' and he can 'tell by his [Dad's] face, I just look at him'. Lanh feels 'like you want to help them ... It makes you feel down ... They're just too old to work hard'.

'You end up grumpy because they're grumpy'

While the nature of the effects is different, children living in higher socio-economic areas are also far from immune to negative spillovers. They are less likely to mention physical effects and more likely to mention *emotional* or *mental* effects like stress, sadness or worry. For example, Rove in a higher socio-economic area describes how his father, a mechanic, 'gets moody' if he's had a bad day. This affects Rove 'quite a bit, because Mum's not home until later'. He deals with it – like other children – by 'just staying out of his way'. The daughter of a couple running a small business whose father also works at a second job as a security guard describes a similar transmission:

> They just come home grumpy and start yelling at you. Not always, but they always just discuss all this crap ... It makes you upset, cause it's just really annoying and you end up grumpy because they're grumpy (Jane, 16, Comfort High).

At Struggle High in Adelaide, Jack notices that his father's anxieties flow on to his mother:

> She takes some frustration from Dad, and also myself, I also get
> frustrated at times … It basically [gets] carried through the whole
> family … You can't get away from it (Jack, 15, Struggle High).

Jack's holidays are constrained and built around the business but, on the positive side, he learns valuable skills and can find holiday employment.

At Leafy High in northern Sydney, Gary describes his mother, a single parent who works as a secretary, as 'always in a bad mood, tired and stuff'. She does not like her job.

Gary can tell over the phone from Asia what kind of day his father has had: 'When I speak to him on the phone I can always tell whether he's had a good day or a bad day, that's just pretty much in a good mood or bad mood'. Peter describes his mother, who works a 12-hour day, as *stretched*. She 'can't hassle me to do my homework' which he says he needs 'deeply'. In the same group, Smithy says:

> [Mum] hates her job … and she wants to get back to singing, 'cause
> when she does it she's happy and she gets energetic. When she
> comes home from work (now) she's always tired and grumpy and
> not in a good mood and all she can think about is getting out of it
> (Smithy, 17, Leafy High).

Smithy wants his mother to change her job to do the work that she loves instead of a job that makes her grumpy. He believes that she 'strayed off her path' for financial necessity: 'sometimes you have to do things you don't want to do'. A good work environment is important for Mike's mother, with dividends for him:

> My Mum has increased her work since my parents broke up. She
> used to be part-time. Now she's full-time … She basically says that
> the environment she works in is really good. She doesn't really
> mind working there because it's clean, air conditioned and she says
> it's just a good environment to be in … Yeah [that makes a
> difference for me because] she doesn't get stressed really (Mike, 17,
> Leafy High).

Changes in working hours sometimes significantly affect young people. However, more hours do not necessarily mean more negative spillover. The nature of the job and its fit with parental preferences are more important. For example, Jacqueline's mother has moved from part-time to full-time work which is positive because 'She's more happy ... She's not as grumpy around the house'. On the other hand, Judith's mother has recently switched from part-time to full-time work with negative spillover effects:

> It's made the household really stressful too because I've never really seen Mum so stressed before. I had seen Dad [who works long hours] but we'd all learned to cope with that, but now Mum is stressed. She says 'Do that!' and she gets angrier quicker, whereas she didn't do that. So we've had to adjust to that. It just makes everyone really stressed and on edge all the time, because they are *both* really stressed out now (Judith, 18, Country High).

In lower-income areas the effect is clear. Once again, it is not *having* a job that is the source of the problem:

> Dad's not really fun. He's mean and bossy. Mum's happier when she's got a job. She's nice. She has depression and she had to stop work. She's happier when she has a job (Kathie, 11, Struggle Primary).

Jacqueline is pleased that her mother has taken up full-time work because 'She's more happy and she knows more people and she lets us do more stuff and when she's gone we can listen to music louder. ... We can do our homework when we want'. However, such freedom holds risks for young people:

> Dad gets stressed. Sometimes he goes out to the pub every Friday night because he's stressed. I'm all right about that because I get to do what I like. I'd rather my Mum work [because otherwise], after school, she always wants to know what am I doing. 'Where are you going? What are you doing?' she asks me (Zoey, 11, Struggle Primary).

The effects of work on parents who bring their stress home in some cases override the benefits of more time with parents as young women at Leafy High in northern Adelaide observe:

> Yes, you notice if they're *stressed* (Chloe, 17, Leafy High).

> Yeah, because the time when they're actually around you, you notice what they are like. So you might be thinking 'Oh my Mum is not here'. But when she is actually there, you're not thinking,

'Oh I'm with my Mum', but 'Oh why is she in such a bad mood?' (Ellie, 16, Leafy High).

Young people easily read the physical, verbal and behavioural signs of a happy or unhappy parent. Most children say they can tell without any difficulty what kind of day their parents have had. There are exceptions: for example, Binh at Strive Primary in Sydney's west says she can't tell because her mother 'always pretends to be happy to me ... But then she hides all the stuff inside. So we don't really know'. Much more commonly, however, young people can tell how work affects parents. Many indicate that there are times when their working parents are 'grumpy' or withdrawn as a result of work stress or tiredness:

> My Dad if he comes home and he's a bit grumpy ... and he wants to sleep that's how I know he hasn't had a too good day. My Mum, she normally just sits there, really quiet, and watches TV and that's how I can tell (Sarah, 11, Strive Primary).

> Well I can tell when they've had a good or bad day. Like they're out of energy or they're complaining about the director because he wanted something then he changed his mind and they had to do it again, and they feel like just not cooking and getting takeaway (Charlie, 12, Leafy Primary).

Bonnie, whose father drives a truck long distances, says she can tell what kind of day he has had: 'He comes home sort of grumpy and when he's had a bad day, he's always on the phone and talking, ringing people up'. She can also tell when her Mum has had a bad day: 'she gets really het up ... she's just grumpy then'.

The negative transmission mechanism

Clear linkages exist between work and home: bad events at work affect parents and then directly affect children. Spillover flows directly from unhappy client to worker to child in both higher and lower socio-economic settings as Bob, 11, describes: 'My Mum works on a phone. She gets crazy people who keep on yelling at her ... and they get really angry at her and then she gets in a bad mood with us cause she's had a bad day at work'.

Kelly notices her father is cranky when he works extended hours which Kelly and the rest of the family dislike. 'When he does overtime, he gets a bit cranky':

> He says 'I just got back from work'. And I say 'Well, I just back from *school*' There are arguments when he has done overtime. He doesn't get to do much with his friends because he works on Sunday sometimes. He is mostly cranky. He is a bit of a control freak. He likes things his own way. If he wants to go out and Mum doesn't want to go out, he has a tantrum. We all [Mum, brother, me] tell him to shut up (Kelly, 11, Struggle Primary).

Kelly assertively challenges the spillover from her father, but she is clear about what makes a 'good Dad': he is someone who has time to play with her like he 'used' to do.

Zac at Strive Primary in Sydney's west says that his Dad comes home 'tired and cranky'. He can tell because 'he yells at us'. When he yells, Zac says 'I just go and play somewhere else, to let him rest'. He removes himself. Of his mother who works in a canteen, Zac says 'She doesn't work a lot and she still earns money and she's not tired'.

These effects are often associated with the nature and hours of their parents' jobs, and their physical and emotional demands. However, there are other important spillovers arising from more occasional or episodic events such as dismissal, redundancy, demotion or reassignment. Where parents' jobs change in negative ways, children are well aware of the change and it often affects them:

> Yeah, my Mum at the moment has to go and reapply for the job that she's got. So she was happy till yesterday and now she's hell stressed and grumpy.
>
> Interviewer: You can tell when she walks through the door?
>
> Yeah 'cause they take it out on everyone else (Chanel, 17, Comfort High).

In some cases the transmission mechanism runs from work to one parent and then to the other, and on to the young person who commonly then withdraws:

> When he gets home he's really stressed, or really tired or he's on
> the phone … It's really hard … then Mum gets stressed, they argue,
> and you just have to go on your own (Judith, 18, Country High).

> He gets really grumpy … He either sits in the lounge room or sits at
> the computer and plays games. He keeps out of everyone's way …
> It affects Mum because she gets grumpy as well. So we stay out of
> her way as well (Candy, 17, Country High).

Other young people described how they work with their
siblings to deflect spillover or 'manage' it with each other. Jack,
15, at Struggle High describes how if his sister gets home first
she takes 'heaps more before I get there … Oh yeah, if Mum's
had a bad day, Anna will find out and she will tell me'. He can
tell his parents' moods 'when they wander in the door', and
when the signs are bad he 'runs away' to his room.

When a parent's work situation improves, children notice.
Rove's mother had changed jobs which meant she now worked
with people she liked: 'She's happier'. His mother had been
travelling interstate each week but she had stopped, with
positive effects for both herself and her son. When she travelled,
'She was really sad about that, she was just sad'. As a result,
'cause we didn't get to see her, we were sad … and now we just
get to see her more' (Rove, 12, Comfort Primary).

Spillover from long or unsocial hours

As we saw in Chapter 3 growing proportions of Australian
employees, many of them with young children, work long or
unsocial hours. Analysis in other places like Canada (Strazdins et
al 2004) finds that unsocial parental working hours are associated with emotional or behavioural difficulties that are suggestive
of stress on children.

Almost all children in our study group whose parents worked
unsocial hours mentioned their parents' hours as 'downsides' of
parental work. With very few exceptions, children perceived
negative spillover effects arising from these hours. Almost half
the children in our study described their parents as sometimes
working long or unsocial hours.

At Leafy Primary in Sydney, Ali, son of a taxi driver, says that he rarely sees his Dad and 'sometimes when he comes back in the afternoon he gets angry at simple things 'cause he's stressed'. Andre's father, an artist in Sydney, is also 'stressed and tired' when he has worked long hours on a painting. Charlie's parents work long hours in the Sydney entertainment industry and experience insecurity in their jobs where 'the industry's kind of push and shove now ... [Mum]'s earning good money, but – like my Dad – it's sometimes long hours and she's all tired and sometimes I have to stay at friends' places because of night shift and stuff'. When this happens for several nights in a row, Charlie can miss 'home a bit and miss seeing Mum'.

Judith's mother works full-time and her father works long hours:

> I know that I don't like the hours that my Dad works because he gets up at 5.30 in the morning and goes to work at quarter past six and doesn't finish work until about 10.30 at night, and he's sitting on the phone for two or three hours getting prices for different people (Judith, 18, Country High).

Like others, Judith sees the phone as an extension of her father's workplace into the home. For some young people, household social organisation is shaped around the phone and their Dad's job. The effect of this extends well beyond formal work hours and into the home: 'We can't watch TV when he gets home because he sits on the phone ... If we do, we have to watch it on mute'. Her father's phone follows them on holidays: 'We might go on two or three holidays a year. He's on his mobile phone, still ringing through, and then we'll visit head office, so he never leaves his job really, no matter where we are ... It's boring'. Similarly, in western Sydney, Melinda's father runs a spare parts shop:

> It is very stressing for him because he is in charge of everything. They all rely on him even when he's not working. They still call him up ... Even when we are on holidays they call him on the mobile, so he's got a lot of pressure on him I think.

Vanessa, whose father works long hours in his own business, which he enjoys, is an exception. She sees that he loves his job.

However, she is not keen to be with him although, approaching retirement, he now wants to spend more time with her. She believes that he regrets 'missed opportunities to be with the family' but she finds his attempts to monitor her movements and be with her inconvenient and intrusive.

Typically, young people see negatives from long hours, for both parents and children. They identify direct negative effects of long hours upon their parents, often describing them as grumpy. Kyle and Robert, both sons of farmers, feel that their fathers get stressed and that this flows on to children. As Kyle describes it: 'You do something wrong and he gets up you'. 'Yeah,' replies Robert, 'he usually comes home in a pretty foul mood and you've got to tread lightly around him'. In the same country area, Kate, whose father is a farmer, declares with passion 'I will *never* marry a farmer'. Her father is not at home very much, and the family has to plan around his work. Kevin, whose Dad works in a rural service business, is angry about his long hours:

> I think his job is crap. I don't want to do it ... It's the amount of work he has to do, the amount of pay that he gets – not all that good for all that much work. You'd [think he'd] get more money (Kevin, 17, Country High).

Young people describe becoming grumpy or sad themselves. Some are protective of their parents; they feel guilty when they disturb parents' sleep, or resent that their parents are not paid better for their extra hours. Candy's father works 12-hour shifts in the wine industry and he lives a 'work/eat/sleep' cycle:

> When he's not on vintage we see a lot more of him because he's not doing 12-hour shifts, two weeks at a time, and he's still up early, but he comes home a lot earlier and sits down and helps us with whatever. [When he's doing] overtime he gets up first, goes to work, comes home and goes to bed (Candy, 17, Country High).

James' Dad drives a truck for long hours. He can't see anything good about his father's job and describes how its effects spillover:

> Money's always going back into the truck and I only see him for a few hours and he's off to bed ... He's very tired, restless of a night.

> Just not as active on the weekends. He doesn't want to do a lot, just wants to sit around and have a beer and watch TV. (James, 15, Struggle High).

Sometimes James goes on trips with his Dad 'so I get to see him'. He has grown accustomed to his father's job and doesn't think the hours 'have a big effect on me ... He's been doing it for four or five years now ... You get used to it. You just adjust'.

Many young people adopt strategies of withdrawal where their parents are grumpy or angry. For example, Bob's father runs a sporting facility and has to work longer hours sometimes, which tire his father and '[When he's tired] if we do the slightest thing wrong, like run around the corridors he will yell at you *really well* [he yells loudly to illustrate]. You try and keep in your room a lot if that happens'.

In a higher socio-economic setting in Adelaide's southern suburbs at 'Comfort' High, Mark describes how his father works two jobs. He has given up a third, which has made him 'happier'. One of his remaining jobs involves night shifts:

> He's incredibly tired, all the time, because he is just constantly going and he gets aggravated. He's not violent, he just yells and he can yell *really* loud. He doesn't do it all that often considering the stress he's under (Mark, 17, Comfort High).

Mark describes a recent afternoon when he inadvertently woke his father from his afternoon sleep. His father shouted at him and he felt 'kind of disappointed in myself because he's under a lot of pressure and we kind of let him down'. Mark doesn't think very much about how this affects him anymore: 'It's not something that I notice any more, because it's been going on for so long'. Mark was quite clear about what he missed as a result of his father's long hours:

> When he is around, we have great times, fun, playing, wrestling, all that stuff and when he's not, it's just not there (Mark, 17, Comfort High).

In the same group, Geoff's father works very long hours which Geoff, 16, resents, observing that his father is 'a great Dad ... but especially when he gets home from work, he seems to be a bit agitated just because he's had a long day and had a lot of people to talk to, and had a lot of stories about bad things that happened'. He distinguishes his 'great Dad' from his agitated behaviour, but also sees that, as his son, he pays a price too: 'It doesn't scar me for life or anything ... [But] I miss out on his company, because he is a great person to play cards with and, yes, just have fun'.

It is interesting how often young men comment upon missing time with their fathers, and reflect on the conditions of their father's work and its impact on their households. Clearly, some young men 16 to 18 years old enjoy their parents' company and look for time (especially unstructured 'hanging time') with their fathers where their fathers are away a great deal or bad tempered because of demanding work. Where fathers are working long hours there is considerable sense of loss and, in some cases, hurt and anger.

Many young people in our study specifically mention the loss of weekend time with their parents. An increasing number of Australians work on weekends. In 1993, 64 per cent of employees worked Monday to Friday. By 2003, this had fallen to 58.4 per cent. Among those employees with young children, the proportion who work Monday to Friday is even lower at 54.6 per cent (ABS Cat No 6342.0 1997, 2003). The shift in working time to the weekends has implications for common family time. Young people care about time when their whole families can be together. For example, Sarah, 11, at Strive Primary in western Sydney would like it if her father had a weekend day off rather than Wednesday because she really enjoys common family time on weekends. Others want their parents around on weekends for more utilitarian reasons, because otherwise 'we couldn't get anywhere'.

Strategies to deal with a grumpy parent

When their parents are on edge or tired from work, many young people adopt a strategy of keeping out of their way. For example, Abraham, 16, feels that his mother's primary class with its 'bad kids' means that she 'is always in a bad mood when she comes home ... I just try and stay away from her' (Abraham, 16, Comfort High).

It seems that young people value some explanation about their parents' moods. Young women in Strive High School in western Sydney described how they don't like their parents being 'shitty' as a result of work, but felt that an explanation of these spillovers mitigated the effect:

> I can tell [what kind of day they have had]. They complain about it. We'll sit at dinner and they'll complain about it a lot and they'll just be overall stressed and angry at society and all that, but they usually eventually talk about it so I know what happened and I know they've had a bad day and why.
>
> Interviewer: So is that better for you – that you understand?
>
> Yeah I like it 'cause it gives me an understanding of why they're so shitty ... at that time. I'd rather *know* than them just being really, yeah, really mean (Melinda, 16, Strive High).
>
> You can tell. Especially my Mum, she's very emotional. She'll come home and she'll be all mad and stuff. She'll be like 'What have you done?' And don't talk to her or she'll bite your head off, you know, but then she'll talk about it during dinner as well. She'll sit down and start complaining and it's like, 'Oh *okay*' (Audrey, 16, Strive High).

Job spillover among mothers at home

Positive and negative spillover from work is not confined to those with paid jobs. While fathers at home are viewed differently from mothers at home (fathers are described as retrenched, retired, sick or unemployed rather than seen as carers like mothers), both parents are seen to experience and transmit effects from their unpaid work in the home. Audrey notices that her father, who is retired, misses his job: 'He wants to get back to work and do something because I think he feels like he doesn't have things to do'. William at Struggle High observes similar restlessness and lack of social connection where his parents, both at home, are concerned:

> Socially it would affect them, they wouldn't get a lot of chances to meet new people. It limits their social interaction. It could lead at times to unrest, disturbance because they're in each other's hair all the time ... [Work] gives them something to do. My Dad is currently injured and he sits around the house all day cause he can

barely walk and he hobbles, keeps himself occupied ... He's used to being extremely occupied at work (William, 15, Strive High).

Many young people with mothers at home, full-time or part-time, appreciate having them around: 'She's always there. She cooks for us'. They see positives both for themselves and for their mothers: 'She gets satisfaction out of it – keeping her family intact', as Aislan, 16, puts it. Many children are well aware that their mothers are energetically maintaining the home and protecting their children from these tasks: 'She keeps the house clean and I don't have to do anything. There's no bad things because she's always happy' say Hayley, 12. Others like Adam, 16, with mothers in the workforce notice that they are expected to do more around the house: 'now she's got a job we have to do more stuff. Dad's not there very often'.

In some families this re-allocation is negotiated and discussed. Once again, the conversation is seen as important:

> Mum sat us down [when she went full-time] and she said 'Okay now things have to change in the house. You're going to have to start doing things. I haven't got the time any more to do the washing a couple of days a week, or cooking. When I get home from meetings, tea will have to be ready, everyone is just going to have to get their own meal, there won't be a set meal'. It's pretty stressful, but we talked about it at the start, about how things were going to change (Judith, 18, Country High).

Being an unpaid worker at home, caring for others, was not without some spillover effects for mothers, confirming the results of other studies (Lewis et al 2001). These include physical and emotional effects:

> [Mum] keeps the house clean a lot and I don't have to do anything at all ... [But] my Mum is getting old and she does everything and my Dad just cooks, and my Mum's hands are getting blisters and cracks everywhere and I think that's bad (Emma, 11, Strive Primary).

Sarah agrees:

> The good thing about my Mum is she always keeps the house clean and I don't have to do anything either, but I just help out round the house because my Mum gets tired because she has to look after my

brother and she has to do all the housework and ... she's got to make the house clean again. Bad thing is she gets really tired, she needs a good night's sleep (Sarah, 11, Strive Primary).

Children of mothers at home observe that their mothers work hard and sometimes get bored. They also felt that their mothers' domestic work was under-valued (including by children), and several mention depression:

[Being at home] can have its good points and its bad points. In a way, [Mum] does all this good stuff, but she's kind of under-appreciated, and I don't imagine it would be easy for her, considering she's had to raise two kids with depression. But if she gets satisfaction out of raising kids then it's good for her all round (Aislan, 16, Leafy High).

Aislan reflects that her mother has built her life around her children's routines and has little time 'for herself'. She has to 'remember everything' and 'she doesn't really get much time for herself, and sometimes she feels under-appreciated because we take her for granted a bit'.

Julia, also at Leafy High, whose mother is at home while her father lives overseas, wonders if her mother would 'feel more competent' if she had a paid job. Vanessa, 16, would like her mother to have a paid job: 'Her house is her life. She just loves cleaning and nagging. So I'd prefer her to be out more. She needs to get out ... I'd rather like it if she was enjoying herself, rather than sitting at home doing nothing'.

Similarly, Melinda, 16, at Strive High, is glad her mother is not at home all the time. She feels that her mother gets bored at home and needs a job to 'give her something to do ... so she is not in my face all the time'.

Binh, 11, whose mother is a widow with six children, sees both positives and negatives from her mother's domestic work. On the positive side she keeps the house clean 'so we don't need to pack up' but when she is not working she becomes 'sad when she thinks about life'. When her Mum is sad, Binh 'feels sad too'.

Job spillover: Good, bad, ugly

These discussions affirm earlier studies suggesting that *it is not whether parents go to work or not, but the state in which they come home that affects children* (Galinsky 1999; Nasman 2003; McKee et al, 2003; Lewis et al, 2001). This 'state' reflects objective characteristics of jobs and the labour market (like hours and intensity) as well as the extent to which parents' work and care preferences match their jobs. The debate about whether to work or not needs to be reframed in Australia, as Galinsky (1999) has argued in the US.

For many children, their parents' jobs are associated with positive spillover. Young people value the money and security that parents' paid jobs bring. Beyond this, they can see that many parents enjoy their jobs, or aspects of them. They enjoy their stories, sense their social connection through work, and see that their parents have fun and feel good about being competent. This confirms the positive views that many adults have about having a job.

But negative spillover is also widespread. It is especially associated with disappointed parental preferences, for example, a parent who doesn't want to work full-time but has to, or a parent who cannot work the shifts they prefer. Large surveys like LSAC tell us that many parents – around a third of parents of infants and preschoolers – want to work fewer hours. Another smaller group – around 10 per cent – want to work more paid hours. These mismatches are associated with unhappy spillover from working parents to home. It is not work itself that is the source of negative spillover, but the gap between *what parents want and what they get* in actual labour market outcomes.

For example, a mother who is happy doing domestic work will have much less spillover than a mother who does such work but is resentful, bored or feels isolated or under-valued. A parent who loves his job and works full-time may bring home less negative spillover than one who works part-time but hates his job and has no say over his hours. That said, long and unsocial hours are consistently associated with negative spillover and the majority of parents who work them appear to children to be sometimes bad-tempered, tired and stressed.

Negative spillover is also associated with some specific job characteristics: risk of physical harm, job insecurity, work overload, or long or unsocial hours which often send a parent home bad tempered. Their mood 'colours' are obvious to young people from physical, verbal and behavioural clues. Children read their parents easily. Negative spillover is sometimes seen as having very significant consequences; at the end of one discussion, when invited to make any final comments about the issues of work, time and consumption, Gary linked his parents' divorce to his father's 'strenuous' job as a stockbroker and the mobility it required. Job spillover, however, does not end with the parents. Both good and bad job spillover is directly transmitted to children. It affects them, their moods, concerns and behaviour.

By and large, young people cannot prevent spillover, although some try: 'I just tell him to shut up'. However, many try to take some action. They respond to negative spillover in - several ways, most commonly by physically withdrawing from a grumpy parent. In the longer term, they distance themselves from the absent or grumpy parent. Some take steps to look after their tired parent: they give them a massage or show concern. Some just worry about their parents, while others dislike, or hate, the contamination of their own emotional states by their parents' jobs. Parental guilt is one further consequence of this spillover and we turn to this in the next chapter.

CHAPTER 5

Guilt, money and the market at work

There is a television commercial formula, familiar to us all, that goes like this: a smiling mother in the kitchen organises snacks for children as they come in from school. She is warm, generous, laughing, prepared. Her children are delighted to see her, well fed, nurtured, reassured by her presence. Her kitchen is clean, well stocked. Whether she is buttering bread, attending a bruised knee, or washing those football jumpers, it is a mother's *time* and *love* that these advertisements speak to. They create a vision of emotional connection with children through products. Her partner is more than likely absent: maternal love and time is being mined for its commercial potential. Maternal love and time are symbolised through consumption: if we buy x, we really care.

Many mothers watching such an advertisement are, on several days of the week at least, unlikely to be able to deliver this reality. They are at work, or picking up children from school and then shopping on the way home, or hoping their child gets home safely. On a good day, they may have stocked the cupboard with food. Many ordinary Australian mothers cannot *be* the woman in the margarine fantasy. However, if they *spend* in the right way, they might just be able to replicate the emotion.

In most cases the fathers of these children will be at work. But these particular ads do not bother to speak to fathers: the terrain of paternal guilt is limited and different. Instead the marketers appeal to men on other grounds, or to well-heeled fathers through glossy flight deck magazines, with a pitch for luxury toy sales on the flight home.

The product our smiling mother is using, promises – beyond clean clothes or satisfied hunger – love. The suggestion is that the products make up for her absence. A truly loving mother will buy certain things, offer particular products and express her love through the market.

The first principle for generous loving mothers and carers in this world of advertising are that they are *there*. They are at home for their children. This is precisely what many parents cannot be for their children. Their feelings of guilt at failing to be *there* are the first fertile ground on which guilt flowers. The second powerful force nurturing guilt lies in the ways work affects parents that make them less than the smiling, prepared carers of the television world. Both *absence* and *mood* are ripe grounds for commercial excavation.

Guilt is easily manipulated through the marketing of expressions of love. But the marketisation of love and guilt has gone much further now. Good mothers buy things for their children. They make sure that children do not miss out or that they are compensated. This guilt is measured in credit payments and pocket money. In many cases, especially in middle- and upper-income households, this compensation behaviour includes sizeable expenditures on extra-curricula activities beyond school: art, drama, special events, music, language and so on.

Materialising love

In the work-spend cycle described by Juliet Schor (1992) increasing income is matched by increasing consumption aspirations. These are fuelled by advertising, creating needs and what Robert Frank calls 'relative conspicuous consumption' – that is, the consumption we do to keep up with those around us (Frank 1999). A sizeable literature now explores the social nature of consumption. Contrary to neo-classical economic theory, 'needs' are not autonomously determined, but socially constructed. An economic system that requires increasing profits and perpetually rising shareholder returns needs both ends of this work-spend cycle: on the one side, the willing worker whose labour produces ever more efficiently, and on the other the voracious consumer-worker who wants more and spends more and is willing to work for it. This drives the work-spend cycle – or squirrel cage, as Schor terms it. This cycle depends on sustained and aggressive advertising and the stimulation of material aspirations: one of our largest and fastest growing industries is devoted to this in the form of advertising.

As we have seen, work provides much more than a pay cheque and pathway to more consumption for many. It feeds our sense of ourselves and our social lives. And the more space it takes up in these ways, the more it becomes a primary source of identity and social life. The more that alternative sources of identity and social connection are crowded out by those created at work, the more these other sources atrophy and are colonized by work, in a work/work cycle where work impoverishes the rest of life, so that work creates a greater devotion to work in the absence of other sources of belonging, competence, social connection and sense of self.

We have reviewed how selling our time in the labour market is a major activity for most Australians and a growing proportion of carers. Many young people are also drawn into their own paid work early in life. We have seen how paid work often gives workers pleasure, and adults believe that their work benefits children. However, we have also seen that many children would like more time with their parents and that many *perceive* and *do not like* negative spillover from their parents' jobs.

Australian parents talk about the guilt they experience arising from their work and its demands. In some cases they recognise that their own earning and their sense of accomplishment and social connection through work affect their children negatively. Many feel guilty and some are well aware that they spend to compensate their children for the parental time they miss (Pocock 2003).

In the US, Arlie Hochschild has analysed the ways in which home has become work (a place of isolated social reproduction) while work has become home (creating strong friendships and social worth), with many emotional and social needs met increasingly through work and less through home. Consumerism is the bridge between these two worlds and it has been the ready midwife of these reversals:

> Consumerism acts to *maintain* the emotional reversal of work and family. Exposed to a continual bombardment of advertisement

through a daily average of three hours of television (half of all their leisure time), workers are persuaded to 'need' more things. To buy what they now need, they need money. To earn money, they work longer hours. Being away from home so many hours, they make up for their absence at home with gifts that cost money. They materialize love. And so the cycle continues. (Hochschild 2003, p 209)

Guilt is an important cog in this machine.

In this world, *purchases materialise love* – or more accurately they are an *attempt* to materialise love. The commercialisation of feelings has accelerated at a rapid pace in recent decades with increasingly sophisticated marketing, which creates strong feelings through scenarios, pictures and dialogue and links these emotions to things, especially commercialised objects and experiences. One portion of this active harvest occurs on the terrain of parental guilt.

Parents who worry about the effects of their paid work on their children spend to ameliorate guilt. Often tired or short of time, they struggle to retain a sense of fair and reasonable boundaries, including financial boundaries, and to consistently apply them. While the challenge of fair, consistent boundaries is not unique to working parents, it is overlaid with the detritus of work in particular ways. Social surveys tell us that Australian working parents feel more rushed than non-working parents. This is likely to have three effects. At a practical level it fuels the purchase of commercial parent-substitutes (care, food, cleaning and so on). Second, feeling rushed means more rushed decisions and less time for planning and careful consideration of purchases. Beyond the effects of being rushed, a third spending impetus is created by guilt.

Growing and harvesting guilt: Advertising to parents

Many working parents salve guilt by buying compensation for their children. Of course, as we shall see, consumption has many stimulants. Children's pester power is important, as is a rising plain of general material aspiration. Together, parental guilt, targeted advertising, youthful nagging and material aspiration are a powerful combination. Among an increasing number of working parents, they drive a hyper-commodification of household life. This is good for marketers and sellers and those who think that increasing GDP is in itself a good thing. Is it good for children?

Several questions arise. First, do young people perceive the guilt that many parents say they feel? Secondly, do young people recognise the material and other methods that parents use to compensate for guilt? Thirdly, what do young people think of parental guilt and commercial compensation strategies? Finally, do these strategies work?

I return to the voices of young Australians in our focus groups for answers to some of these questions, considering the links between parental guilt and consumption, what young people say about parental guilt, and whether guilt stimulates participation in the labour market. The market is implicated in the compensation strategies of parents who work. It turbo-charges a work-spend cycle that increases consumer spending. This often leaves both spender and recipient feeling empty and unsatisfied.

Advertisers are alert to guilt as a marketing opportunity. Marketing magazines and documents suggest they deliberately *create* and *milk* guilt, recognising it as a powerful commercial ally and spending stimulant. Guilt is a soft emotion that they provoke, work over, and seduce to the cash register.

Mining guilt: Spending our way out of guilt

The phenomena of working-parent-guilt and its relationship with buying are now widely recognised in the commercial world. Changing demographics and smaller families mean that corporations seek new ways to expand parental spending on a shrinking population of children. Preying upon guilt is one means of stimulating consumption. A prime target is the parent of the 'priceless' child (Zelizer 1985). Marketing experts are explicit: they see parental guilt as a 'major motivator' for parental spending and some set about burrowing into parental wallets by means of their children who are seen as a major commercial force: 'the goal is to target children in such a way they pressure their parents or others adults into spending.

Adults buy into it for a number of reasons. But a major one is guilt' (Braddock 1998).

Market researchers analysing the changing demographics in the UK and the US reach similar conclusions: higher-income parents have smaller numbers of children and, with more of their mothers at work, the 'guilt factor' is increasing, with some parents 'tending to buy things for their children to make up for spending less time with them; they may also spend more on treats, such as meals and outings, in an effort to procure quality time with their offspring' (Key Note Publications 2003, p 1).

The connection between parental time and spending is evident in US research which finds that parents who spend more time at work also spend more upon inessential things such as toys, videos and books for their children (Schor 2004, p 25).

Marketers targeting the Baby Boomer female demographic are exhorted to be attentive to their 'sandwiched and stressed' state and to be aware of their guilt – guilt that can arise not only in relation to their children but also in relation to the arrangements they make for their aging parents:

> Between work, parenting, eldercare, and their own needs, [Baby Boomer Women] are a busy group ... Stresses associated with being sandwiched between eldercare and child-care include financial strain, time poverty, and emotional concerns (such as guilt over lacing parents into assisted-living facilities). (The Mature Market 13 June 2005)

Some point to the rapid increase in disposable income in the control of children and teenagers, especially in the US. One family therapist describes the increasing funds available to US teenagers as a form of monetarised apology:

> We are overwhelmed trying to balance our work and family lives. It's 'I'm sorry that I'm not home more' money, 'Sorry that we don't eat dinner as a family' money and 'Sorry that I don't really know much about your life' money. We feel just plain sorry ... and guilty. (Kendrick (no date))

This money-for-guilt takes several forms, including buying compensating 'experiences'.

The compensating commercial experience

In the face of a squeeze on family time, parents are encouraged by advertisers to create family experiences that are special – 'special' meaning commodified and preferably 'expensive', the more expensive the more special. At the upper end, this is represented by a visit to Disneyland or to 'the worlds' on the Queensland Gold Coast. At the lower end it is represented by a trip to the movies or out for dinner. These opportunities are what one marketing magazine calls 'experiential marketing opportunities'. The family experience is materialised through the market. It is commodified. This is the opposite of an earlier 'cocooning' approach adopted by corporations which aimed to encourage spending in the home, making the family enclave a special and safe 'haven'. Now 'family feelings' are created by commercialised experiences outside home, a commodification that is readily stimulated by parental guilt, as market analysts recognise:

> [W]ith both parents working, a sense of guilt causes many parents to buy children things as replacements for the lack of experience shared together, even inside the home (Young 2004).

Canadian marketing researcher Michael Adams notes that family members now make 'a date' outside of the home, creating a large market for these experiential family experiences: 'they are looking to buy quality time' (Young 2004). Smaller families encourage spending on the single 'sacred' child and the creation of a sense of family through the commodified joint experience.

Compensating stuff: Food, clothes, toys, stuff

Some parents compensate for their absence or the effects of their work by buying food, clothes, toys or other gifts for their children.

This may partly explain the increase in consumption of fast food in Australia. Australians eat out at a takeaway restaurant more often than the international average. An AC Nielsen poll in late 2004 found that 30 per cent of Australians eat at a takeaway restaurant at least once a week and almost two-thirds eat out at least once a month. While this is less frequent that in the

US and Asia, it compares to a lower global average of 24 and 51 per cent respectively (AC Nielsen, 2004). The turn to take-away has many causes, but is partly explained by a parental time squeeze and its combination with guilt. A US study found an association between maternal employment and obesity: more hours of weekly work were positively associated with obesity (Anderson, Butcher and Levine 2003). The association found in this study was more pronounced amongst mothers in higher-income households, suggesting that obesity in lower-income households (where it is more prevalent) has other sources. The study did not explore the effects of paternal employment because of data limitations so we do not know how or whether fathers' work is associated with children's obesity.

There are several mechanisms which might explain this association: higher-income working mothers may use take-away food more than mothers who work less, they may supervise their children's eating and exercise regimes less actively, or their children may exercise less or be influenced by junk food adver-tising more. They may also be more prone to compensation strategies that involve unhealthy food. These ideas remain untested in Australia.

However, some parents may compensate for their work and its effects through bought food including take-away food and, as we shall see, children readily perceive this tendency and some work on it.

Do young people perceive parental guilt?

The majority of young people in our focus groups perceived that their working parents felt guilty about their work and/or towards their children. They describe many direct signs of parental guilt. For example, Bonnie says of her mother 'She tells me'. She knows her father 'feels guilty when he can't be there for things':

> I talk to him on the phone. He always keeps on talking about saying sorry and things like that. (Bonnie, 11, Country Primary)

Others can 'just tell' or notice because their parents try to make it up to them by being 'extra' nice. Guilt was recognised by young people in both Years 6 and 11, in the city and the country, in high- and low-income areas, and in single-income, dual-income and sole-parent households. It was less prevalent in households where parental earnings were seen as essential and where income was lower. In these homes, economic necessity overrode guilt, just as it undermined children's hunger for parental time.

Sometimes the perception of guilt affected one parent, usually the mother, more than the other:

> When Mum had to go to Canberra every week, she felt guilty. It was okay. We didn't blame her for anything. Cause that was her job ... Dad doesn't feel guilty. Dad, he just *can't* feel guilty. No, he doesn't feel guilty about anything. (Rove, 12, Comfort Primary)

However, many children of fathers who work long hours felt that their fathers were affected by guilt. Sebastian's father, a boilermaker, sometimes works long hours:

> Just as an example, my Dad just comes home pretty late. He feels guilty, he demonstrates it to us. He wants to spend time with us... They give him overtime. He feels guilty so he wants to take us to the soccer field. He makes it up by taking us out shopping as a whole group, or he takes us out to dine somewhere... (Sebastian, 17, Strive High)

> Interviewer: And when he does that, does it work, does it make it up?

> Yeah it works heaps ... Being together, you just feel happy enough spending time together, quality time together. You never know, something could have happened to them at work. Or I don't know, you've got to cherish that time I suppose.

Sebastian enjoys soccer with his father and values the time his father takes to compensate for his absence. Jack at Struggle High says that his father feels guilty 'a lot'. He can tell because:

> When I'm doing something and, just out of the blue, he'll come over and start talking to me and I just don't want to ... He feels guilty because he's had long hours at work and he wants to come home and talk to me. But I'll be doing homework or something. You can't get away from him! (Jack, 15, Struggle High)

Jack obviously does not always welcome his father's intensive, compensating attention.

At the other end of the economic scale, at Leafy Primary in Sydney, young boys also identified parental guilt easily, along with various compensating strategies. They mostly mentioned fathers, reflecting their longer absences from their children. Andre's father is an artist who, when his paintings sell, promises special treats, like a plane trip, to make up for his absence. Another classmate says his father 'feels oh so sorry for not being around 12 or 13 hours a day'. Matthew's father takes him to the movies to make up, while others in the group talk about their fathers coming to watch them play sport or spending extra time: 'He does make it up by spending more time with me'.

In some higher-income homes there is an acceptance of life as it is:

> I think, my Mum or my Dad, it's not that they don't feel bad, because it's just been like this the whole time, not being there, so there's no apology needed. It's something that has to be accepted. (Vanessa, 16, Leafy High)

> Yeah, I can remember my Dad was away three years in a row for my birthday and I just went kind of angry at him each time but he just [says] 'There's not much I can do. It's work, I have to do it'. But he didn't really apologise or anything. It's just that's what he has to do. It's part of his job. (Peter, 16, Leafy High)

Some young people do not perceive any parental guilt, and this was linked to, first, a lot of time with parents and, secondly, the absence of choice. Where parents' work patterns were imposed on them or seemed involuntary, young people were more likely to believe that their parents did not feel guilty, as Geoff and Louise illustrate in higher- and lower-income areas respectively:

> My Mum [doesn't feel guilty] because she has taken it easy. She sees us a lot of the time. But my Dad probably, I don't know if he feels guilty but I think he would prefer less hours and more time with us. I don't know if it's guilt ... I think he'd much rather be with us than work but I think he sees that he doesn't have much of a choice. (Geoff, 16, Comfort High)

> I don't reckon my Dad feels guilty because he's making money that will pay for the bills and pay for the stuff, like the telephone,

which he won't shut up about cause we use it too much *apparently*. And so I don't reckon they feel guilty cause they're there when I need them and stuff. (Louise, 15, Struggle High)

Mark, living in the same area as Geoff, shares his perspective: 'I don't think [Dad feels] guilty because he can't help it and he knows that and so there's no guilt'. Where work patterns are seen as unavoidable, guilt is less obvious. However, for many mothers, the question of choice is more ambiguous, especially where their paid work is positioned in public or family discourse as less essential than their partners. Perhaps this explains the high level of guilt that women report.

In some cases, young people think habit 'wears' paternal guilt away. Bob, 11, at Comfort Primary considered that his father 'probably' felt guilty when he started his job in a sports facility five years ago:

[B]ut it has worn in so he doesn't feel that guilty any more.

Often perceptions of parental guilt are followed by ready recognition of why parents work. As Rove said 'She was doing it for us'. The following exchange between young women at Comfort High illustrates their recognition of the limits on parental choice. In this context, guilt is out of place in their view:

No [they don't feel guilty] cause they're working heaps hard and earning money for the family and stuff. (Sarah, 16, Comfort High)

They don't really have a choice. (Jade, 16, Comfort High)

It's not like they're doing it on purpose. (Mary, 17, Comfort High)

It's not like they go out every night to party and then come home and go 'Oh, we don't have any money. I don't want to go to work'. (Susie, 16, Comfort High)

Some older teenagers felt that their mothers made too much of guilt: 'she always makes a bigger deal of it', as Gary (16, Leafy High), puts it. Thanh also finds it annoying:

You can't see it through her behaviour, but she just says it. She just says like 'What do you think of me working so much?' I just [say] 'I don't mind.' I don't want to put her under any pressure. (Thanh, 16, Comfort High)

Interviewer: So when she says she feels guilty you'd rather she didn't feel guilty?

Yes! It gets annoying.

How do parent's ameliorate guilt?

Young people, whether in low- or high-income households, in the country or in the city, can readily name the things their parents do when they feel guilty. Four main strategies are obvious to young people: first, parental talk and apology; secondly, compensation through time; thirdly, compensation through 'stuff'; and, finally, compensation through 'time and stuff' or 'experiential consumption'. I consider these in turn.

Strategies that involve talking and an apology are described by a number of children whose parents discuss the squeeze on their time and explain their absence:

> She tries to hang out with me and she tries to play games with me and talk to me. (Eddie, 11, Struggle School)

> My Dad feels guilty if he's not there and I'm just at home. He'll ring me on the mobile and say 'I'm sorry for not being there, and I'll try and be there next time'. (Matt, 12, Leafy Primary)

Some parents compensate by making extra or special time:

> Well my Mum tells me when she feels guilt and just apologises, so then I know what she's feeling. Then she tries to make up for it just by being there a bit more. (Mary, 11, Comfort High)

> I think my Dad feels guilty for never really ever coming to watch me play tennis. He does make it up by spending time with me. (Ali, 11, Leafy Primary)

Some children are well aware of how their parents attempt to influence their working hours to be with their children and avoid feeling guilty. For example, Sarah knows her mother does her best to be with her:

> My Mum usually tells me [if she can't be there]. If she's working five or seven nights in a row, I'm left by myself all those nights, she feels really guilty, but she can change her shift sometimes, even though heaps of people don't want night shifts, so if she can she

does and I know she's trying and she tries to spend more time with me. (Sarah, 16, Comfort High)

These time compensations are not always welcome:

Doesn't really matter to me. She feels guilty but she doesn't give us extra stuff or anything just because of that ... She comes and watches TV with us which is really weird. (Jill, 17, Comfort High)

In other cases young people identify material compensation: parents making up through bought 'stuff'. As Eddie, 12, put it: 'He buys stuff and he can see you feel sad'. When Ricky's mother couldn't make it to his football game she compensated with money and relaxed limits on curfews: 'She gave me money and let me go out late' (Ricky, 12, Struggle Primary). In the same lower-income area, Olaf's Dad 'misses out on seeing us. He wants to see us heaps and heaps to make it up'. Kelsey, also at Struggle Primary, has a father who says he is sorry for 'being out late' and takes them out for movies, tea and mini-golf. Kelly's mother 'feels guilty' and she takes Kelly and her friends out to movies and for holidays. Melinda's father feels guilty and compensates by taking the family to their holiday house: 'He works every second weekend. And I think he would like to have the weekend off, but we can't afford it. He needs to work, so he feels guilty about that'. For her father, guilt lies in the gap between the time he would like with his family and the time he must give to work. Melinda is not at all confused about why he works when he does.

Buying time:
Can 'stuff' substitute for parental time?

Many parents attempt to substitute stuff and commercialised family experiences for time. It does not work well with children. They don't mind getting the stuff, but they don't see it as a substitute for parental time. When invited to choose between compensating *time* together or *stuff* (like a CD), Sebastian, 17, chooses 'both the present and the time going out together', 'because they're giving you something as well as time ... Two for the price of one'. But he is clear that the gift without the time is inferior and is not his choice.

Some young people clearly feel, and regret, the distance that results from not enough time with a parent, often as a result of long or unsocial hours. Two examples illustrate this with poignancy. In both cases the long-term closeness of daughter-father bonds are made precarious, one in a higher-income area for an 11-year-old, and the other in a lower-income area for a 16-year-old. At Leafy Primary, Brittany describes her father's truck driving hours and how they affect her: 'He drops me and my sister down to school at around 7.30 and he comes back home at around 12 at night'. She says he feels guilty:

> Because he works full-time and he knows that he can't spend time with me and he knows that I really like to spend time with him. And once I had a lot of trouble and I didn't come to school for a couple of days because I just wanted to stay with my Dad as long as I could. (Brittany, 12, Leafy Primary)

> Interviewer: What do you like about being with Dad?

> My Dad, he understands me better than my Mum ... And I always know that if I have something to talk about I can always tell my Dad.

> Interviewer: And when you say your Dad feels guilty, how can you tell?

> Because once I saw him crying and talking to my Mum, saying that he didn't want to work at the job he's working at now because he knew he was missing out on my younger years and he knows that when I grow up I might go out of the house and he won't have a chance to share as much time as he could have.

> Interviewer: Does he do anything to make up for not being there?

> Yeah. Sometimes on the weekend he takes me out, just me and my Dad, and we go out to dinner or we just go out to late night shopping.

> Interviewer: And what do you think about him making up to you like that?

> I think it's good because I get a chance to talk to him.

Interviewer: If you could choose between a new thing, like a CD, and time with him, what would you choose?

Spending time with him.

Brittany does not hesitate in her answer. She wants her missing father and, like him, she doesn't think that time later will substitute for time now. She sees the quality of her close relationship connected to time with him. She fights for time with him, 'staying away from school for a couple of days' to be with him. She sees his sadness.

At Strive High, Audrey, who is 16 years old, reflects on her relationship with her father, both when he ran a driving school when she was younger, and now that he is retired:

> He felt guilty because I know I got spoilt really, really badly when I was little, by him, and I remember I hardly ever saw him. It was usually just me and my Mum at home, but then when he retired my Mum went to work and I still see her cause she's usually only school hours and my Dad's at home. I think my Dad feels guilty because he missed out a bit on my childhood when I was growing up, so maybe that's the reason why I'm not that close to him. I'm close to my Mum. (Audrey, 16, Strive High)

Audrey, having missed his presence as a child, has not become close to her father later in her adolescence despite his full-time presence at home in retirement. Her father's strategy of substituting stuff for his time has not worked; it has not 'made up' for his time. Indeed, she says she didn't need it and is critical about being 'really, really' spoilt as a consequence:

> When I was little, you don't need all this stuff. I had heaps, the handbags, all these hats and dresses and stuff. I was really, really, really spoilt by him when I was little … I had everything that I wanted when I was a baby. (Audrey, 16, Strive High)

At Comfort High, Mark's mother brings back little presents and things when she comes home from work trips: 'It's not necessary. An act of good fun' he says. Susie at Comfort High agrees: 'They try to give you things and they're all nice'. She likes this situation: 'It's nice to make them feel guilty! So that Mum becomes 'overly nice'.

In leafy higher-income Sydney, Aislan also identifies the purchase of goods as compensation and an attempt to materialise love:

> I actually think he covers up his guilt with material things. You know he feels guilty for not spending time with us, but he will make it up to us by buying us something ... Like, we just got this big screen TV and I think it might be his way of saying, 'Oh, I'm not with you, but kind of look what my job is doing for us, we can get this stuff'. But I think we all understand that he has to work for us to have those things. I think all of us are old enough to understand that now. (Aislan, 16, Leafy High)

Aislan thinks it is 'kind of cool' getting things. She is now so accustomed to her father working a lot and receiving gifts as compensation that she says: 'Honestly, I've just become so used to it that I don't really know what I think of it'. When asked her advice for parents who compensate for not being with their children, she said that she would probably suggest to parents who are 'never there' that they spend more time with their kids because 'it can affect them'. In the same Leafy High school, Ellie's Dad 'wants to spoil us' when they get together 'because we haven't seen him for so long and he wants us to know that he's still there and he can still do things for us'.

In the country, Judith's Dad who works very long hours is a soft touch for stuff because of his guilt. Judith sometimes works on the weakness:

> I'll get [shopping] out of Dad cause he'll feel guilty and I go 'Come on Dad, I need it and I want it'. But getting it out of Mum [who works part-time] – can't do it. (Judith, 18, Country High)

Other parents who are away a lot, bring gifts home:

> Well, when my Dad isn't there he brings home presents to make up for not being there ... just little things, he buys me clothes and sunnies ... He bought me a watch. He just buys me little things but they're good. (Jade, 16, Comfort High)

Parents often make up for not being there by spending special time with children and doing things that involve both time and money:

Well, sometimes if he feels guilty he normally tries to make it up to us and then we play, we go places and stuff ... He takes me shopping and to the beach if I want to go, or the pools, or the movies. (Hayley, 12, Strive Primary)

Mum doesn't really [do anything] but Dad would like to take us out to speedways or something or to the cinemas or something like that. (Candy, 17, Country High)

Dad doesn't but Mum does. She takes friends to movies, friends to holidays. Takes me to movies. (Kelly, 11, Struggle Primary)

These strategies vary between city and country. In the country group where most mothers are at home during school hours, young people recognise parental guilt and see the main compensating strategy as time and physical contact. They are more likely to discuss guilt in relation to absent fathers than mothers, and this guilt is less likely to manifest itself in commodities or spending. It is more likely to result in an apology, a hug or time in an activity they like.

What do young people think of parental guilt and compensation?

Young people enjoy the compensations that flow from parental guilt whether in the form of time or stuff or both. Where there is no open recognition or contrition about absence, some express resentment and hostility and others define their own futures *against* the inadequacies that they see in their parents' working lives: 'I will *never* work like him. I will *never* marry someone who works like him'.

Young people like parental acknowledgement of regret about missing significant events or being absent for long periods: 'he just tells me that he is sorry'. Many do not look for anything more. Many love family time and being 'all together'. Others are not averse to the fruit of parental guilt, whether time or money or both. This is less obvious among older young people (16 to18 years) in Sydney ('we don't really want to hang with our folks so much any more') than among those in lower-income areas, the country or younger people. However, significant numbers of young people enjoy compensating time and accept it as a good 'make up' substitute.

Young people especially like 'experiential compensation' strategies that give them *time and money*, going out for a family meal, to the movies or shopping with a parent (and their wallet). In general, 'make up' compensating time with parents and the whole family is preferred. If it comes *with* consumption, well and good, but the *time together* element of this package is critical. While many children giggled or laughed about the stuff that parental guilt bought them, they obviously preferred the time. When Jade was asked whether she thought her Dad should buy gifts to compensate for being away, she said:

> Oh, yeah, why not? But I'd rather him be there than buy presents, · but there is not much I can do about it. (Jade, 16, Comfort High)

Jade would have preferred that neither the guilt nor the compensation were necessary. Smithy in Leafy High in Sydney felt the same:

> My Dad always apologises for not seeing me much and ... sometimes he will call me at the last minute, and [say] 'I'm sorry I can't see you' and he'll try to make it up to me somehow ... He'll take me out to dinner ... [I say] 'Don't worry about it'. (Smithy, 17, Leafy High)

> Interviewer: So when a parent uses a making up strategy like that, do you think they should?

> I don't know. It shows they care. I don't really ever take up the offer ... I'd prefer them to make that effort because it shows that they actually do care, and I like that. I'd prefer them to show up in the first place.

Guilt, time and money: The cure becomes the disease

From these discussions with young people in higher and lower income areas, many perceive parental guilt about how their work affects time with their children. However, the perception of guilt is far from universal. In cases where parental work does not intrude overly upon family time, or parents are reconciled to the necessity of work patterns, young people are less likely to perceive parental guilt. However, in many households, parents' jobs do intrude and such reconciliation is not complete. In these households, guilt is obvious to children. It especially affects parents who work long or unsocial hours or spend extended periods away from their children. Both mothers and fathers are affected. Often one parent will not feel guilt while the other clearly does.

The signs of guilt are obvious to young people and go beyond the symptoms of tiredness, injury and stress that afflict many parents as a direct consequence of work. They arise from a mismatch between the way parents *are as workers* and the way they *want to be as parents*. Many young people see parents' jobs and hours as immovable objects. They accept this, but they are affected by the guilt they notice, and are concerned about their parents' feelings of guilt. Others find it annoying, over-played and some resist the intensified, compensating parenting that it sometimes stimulates.

There are several common parental reactions to their feelings of guilt, in the eyes of young people. The response of 'talk and apology' is utilised in both high- and low-income households and is more common in country than city households. Many young people respond positively to the straightforward acknowledgement of regret or that their parents' preferences for time with the family are being frustrated. They appreciate the information and the discussion about the household implications. Children and young people remember when their parents have expressed their regret, sadness or frustration about missing them and can readily quote these exchanges. Some young people prefer that this verbal acknowledgement not be 'over done'.

In addition to talk, many parents spend extra time with their children. They go to the park, kick a ball or hang out with them. Some make sure they spend the weekend together. No child in our study had anything negative to say about these times, but a few of the older ones felt the 'closeness' timetable was set by parents, was artificial or too intense or cut across their own schedule or time. However, most young people, even older teenagers, appreciated these special times.

Much more common than simple verbal acknowledgements of guilt or make-up time are 'time and stuff' strategies on the part of parents, who make up by trying to spend both extra time and money on their families. Young people quite like this 'two for the price of one' approach. If they have to make a choice, however, they choose time rather than stuff. The substitution of stuff does not compensate.

Many young people have a high level of understanding about the necessities and demands placed upon their parents. A large proportion enjoy make-up time but they are not always on the lookout for material compensation and some are sceptical about it, seeing it as unnecessary.

Some young people see how commodified compensation contributes to a work and spend cycle. It is obvious to 11-year-olds like Danielle:

My Mum always tries to work in the morning, so she gets more time with me and then she always feels guilty when she is working in the afternoon ... (Danielle, 11, Leafy Primary)

Interviewer: So does your Mum do anything when she feels guilty?

Yeah, she sometimes takes me shopping and the other day she took me to find my dress for the formal and then she spends lots.

Interviewer: And what do you think about her spending on you when she feels guilty?

Kind of good, but I think she should save some of her money so she won't have to work that much.

Interviewer: If you could choose between a new thing, like a CD, and time with her, what would you choose?

More time.

Danielle sees that her mother's efforts to compensate for her guilt lock her into more work and she would prefer a different approach. Danielle's preference for time is quickly and emphatically volunteered, just like her classmate Brittany, who says that being 'really, really, really' spoiled is no substitute for her father spending time with her. Neither hesitates in their assessment.

As Danielle understands, this 'compensatory consumption' drives new levels of work to pay for the compensation. Parental guilt acts as a stimulus to inessential consumption like meals out, movies, trips, 'stuff' – exactly as advertisers and corporations observe and work to expand. They are on firm ground when they stimulate parental guilt. The implication that guilt can be satiated by stuff and spending finds ready support among parents who hope they are materialising love, even if unconsciously. The suggestion that stuff signals love and can substitute for it has many parental supporters.

In this way, parental guilt feeds consumption, creating fertile commercial terrain. However, the expression of 'contrition through spending' appears to work better for parents and the market than for young people. Children are not so convinced about the merits of the trade. Many want their parents' time, not compensatory stuff. Some see it as cool, but most we spoke with do not actively seek it and few manipulate guilt to get things. It therefore seems sensible for parents to avoid compensatory spending in favour of 'talk and time' where possible. For many young people 'stuff' does not deliver and, most importantly, more stuff and spending requires more money to finance it and consequently more hours of paid parental work. The 'cure' becomes the disease.

Many young people are aware of the slippery fraud of offering stuff for time. As Smithy puts it: buying the stuff 'shows they care' but, like most, he prefers the time because for him 'it shows that they actually *do* care'. The 'monetarised apology' lacks authenticity.

In this respect, our smiling television mother with her margarine and clean football clothes is an exercise in emotional fraud: she promises the successful substitution of products for maternal time. This might work well for the retail market and its commercial bottom lines, but the human appetites of guilt and desire for time are not so readily fed. 'Things' do not substitute for parental time. Shared experiences might – but the kinds that young people value do not depend on 'experiential consumption' so much as the spending of time and conversation.

And our smiling advertising mother is inadequate on another score: she cannot make up for the father who is missing from the kitchen and home. It is this figure, whose long hours often make him the more absent parent, who many young people miss, and no amount of 'special' compensatory stuff can quite make up for him. Indeed it can 'spoil' children, as some observe. What is more, a lot of father-time later in childhood does not necessarily make up for much less of him early on. Finally, the work-guilt-spending cycle is less pernicious it seems, where parents get a satisfactory match between how they feel they should work and the reality of their work patterns. Where they must work differently than they want, their guilt is exacerbated, and their commodification strategies most active and perhaps least satisfactory. The labour market both creates guilt and offers a means towards its commodified salve, but in doing so it feeds more time-taking work. It feeds and eats simultaneously.

CHAPTER 6

Future work and households: Transitions and sharing?

The demographic future of Australia is under the microscope, with predictions of declining population growth (resulting from low fertility rates, constrained immigration and growing life expectancy). Unforeseen events aside, this combination will result in rising dependency rates and budget strain as taxation revenue struggles to meet the costs associated with an aging population in the presence of a smaller active labour force. According to the ABS, the median age of Australia's population will probably increase from 36 years in 2001-02 to between 40 and 42 years in 2020-21, and to between 46 and 50 years in 2050-51 (ABS Cat No 1301.0, 2005).

How will young people's future work and reproduction plans play out in this environment? In this chapter we consider two issues: first, young people's plans for work and children and, second, the allocation of domestic work that they anticipate in their adult households. Our focus group discussions suggest that many young people already have plans for their own work and home lives as they leave study. Most expect to have children. Some, especially young women, have clear ideas about the number of children they will have, and readily discuss the days they will work and what periods of leave they will take off from work. All the young women we spoke with anticipate working for money, although many expect to take some or primary responsibility for children, generally with their partner's active support. Many young women adopt a 'time off from paid work' approach to their projected parental care and work futures: that is, they expect to hold paid jobs both before and after having children, and to fit their work and motherhood together over time. Maternity leave is an integral part of many young women's expectations. Many plan to care for their children on an equal basis with their partners. However, their plans for children depend upon their economic and housing security. Many see being 'established' in terms of housing as a critical precursor to having a family.

On the whole, however, they expect to study, work, earn, reproduce, and then return to work – in that order, and have a lot of fun along the way. Young women do not anticipate economic dependency on a man.

Many young men anticipate work patterns that are different from their own fathers', and define their plans against their own experience as children. They talk of spending a considerable amount of time with their children, taking care not to miss weekends and evenings or to let their jobs overwhelm their parenting. They know what a workaholic is, and they don't plan on being one.

Of course youthful expectations and intentions are a long way from future realities. These young people will find themselves in unexpected jobs and household types, and larger and smaller families than they predict. They will divorce, recouple and be sole parents. Many will probably spend parts of their lives in sole-households, distant from their family of origin. However, they take to their life trajectory a set of assumptions, intentions and aspirations. These may prove fragile in the face of institutional reality and life's fortunes. Nonetheless, it is useful to weigh them against present institutional realities. While public policy can do little about life's fortunes, it can meet predictable life events and transitions in better or worse ways.

Having a job

Young people expect to work for much of their lives. All the young men and women we spoke to plan to have jobs when they finish studying. None said they planned to depend on someone else in an ongoing way rather than have a job of their own. 'Breadwinners' and 'carers' were not concepts they used – except perhaps when children were very small, or to reject them as Judith does, saying that men now share earning with their partners and should therefore also fairly share housework. Most of those we spoke with could name an occupation they were interested in, and most envisaged a partner.

They are very positive about their future jobs. They antici-pate being skilled workers who will enjoy their future work. Given steady increases in young people's appetite for qualifi-cations, especially degrees, their anticipation of being skilled workers is not misplaced. In 2004, 27 per cent of 25-34 year olds in Australia held a bachelor degree or better, almost double the level in 1994 (ABS Cat No 6227.0, 2004). Young women have especially embraced education, particularly higher education. In 2004, women made up 55.3 per cent of enrolments in bachelor degree or higher degree studies in Australia, up from 45.5 per cent in 1981 (ABS Cat No 6227.0, 2004, p 9; Preston and Burgess 2003, p 503).

Many young people have witnessed their parents' positive enjoyment of aspects of their paid work, especially their social connections and friendships and the pleasure they take from applying their skills and experience, and making a contribution. As we have considered in Chapter 4, many young people are also aware of negative spillover arising from their parents' jobs, but most hope to take positive pleasure from their own future jobs.

Despite a few concerned about being 'locked up' in a job later in life, most emphasise the importance of enjoying their future work. For example, Vanessa describes her Dad, in the insurance industry, as a workaholic, but she has no intention of following his example:

> It's his whole life ... he puts so much emphasis on it, and from seeing that, I don't reckon I'm going to get locked up in my work. Hopefully I'll find something that I want to do, so it won't be like working. It will be just like having fun. (Vanessa, 16, Leafy High)

Young people in both high and lower socio-economic areas share the hope of finding rewarding work and a job they will enjoy. Many expect to be skilled. Where they have had a 'workaholic' or very hard-working parent, they often define their future work patterns *against* those of that parent, hoping for work that allows them to have fun.

Plans for children

The overwhelming majority of young people we spoke with are also planning to have children, in line with national and international survey evidence of reproductive intentions.

Eighty-four of the 93 in focus groups expect to have children. Some are very specific ('two girls and one boy'), while others are vague and some mention concerns about money and the difficulty of affording children. All of the younger children (10-12 years old) expect to have children, while some older children, most of them women, were ambivalent.

Of those young people who do not readily anticipate having children, one boy was definite about his decision, while two young men and six young women were unsure, saying 'maybe'. Only two of the nine who were uncertain about having children or had decided against it, were from lower socio-economic areas. The remainder were from higher socio-economic areas, in line with evidence about lower fertility outcomes in higher socio-economic groups. Uncertainty was higher among young women: six of the nine who were uncertain or negative were female and all of these were from higher socio-economic areas.

Large surveys in Australia confirm that only small proportions of young people do not expect to have children. Surveys of people of childbearing age in Australia in 1981 and 1996 suggest that only 3 to 7 per cent did not intend to have children. The intention is lower among those with qualifications and no religious affiliation (Weston and Qu 2001). The evidence suggests that some of these intentions will be thwarted by reality. McDonald's analysis of the Negotiating the Life Course survey shows that among Australian women with post-school qualifications the expectation of having children drops sharply as they age and their 'expectations are modified by the reality of institutional constraints' (McDonald 1998, p 2). On average, Australian women 20-24 years old expect to have more than two children (2.33), but they fall short of this, with the gap being wider among more highly-educated women (McDonald 1998).

More recent results from the HILDA survey find that expectations of childlessness are increasing among young people, with 24 per cent of 18 to 24-year-olds in the 2001 HILDA wave expecting to remain childless, compared to 17 per cent of 25 to 39-year-olds (Fisher 2002, p 8). Childlessness among women is associated with higher levels of education, paid work (especially full-time work), income, employment satisfaction, and greater emphasis on work and employment (Fisher 2002). They are also less likely to believe that they have 'a secure future in their jobs' or be satisfied with the hours they work in their job: for women, both labour market insecurity and a poor fit between preferred hours and those worked are associated with more childlessness (Fisher 2002, p 10). Both women and men who expect to remain childless are less likely to own or be buying their own home.

The gap between intention and outcomes around family size has been much debated. However, the rate of childlessness is expected to continue to rise in successive generations: estimates place it between 20 and 28 per cent over the life-cycle among those who are 20-24 years old at present (ABS Cat No 3222.0, 2000; Merlo and Rowland 2000). Given that the proportion of those who *intend* to be childless is lower, the gap between fertility expectations and outcomes is sizeable. And the fall in fertility cannot be traced to intentions alone: these remain firmly in favour of having children, it seems, at least until the late teens and the early twenties.

Preferences in favour of having children among our focus group participants seem likely to be eroded by experience, and to result in unanticipated levels of childlessness. Early in their lives, young people do not have the 'one-in-four' preference for childlessness that may emerge as their reality. The robustness of the gap between *predicted* and *preferred* fertility, and the factors that might explain it, are of considerable interest to the current fertility debate. It is clear that many of these young people will await the end of initial education, travel and career establishment, as well as finding housing security, before having children. A growing number of women in this cohort will have higher education qualifications and be in paid work – in many cases for a decade – before they have children. Both of these factors are associated with higher rates of childlessness and smaller family size. The pursuit of qualifications and labour market participation increase the age at which young women, in particular, have their first child, which is in turn associated with a lower fertility rate.

In the US, Shapiro Barrera has argued that young women are reacting to their mother's juggle of work and care, in favour of being home-based mothers supported by well-off partners (Shapiro Barrera 2004). In our study there are few signs of this. Although a couple of young women were concerned that their working mothers have little time to themselves, no young women we spoke to had plans to rely upon a high-paid partner/earner in an ongoing breadwinner arrangement. At this point in their lives at least, the next generation of young women are not planning to find a wealthy breadwinner as a way of avoiding a work/family juggle. It seems, on the contrary, that many young people are well aware that relationships and household shape can change, making long-term reliance on a partner's earnings precarious.

Uncertainty and security

Some factors contributing to declining fertility are evident from young people's discussion about having children. Many are tentative about future parenting, even those who expect to have children. They mention financial concerns, a desire for stability before having kids, concern about the loss of time for themselves or with their partners, risk of loss of their careers (especially among women), and concern about the end of 'partying' through parenthood (as one young man put it). Financial and security issues are especially to the fore, reinforcing the HILDA survey results showing a link between security and family plans: in the 2001 wave fewer women who were childless agreed that they had a secure future in their jobs than women who expect to have children (the difference was smaller but in the same direction among men). As one of our focus group participants put it: 'You need to be established first'.

Mike from Leafy High on Sydney's north shore was very clear about financial issues. His father had told him that each of the three kids had cost 'about $250,000'. Mike was initially scathing about having children because he wanted to 'be rich' instead. Even he, however, felt that children were not entirely out of his picture. However, like many young people, especially those in Sydney, he was concerned about money:

> Basically you wouldn't want to have kids for the first few years of your adult life because you need to get yourself started, you know what I mean – house, wife, furniture, all that other stuff – and when you've got kids, where are you going to put them? You've got to pay for babysitting, pay for all this crap. (Mike, 17, Leafy High)

In the same Sydney higher-income group, Smithy plans to defer having kids until he has 'done partying' which he knows he can do for a lot longer than his female peers: 'until I'm 50'. Young women in the same northern Sydney group mention concerns about being financially secure before having children, and young women from the western suburbs of Sydney agree, as did young men like Jack from western Adelaide:

> I don't want to start too early … Anytime after 25 is good. Get yourself settled down first. And then think about it. (Jack, 15, Struggle High)

A number of young people expect to make their work and fertility decisions mutually with their partners, and this will affect their choices:

> I'd have kids. I don't know I'd probably still want to work if I had a job which I liked obviously, and, as for my partner, I would not want to make any kind of decision [for her]. (Claus, 15, Struggle High)

Claus and his partner would work it out together, and William concurred, wondering whether he needed children if he and his partner were already happy:

> Very much the same as Claus: make decisions together. That's if I was to have children, which – I don't know – they just seem a bit too much. I don't know. Really they become a financial issue … And if you're happy in your life as it is with your partner, and with a job if you love it, which I hope I would, why would you need the extra satisfaction for raising new life? Be quite happy [as you are]. (William, 15, Struggle High)

Most of these young people – at least early in life – have an expectation of having both a paid job (which they expect to enjoy) and children. This is fairly consistent between sexes and across income groups. Some hesitancy about having children is already evident among young women as they approach their twenties, and among those in higher socio-economic areas and higher-cost cities like Sydney. This suggests that combining paid work with care of children is going to be a significant issue for a new generation of workers and carers, most of whom anticipate a dual-earner couple household.

Having children: Juggling jobs and care

We asked the young people in our focus groups to consider how they would care for children given their ambitions to combine paid work with raising a family. Five approaches emerged, as set out in Table 6.1.

Table 6.1. Young people's plans for care of children (per cent)

	Males	Females	Persons
Sharing between partners	39	40	40
Intermittent maternal care	15	28	23
Traditional maternal care	36	16	24
External care by family or formal institutions	9	14	12
Paternal care	0	2	1
Total	100	100	100

Note: Total number of young people whose plans for care of children were known = 83.

Source: Focus groups. This table excludes ten young people whose preferences are unknown. While these are the dominant forms of care indicated through discussions, many young people plan to supplement their main option with others, for example, shared parental care might be backed up with formal external childcare (see discussion below).

This is a very small sample but it is suggestive about future care patterns. For the 83 young people whose preferences are known, the most commonly mentioned form of care is shared parental care. This is the preference of 40 per cent of both young men and young women in the group.

A similar sized group of young men would prefer traditional maternal care: that is, their female partners at home caring for their children while they work (the male-breadwinner model).

A much smaller group of young men have a preference for 'intermittent' maternal care: that is, their wives working and taking leave around young children and work, 'backed up' by male partners, childcare or extended family. This represents a 'modified traditional' household type.

Similar proportions of young women share young men's main preference for shared care. However, there is not an equivalent female group with a preference for traditional maternal care: only a small number of young women nominate traditional maternal care as their preference (eight of the 50 young women). They are more likely to see themselves as intermittent carers, who take time off work with babies for example, and perhaps work part-time in the preschool years or rely on the support of their own mothers and childcare.

Care by others outside the family is less preferred by both sexes with most young people favouring familial care, though a few would seek to combine this with some external care. Only one young woman expects her male partner to care for children while she works, and no young man envisages this.

Shared care between partners: how it might work

The sharing approach to work and care involved contributions from both partners. It might be accomplished by alternating care with a partner, or by both taking time out of paid work, as Smithy imagines:

> I think it will pretty much depend on the financial situation. When I have kids I would love to be able to take a few years off and not work and spend it with my kids and with my wife and just starting a family and being there for my kids for the first few years of their life. But then I'd definitely go back to work when they start school,

but I'd make sure I was there for them in the evenings, help them with their homework and on the weekends, take them to sporting activities and all that, and when they're older and think I'm just boring and not cool, let them do their own thing, but still try and sneak in some quality time. (Smithy, 17, Leafy High)

Adam has similar hopes:

When they're young you could probably try not to work as much, so someone is there most of the time to help. When they're older you can work more after they've developed I suppose. (Adam, 16, Country High)

Some preferences are contingent. Smithy says that if the financial situation is right, his preferences *may* be relevant. Similarly, Adam will 'try' not to work too much. The provisional nature of the preferences of these young men is echoed by others, suggesting that Adam and Smithy are aware that their preferences could be constrained by finances or workplaces that make achieving them difficult. These young men, like many others, are keen to be active fathers. However, they plan to *lean against the door* to workplace flexibility (for example, seeking time off their jobs or part-time work) but where it does not fall open – and they expect it may not – they are ready to concede. Their participation in caring is *contingent* – '*If* I can do it'- and fragile preferences may fail in the face of even moderate resistance. The default is female care.

Some young men do not think that they can reasonably rely upon their partners to stay at home and 'do it all' and, like Smithy and Adam, express a strong desire to be active fathers. Kevin from the country plans to spend time with his children and to share care and housework, on the grounds of fairness and mutual decision-making:

If the children are younger, you probably want to spend time with them. I guess later you wouldn't put it on her that she has to sit at home and do all the housework. If she's got a passion or a desire to do a job, that she wants to do, then fair enough, she can make that decision herself. You can't rule over her and say 'You stay at home and do this housework before the end of the day, look after the kids'. You've got to share the workload so she can do what she wants. (Kevin, 17, Country High)

In Sydney, Peter also favours shared care, but on the grounds that children need 'both genders':

> I believe that both Mum and Dad should cut down [to] the same amount of hours so it's not just one side giving all their love and then just the Dad or the Mum on the side: they come in every night or something. I don't think that really works. I think while they are growing up they need both sides of genders put into the kids. (Peter, 16, Leafy High)

In Adelaide Karl, a younger boy, wants to share responsibility. He 'hopes' for flexible working time, both for himself and his partner:

> I suppose I would work and try and work hard so I can have flexible time so I could spend time with kids and if my wife does work I would hope it would be flexible so she could also spend time with the kids while I'm working and vice versa. And hopefully not make them walk home from school too much. (Karl, 11, Comfort Primary)

Zac, 12, is also unsure about how much flexibility he will have to undertake the kind of alternating care he would like: 'If I could, I'd try and work when she's not working'. At Strive Primary, three of the five young people plan to share care, while one expects to work while her husband stays home because 'I don't like being stuck at home sometimes'. Lee, a young woman in the same group, intends to work on weekends while her husband works during the week, with both doing housework when at home. Koco, 12, also proposes to alternate both paid and unpaid work.

Plans to share care are common in both Sydney and Adelaide and across income groups:

> I would work and my children would be at school or at a childcare place, and then my husband would work in the mornings and then we'd have the nights together. (Danielle, 11, Leafy Primary)

> If I had children under five then I'd probably just rearrange the times if my husband and I were both working. We'd have separate times so one of us was always home with the kids unless they were at kindy or something. (Sarah, 16, Comfort High)

Many young people from higher-income areas plan to maintain a connection to the labour market, believing that women outside it are bored. They want to use their skills and education, earn and enjoy paid work. The effects of such preferences are already clearly evident among older cohorts: educated Australian women who are 20-40 years old and live in higher-income households are already more likely to have smaller families, delayed motherhood and higher levels of childlessness. Danielle and Sarah's plans to interleave care around their jobs, and to share it with their partners, reflect their desire to avoid boredom, make the most of their education and have a career. These concerns affect the timing of their children, as Amy says:

> The same as Sarah. I wouldn't want to drop my job completely ... because after studying I wouldn't want to drop my whole career just for kids. So I probably won't have kids heaps early. (Amy, 17, Comfort High)

Amy's group go on to discuss the dilemma when 'you love your job and you have kids':

> What if that's your ideal job and you want kids? (Susie, 16, Comfort High)

> It depends how much you love it. (Amy, 17, Comfort High)

> And if you can't get your job back, then you're screwed. You have no money and then, you might get a job you don't really like. (Susie, 16, Comfort High)

> Interviewer: So it depends on how much you like your job?

> And how much you like your children! (Channel, 17, Comfort High)

Melissa at Leafy High in Sydney does not want to 'give up all my dreams of a career because of children'. Most of the young women from higher-income areas intend to have professional jobs and either to share housework or find outside help with it. They are less certain about having children and they are much more concerned about these factors than young women from lower-income areas. They also have much lower expectations of help from their own parents with childcare.

Intermittent maternal care: How it might work

Many young men in these groups think that their female partner will look after their children 'around' her job, and some young women also adopt an 'intermittent' approach to care. For example, Ellie at Leafy High, who loves cars and expects to marry a mechanic, plans to follow her mother's path of being at home when her children are little and then doing part-time work when they go to school, working up to full-time. She assumes her husband will be working full-time: 'he'll be doing the cars'. When it comes to housework, Ellie is clear that her husband will not be doing any and she is planning on hiring a cleaner.

Many young women at Strive Primary expect to work 'around' their children, and they expect their own mothers to take over when they return to work. Binh would work out which days she and her partner are able to devote to care and 'when we're doing our job, we can give it to a relative to look after'. Emma, 11, would 'make up a roster or timetable so then it will be easy and our parents will look after the kids'.

Young women have clear ideas about maternity leave:

> I'll have a year off or something so I can look after them. (Sarah, 11, Strive Primary)

> I would be working and he could work as well, and then my Mum could look after the kids as well … When I first have the kids I can just be on maternity leave for a year or something so I could look after them. (Haley, 12, Strive Primary)

These expectations, if they rely on paid leave, are in advance of current Australian standards, which give a year of unpaid leave to those with at least 12 months continuous service with their employers. Paid leave is available to only around a third of Australian women, most of them in the public sector or working for large employers, and usually of only a few weeks duration in the private sector.

This intermittent plan for care places initial responsibility at least with wives or mothers. In these households, maternal care is assumed to be the automatic default if men cannot get the flexibility they seek. For example, Rove hopes to alternate care with his partner, though if that is not possible, his wife will do it:

> If I could work part-time then I would look after the kid or kids
> sometimes, and my wife would look after [them]. But if I was full-
> time, my wife would probably look after them. (Rove, 12, Comfort
> Primary)

Thus, Rove's plans are contingent upon flexibility at work, and
he anticipates that he may not be able to get part-time work.
Many such plans are reliant upon flexibility at work for *both*
partners, but if it fails to materialise, then, once again, the
default is maternal care. The implication is that, without
improved workplace flexibility for women *and* men, maternal
care will persist as the dominant type, regardless of maternal
paid work patterns and regardless of the predilections of men
and women. Thus the preference is shaped and made contingent
by institutional possibility. It is likely that institutional
limitations in workplaces, labour law and so on will dominate
these preferences if current patterns are any indication. Young
men's wishes to be active fathers and share care may be wistful
hopes in the face of realities.

Traditional maternal care: How it might work

As we have seen, young men are more than twice as likely as
young women to nominate the traditional breadwinner model
of care. Bob, 11, is clear that his wife will be the primary carer,
though he hopes to 'be there' for his kids 'as much as possible'
and he hopes that half-time care might be a possibility for him.
Sebastian opts for the traditional, but knows that he may need
luck on his side ('fingers crossed', as he says):

> Fingers crossed – in my situation – I'd probably, with the kids, let
> my wife be at home, be a housewife so when I come back from
> work she'd have the food ready, the house nice and clean just for
> me to relax and spend time with my kids and all that. (Sebastian,
> 17, Strive High)

Even Sebastian, however, wants time with his children – in a
clean house and after everyone has been fed.

Some young women also prefer traditional maternal care
when children are very young:

> I'd like to be able to stay home with the kids when they're young, in the first years of school, so I can take them to school and be there when they're vulnerable and little. And then have my husband working. (Sarah, 15, Struggle High)

However, such acceptance generally anticipates some maternal attachment to the labour market. At Comfort High, Ann doesn't want to use childcare. Her children could be looked after by whichever partner 'actually wants to' but in the end it will probably be her:

> I would be happy enough to stay home if I could be secure that my job would still be there. But if it wasn't going to still be there, I'd just have to work part-time or something. (Ann, 16, Comfort High)

Like others in her group, she is concerned that her job remains open; if it is not, then she will work part-time. Once again, her preferences foreshadow institutional limitations. In this case, refusal of extended leave would keep Ann in the labour market part-time when she would prefer to be at home full-time. Amanda is also concerned to keep her foothold at work: women who lose this foothold 'get really bored ... Work fills that up' (Amanda, 16, Comfort High).

Most girls and young women in this study are clear that they will be in the workforce and will only be taking short breaks when their children are babies or very young. Their choices will underpin a continuing rise in the workforce participation rates of women with babies and young children.

A consistent preference for an 'intermittent' approach to child rearing years is evident, whether their own mothers worked or not, and in both higher- and lower-income areas. For example, Amy in Adelaide plans to organise her work around her children, and is committed to putting her qualifications to work, and Melinda from a lower-income area in Sydney's west is also committed to a career around her children – both in the interests of stability and a life 'of my own':

> I'd take a year off maybe to get settled in and used to it, then I'd go back to part time if I had a job beforehand. My partner would be full-time so for stableness and you need money to support the

family so I'd be at work. I'd still want a life of your own, not just the kids, so I guess I'd work. (Melinda, 16, Strive High)

External care by family or formal institutions: How it might work

Most young people felt that it was important that one of the parents or grandparents be with the child when they were very young, although views about childcare were conditioned by experience itself, as discussed in the next chapter:

I'd just try and use friends and family. (Judith, 18, Country High)

Many would only consider childcare as a 'last resort'.

Oh yeah, [I'd use childcare if] I had to, I suppose, yeah. If myself and my Mrs was working ... (Robert, 17, Country High)

Interviewer: If you had to ... ?

Yeah, probably wouldn't want to though. Yeah, it would be last option. (Robert,17, Country High)

Interviewer: Last option after?

My parents. (Robert, 17, Country High)

Many nominate grandmothers or very close friends as their preferred care option, some believing that this would be good for grandparents because 'They will get to spend more time with the grandkids' (William, 15, Struggle High). For example, Audrey plans to work full-time like her partner while her mother cares for the children:

If I ever had kids, I don't think I'd even take a year off, I'd take what I needed and go back to work. And I would be full-time, I wouldn't stay at home ... . I'd be a 9-5 worker, my husband will be 9-5. (Audrey, 16, Strive High)

Interviewer: And what [would be] happening with your child?

My Mum. ... Yeah, I've already worked it all out. ... No, she doesn't know yet.

Other young women are also already planning this for their mothers, optimistic that they will readily offer:

> If I decide to be a physiotherapist I'll be working a lot, so I'll have the weekend off, so during that time, if I have a partner, we would work, my Mum would be the Nan, she said she will mind the children for me. (Sarah, 11, Strive Primary)

Young people, especially 10 to 12-year-olds from lower socio-economic and non-English speaking backgrounds, have high expectations of support from their own parents when they have children. Some believe they already have agreement from their parents for this back-up. Some of these plans are based on experience: many young people in western Sydney in our focus groups spoke of the role of extended family in their own households.

However, these plans depend upon several factors. First, grandparents must be available for childcare, rather than in the labour market themselves. In fact, the workforce participation rates of many older Australians are likely to rise in coming years. Secondly, grandparent care relies on geographically stable, extended families. The high mobility of Australian households will disrupt this for many. Thirdly, grandparents will need to make themselves available. Many may have other plans after years in the labour market. They may not be easily recruited into regular and sometimes extensive hours of grand-childcare. Indeed, qualitative research among Australian adults suggests that some are already resentful of involuntary grandparent care and the element of conscription they experience (Pocock 2003). In this situation, many young people may find themselves using non-familial childcare more than they anticipate.

Non-traditional male care: How it might work

Only one young woman planned to keep her job while her male partner looked after their children. Susie plans to be a politician – perhaps President of a republican Australia – and to have one child:

> [In my imagined future] I have a job and my husband can stay home and look after the kids. (Susie, 16, Comfort High)

The group discussed what will happen if he can't cook: 'Well he'll just have to learn how to cook. Or I'll marry Jamie Oliver!'

Susie agrees it would be hard for her as a political leader when she has her child:

> It would be a bit hard [to work part-time] ... Can I just quit for a year? But I want my job back immediately after!

No young men expected to stay at home on an ongoing basis, although some, like Matt, 12, anticipate it for a limited period or believe that working from home might be an option: 'I'd like to work at home so I could have time with my kids, whenever they want, help them out'.

Several others agreed with Matt, seeing value in working part-time or school hours so they see their children and share care with their partners. Olaf from Struggle Primary is very keen to be a full-time father, though sharing care by alternating work with his partner would also be 'really good'. Jack at Struggle High is clear that his plans to share care are dependent upon whether 'you can adjust the hours to allow that to happen'. He says that he would use childcare:

> If you're both working full-time and you're unable to adjust your hours, yeah. If your office has got a crèche thing, use it. That way if you need a break [from work] you can go and talk to something that doesn't talk back. (Jack, 15, Struggle High).

The plans of many young men are contingent upon what might be possible from the point of view of their jobs. Their caring depends on their jobs and whether they can fit childcare around them. The desire of many young men to be active parents, to take 'time off' to be with their children and to share care with their partners, is widespread and a strong preference – but one they expect may be contested.

Future care:
The disappearing breadwinner household

If the preferences revealed in this small group are realised, present trends away from male-breadwinner households to dual-earning households will continue. Male-breadwinning households, currently a third of all households with children, will shrink while dual-earner households with children, around

61 per cent at present, would increase to reach perhaps three-quarters of all households with children.

There are no signs from these discussions that the pressures of combining work and family, which rise with the growth in dual-income households, will moderate in the years ahead. Indeed it seems likely that they will extend to a growing proportion of households in Australia. The pressures on work and family balance are likely to intensify rather than moderate.

Gender tensions may also increase, given that half as many young women as young men in the groups we spoke to favour the male-breadwinner structure of maternal care. There is a significant mismatch between the genders on this issue. If these inclinations hold in the larger population, a contest between preferences is probable in many households. These might be exacerbated by domestic tensions around housework which we now turn to.

Housework

What do these future plans about paid work and care mean for domestic work? Australian women spend many hours in unpaid work. Two-thirds of Australian women 18 years or over living in couples spent 11 hours or more per week on housework in 2001, compared to 14 per cent of men (HILDA wave 1; Fisher 2002, p 27). Many women are aware of the inequality in sharing domestic work and it rankles. Sixty-three per cent of women in couples in the 2001 HILDA survey agreed with the statement that they do 'much more or a bit more than my fair share of housework per week', compared to 18 per cent of men. This 'double shift' has significant effects on women's ability to rest and take personal care of themselves: 30 per cent of women in couples said they 'never have spare time that they do not know what to do with'. The pressures are most intense on women who work full-time, 41 per cent of whom said they 'never have spare time that they do not know what to do with' (Fisher 2002, p 27).

Australian studies suggest that the majority of Australian men and women believe that housework, childcare and shopping should be shared equally between the sexes (Bittman and Pixley 1997). However, this preference for equality is difficult to reconcile with reality and persistent inequality in the distribution of unpaid domestic work. According to Bittman, this reconciliation might be explained by two theories: either 'lagged adaption' (whereby the change to genuine equality is imminent) or 'pseudo-mutuality' where people kid themselves that equality actually exists. The latter is achieved by an 'ideological embracing of mutuality without any adoption of mutual practices' (1998, p 32). Bittman sees little evidence that a male take-up of domestic work is underway in Australia, thus discounting the theory of 'lagged adaption'. Indeed, he finds much greater and faster adaption among women as they turn to the market for help. He considers that the explanation for the disjunction between values and behaviour around domestic work lies in 'pseudo-mutuality': 'a regular and relatively stable outcome' as Australian men inflate the size of their actual domestic contribution, and understate women's, sometimes with women's collusion.

Discussions with young people in our focus groups suggest that a youthful gendered pseudo-mutuality is at work, with only weak signs of 'lagged adaption' among some young men. While both young men and women espouse the values of equality around sharing paid work and unpaid domestic work, this value is more common among young women, with a sizeable group of young men paying it no heed at all, expecting their working wives to do most of the domestic work. While this group of young men show little 'lagged adaption', in line with Bittman's analysis of adults, young women look likely to continue the adaptive behaviour of their mothers, turning to the market for help.

Who will do domestic work?

Three distributive models of housework allocation are evident among the young people we spoke to, with the most common being 'sharing'. Next, and a long way behind, came paid help (whether cleaner, maid or a paid parent). The third I call 'male minimisation' (or 'my wife will do it'). Needless to say, this last model is more prevalent among young men than young women.

Support for these models is highly gendered. It was occasionally futuristic: when asked who will do housework in his

Table 6.2. Plans for the allocation of housework (per cent)

	Males	Females	Persons
Sharing housework	47	59	55
External help will do it (cleaner, maid)	6	23	17
My wife will do it (males only)	41	0	15
I will do it (females only)	0	16	10
My husband will do it (females only)	0	2	1
Other (eg, robot)	6	0	2
	100	100	100

N=83

Source: Focus groups. The table excludes ten young people whose preferences are unknown.

future home, Jack, 15, at Struggle High nominates 'robots' (which he predicts will do all housework in 'about five years'). The distribution of these different allocative plans is set out in Table 6.2.

Table 6.2 shows that, beyond sharing, the sexes divide. A surprisingly large proportion of young men are hopeful that their wives will do the housework. They are joined by a significant, but much smaller, proportion of young women who anticipate doing it themselves. Less than two in ten young women intend this – half the proportion of young men who expect it of their wives. This is a significant mismatch of preferences.

Sharing housework

Almost a quarter of young women plan to use a cleaner, a much greater proportion than young men. Young women strongly favour shared housework, and many young men agree. However, 'sharing' for some young men is not even: they allocate lesser shares to themselves, or plan to share 'not quite evenly' as Kyle, 16, from Country High puts it.

An assertive approach to housework is exemplified by conversation in a group of three young women in a lower-income area:

You know, I'll be helping full-time [in paid work], I expect shared responsibility. I am not going to do all the housework and look after the baby by myself. He will be doing it as well. No more the woman's work, you know, it's going to be a shared household. (Audrey, 16, Strive High)

Interviewer: So, 50/50 shared?

Maybe 60/40. (Audrey, 16, Strive High)

Yeah I agree with that. I think we shouldn't be stereotypes, we should both do an equal amount of work and bring in money as well as manage the household. (Melinda, 16, Struggle High)

Well it depends on how much money we have, but I'd hire a cleaner. But if not, it's 50/50. Just because we are female, why should we be in the kitchen? (Tanya, 16, Strive High)

Young women in higher-income areas agree, as Vanessa, 16, puts it: 'It shouldn't be all the girls get to stay home while he gets to work and have fun'.

These young women have a lively and assertive expectation of equality – but a vision of equality that is backed up by market support – or a retreat to 'maybe 60/40'. They are keen to avoid gendered stereotypes about 'women's work'. However, alongside this preference for equality is a similar sized group of young men who actively plan to minimise their housework.

Women do it while men minimise

These young men see housework as mainly their wives' job. They are open minimisers, intent on doing as little as possible, or as little as they can get away with, discussing their strategies in a good-humoured but sometimes wily way. Four in ten young men in the study group were straightforward about their desire to avoid housework and leave it to their partners, as Smithy, 17, exemplified: 'Either I suggest my wife is a good cleaner and does all that, or she hires a cleaner, because I'm not doing anything'.

Interestingly, Smithy is very keen to take time off paid work when his children are young to share their care with his wife, but he is unswerving about housework. His classmate Mike at Leafy High agrees: 'My lady is doing the cleaning. I'll just be on the porch having a beer!'

'Welcome to the 1950s!' comments one of his female class-mates. These young women see that it may well be hard to get a fair balance. They anticipate getting on with it themselves, and the prospective demand of being 'superwomen':

> It's the hardest thing to balance ... (Hannah, 16, Leafy High)

> [You have to be] like superwoman or something ... I think, in the end, if he didn't contribute I'd probably end up cleaning it because I can't stand mess. It annoys me. So I'd get around to probably cleaning it myself. (Vanessa, 16, Leafy High)

Karl and Bob, younger boys from Comfort Primary, expect their working wives to do the housework, although they would quite like to do some cooking which they enjoy. Karl, 11, supposes that he 'would have to' mow the lawn, because his love for his wife would make him vulnerable to 'exploitation': 'Well just the fact, that if I love her, and I could see she would probably try to exploit that from time to time'.

Girls in the country – who all plan to have jobs – expect to be doing the housework though they plan some help from their children and a little from their husbands: 'I'd make him put his dirty clothes away in the basket' (Bonnie, 11, Country Primary).

There were exceptions: Judith at Country High is convinced that things are changing, though male resistance is strong. Abby agrees and points out that mothers do not always support daughters in the face of male refusal:

> My Dad can't cook. My brother refuses to cook. Mum will say to him, you know, do something, get some wood for the fire or something and he'll say 'no', so Mum will say 'Oh Judith, will you do it?' ... I think it's a guy thing, you know, he won't do it, and he thinks that this 200 year old 'women-need-to-do-everything' thing continues. Well, it is starting to stop. (Judith, 18, Country High)

> That's interesting. My brother is 12 and Mum's not really scared of him, but she won't force him to do anything, but she'll yell at me if I don't do it. Because I won't do anything else like scream the house down or anything. (Abby, 16, Country High)

Several young women in the country expect marginal help from men, most of which they would direct. Their male peers support their willingness to do more housework: when asked who will be doing housework in his house of the future, Daniel, 11, says 'Not me … I hate it. I'll probably have to do some things, like the lawns and mowers and things like that'.

Paid help: A continuing turn to the market

Among our participants nearly a quarter of young women, and a couple of young men, plan to use some form of paid help. A few plan to use their parents ('I'll pay them of course'). When faced with a partner who does not do housework, as Ellie anticipates of her mechanic husband, she will hire a cleaner.

For a few at Comfort High, this option was rejected because of 'high standards' that a cleaner could not meet, while another felt you should not pay someone else to clean. In the face of steady male resistance to sharing, young women will continue the trend established by their mothers of turning to the market to buy help with housework and cooking, to supplement their own efforts. Many recognise they will need help and that their husbands cannot be relied upon, despite the persuasion that they plan to exert.

The resistance to sharing among young men was surprisingly persistent and widespread. It gave many young women pause. Most young women are not sure how easy sharing will be, in practice, especially when they think about their brothers and peers. Some placed optimistic hope in their own capacity for persuasion, careful partner selection or blackmail, as well as young men's gradual maturity:

> I was having a discussion with one of my guy friends and – I think he was joking – he was saying 'I'm not going to clean, you'll have to do that'. That was a lot of them actually, but he works in a restaurant, so he cooks and cleans, you know. I'm expecting my husband or my partner to help me out. (Tanya, 16, Strive High)

> I have this guy friend who believes girls should be in their place – the laundry, the kitchen, the bedroom … yeah, just the traditional stuff, and I told him right off. (Audrey, 16, Strive High)

> Yeah, he's been asking me too, and I said we don't put up with that. (Tanya, 16, Strive High)

Interviewer: So you're not going to put up with that. So what does that mean? You're not going to choose those people as your partner or ... ?

I think we'll make them come to an understanding. You know, it's either help me out or, you know ... (Tanya, 16, Strive High)

Yeah. Right now they're still young ... (Melinda, 16, Strive High)

I think they'll change. Maybe. (Tanya, 16, Strive High).

Girls in Adelaide had little confidence that their male school peers would easily share the housework. They hope for 'maturity' among young men, backed up by their own powers of persuasion and use of 'incentives':

Interviewer: So when you think about your brothers, and the boys you know of your own age, who will be your partners, how easy will it be to get them to share the housework?

Not very! (Ruby, 11, Struggle High)

The guys we know? [She rolls her eyes] (Brittany, 12, Struggle High)

They're just lazy. (Chloe, 16, Struggle High)

After they mature, they might mature ... (Alana, 16, Struggle High)

If I was in a relationship and they said no, if I asked them to clean, then I'd be very mad ... Like I wouldn't be mean about it. If you just said, 'Can you do the vacuuming this afternoon?' and they didn't do it, then I'd be angry. (Alana, 16, Struggle High)

Sarah feels that her boyfriend is 'really grown up and mature' and that he would help. But her friends agreed that young men 'need incentives'. They giggled at the various incentives that they might try, including withholding cooking and caring.

Concern about the challenge of sharing crossed income levels, with young women on Sydney's North Shore agreeing that 'it will be hard' to enforce sharing. Their strategy was to 'pick the right guy': 'Well, try our best to do that, yeah!' (Melissa, 18, Leafy High). Like their peers in Adelaide, their confidence is fragile and their scepticism palpable:

No, I don't think [men] will do as much as the women do. (Abraham, 16, Comfort High)

They'll help if they're forced into it. (Ann, 16, Comfort High)

At Comfort High, the consensus is similar:

Interviewer: Thinking about the boys you know, do you think that it is going to be easy to share housework straight down the middle as you plan?

No way! (Channel, 17, Comfort High)

My brothers will be hopeless in the future. They already are! ... They don't do the domestic type stuff. They work for my Dad with the papers and all the physical stuff. (Mary, 17, Comfort High)

Most young people recognised that the housework done by their parents was highly differentiated by sex, with rare exceptions. Some intended to replicate this and to avoid certain jobs:

Interviewer: Would you clean the toilet, Claus?

Um. I might hire someone. (Claus, 15, Struggle High)

Gender tactics

In the face of male resistance, young women have considered their strategies. Young men have also considered their approach. These gendered tactics suggest that young people already recognise, or have themselves witnessed, some heat around the issues of housework. Tactical planning is well illustrated by conversation among young people in the country. The young men optimistically hope their wives will 'relax' about sharing as time goes by, while the young women are determined not to marry anyone who won't help, and recognise that they will have to start strong and stay strong if they are to avoid repeating the 'disgusting' imbalance they currently witness. As the boys put it:

You've got to share, otherwise she'll divorce you. You should be able to help for the first few years [of marriage] then it might wear off ... (Kevin, 17, Country High)

Most girls today, they're not as into doing housework as 60 years ago. It was expected that housework would be their whole job, but I suppose nowadays they're not as 'Oh yes – I'll do the housework'. It's sort of share, work rate evenly, sort of thing. Maybe not quite evenly. (Kyle, 16, Country High)

Interviewer: So do you think you'll be sharing but not quite evenly, is that your plan?

Yeah, we hope we do. (Kyle, 16, Country High)

Their female peers, who want to share housework, anticipate their strategies:

There needs to be a balance. I think it is disgusting the way it is. (Kate, 16, Country High)

I was thinking the other day ... I didn't want to end up like Mum, having to do everything so ... if they are good at home economics or something, they can cook maybe three times a week and I'd do the other bit, and make it balanced. (Judith, 18, Country High).

[You need to share] from the start – because my parents started [not sharing] as they are from the start ... I'm not marrying him unless he does the dishes. (Kate, 16, Country High)

Judith in the country, like her peers in western Sydney, uses the language of fairness and contests the idea of the male breadwinner, although she does not underestimate the challenge:

It is still going to take a couple more generations for men to start realising they have to do something. That women are now going out to work and they are bringing home money and [men are] not all the time the [male] breadwinner of the family but [women] are contributing equally as the men, so they need to. They're bringing in half the money, the guys are bringing in half the money, so they need to share the work around the house as well. (Judith, 18, Country High)

Interviewer: Looking at your brothers, do you think that is going to be easy?

No. My brother is incapable of doing anything for himself. He can make chips – that's the frozen ones. (Kate, 16, Country High).

Socio-economic background and the allocation of housework

Several of the young women at Leafy Primary live in households with cleaners at present and hope for a maid in the future. At Strive High, some young women also hope for a maid, suggesting that hope for help from the market is not confined to higher socio-economic areas. However, there are some important socio-economic differences. Young women in lower-income western Sydney and the country, talk of strong persuasive tactics and angry rebellion if their partners don't do a fair share of house-work. Young women from higher socio-economic areas in both Sydney and Adelaide are more likely to accommodate the imbalance and to 'pick up the slack' themselves:

> I think cleaning sort of cleanses your soul, sort of thing. (Mary, 17, Comfort High)

> I wouldn't trust a cleaner. I don't mind cleaning myself but I wouldn't pay someone to clean, if we keep the house clean all the time it shouldn't get that dirty anyway, so I'd clean myself. (Amy, 17, Comfort High)

This may mean that young middle-class women who believe that their partners should share domestic work, will nonetheless do more than their partners. Their accommodating approaches may reflect a specific culture of motherhood, and an internalised hope of fulfilling an ever-competent, able and caring standard of proper middle-class motherhood, while being paid workers. Doing their own housework to a 'decent' standard, and vir-tuously enjoying it, may be part of their expectation of working motherhood. However, it sits uncomfortably alongside a busy household and paid job, and perhaps a male partner who is resistant to doing housework.

Working class and country women are more likely to talk about vigorous resistance, or go for an efficient, pragmatic solu-tion. Ellie and her tradesman husband will have a cleaner because 'of course' he won't be doing housework, while in western Sydney Tanya, Melinda and Audrey will insist on help or their partners will pay a price. The picture is of flinty determination among young working-class women as they push

for fairness, contrasting with a more resigned, virtuous willingness to do more, rather than risk standards, among young
women from higher socio-economic backgrounds.

Pseudomutuality or 'lagged adaption'?

Among young men, 'sharing' has some traction for a significant
group in both higher- and lower-income groups, but is tempered
by an open, wily evasiveness – one that some brothers are
already practising on their sisters and mothers. They hope that
they can find a wife who will do the housework, that women
will not notice unequal sharing, or that their monitoring and
demands will weaken with time. A pragmatic willingness to
employ others as a means of avoiding the problem is evident
across income groups, especially among women.

The over-allocation of housework to women has its supporters among both young women and men, though men
outnumber women more than two to one. The match of preferences is better around sharing, but this sharing is tempered by
some deviations from 50/50, all to women's disadvantage. Many
young women expect young men to resist doing housework,
based on their observations of their brothers and male friends.
They see that young men will resist doing housework. Young
women are already resentful about this, across the socio-
economic spectrum. The gender struggle over unpaid housework seems far from over, based on these conversations.

This account provides some support for an enduring gendered
discourse of pseudo-mutuality, where young women's hope for
equality jostles with their perceptions of their peers. However, a
sizeable proportion of young men do not pretend that they
intend to share: they want women to do it. The theory of 'lagged
adaption' and the hope that sharing is in the intergenerational
pipeline finds little support here. Instead, as Bittman (1998)
describes, the adaption is by women who seek support from the
market. The failure of a gendered redistribution of the work of
private sustenance to men and away from women thus drives a
turn to market sustenance as a source of support. The market
offers a gender-neutral route to goods and services. It welcomes
over-worked women who cannot thicken up the sources of

sustenance from their male fellow-householders, whether sons or partners.

This commodification means more spending on domestic labour substitutes (childcare, pre-packaged food, gardening and cleaning services) all of which have shown strong market growth in recent years. This in turn drives the work/spend cycle at a faster pace, putting upward pressure on labour market participation rates.

However, the growth in the market for domestic services may have implications for labour market equity if it fuels growth in low-paid, insecure, 'black market' feminised employment. Without decent minimal labour market standards and protections, commodification is underpinned by widening gendered inequality in the labour market for household services like childcare and cleaning. Ironically, women's increasing need for commodified support drives increased gender inequity in the labour market.

A challenge for public and private sources of sustenance

The qualitative data reported in these conversations suggests some interesting trends. It confirms a significant fertility gap between the plans of some young Australians and their predicted fertility outcomes. It suggests that the declining birth rate is not explained by early decisions against reproduction, but rather by uncertainties about security, housing, financial stability and workplace experience, in the context of rising personal aspirations.

There is little sign in this group of young women turning away from paid work in reaction to the double-day they have witnessed among their mothers. There are, however, signs of this in the minds of some young men who hope that their wives will run their households and do much of the housework as well as earn money.

A continued long-term decline in male-breadwinner households (with children) and the growth of dual-earner households is implied in these plans. This suggests that tensions around work and family, that are most intense in dual-earner house-holds, will increase rather than diminish.

It seems that many young people show a predisposition to share earning and caring for children with their partner. This is the dominant preference, backed by the extended family. Given these signs of a strong interest in active fatherhood, why do men's preferences have such weak purchase later in life? The low proportion of Australian men who take extended leave from jobs to care for children, and their low participation in part-time work, point to the power of institutions or cultures to overwhelm young men's preference to care. Certainly, the contingent nature of young men's plans to share care is very evident. They know that active parenting may be difficult in their future jobs.

The implications for young women are clear: they are the default domestic workers and carers when men's preferences to share fail to be realised. This 'cascade of care' to women suggests that maternal care, through modified traditional household structures that interleave maternal care around mother's jobs, is likely to remain the dominant family form well into the future.

For this next generation, the workplaces, laws, childcare provision and social supports that shape their labour market and care transitions will be critical to outcomes. A supportive public framework of parental leave, integrated quality part-time work and quality, accessible childcare is of great significance. Without supports that facilitate these transitions, women's responsibility for an overloaded system of private sustenance will leave them shouldering higher labour market risks (including limited retirement incomes) and care decisions that are constrained by limited options. They may pay a high labour market penalty in terms of earnings and job rewards. They may experience high levels of private anxiety about the quality of care for children and equality in relationships. If they rely on cheap 'outsourced' domestic services that pay poorly or lack decent labour con-ditions, their reliance on the work of other women may contribute to widening labour market and gender inequality.

There is a wide gap between the kinds of support that many young women and men will seek and the labour market, workplace and social supports provided by the existing fabric of public support. These conversations provide little support for the optimistic hope that the allocation of unpaid work is moving briskly to a fair division between the sexes, or that this discussion will be less heated than among earlier generations. Private sources of sustenance and their gendered allocations will be sources of disruption, divorce and discomfort into the future – affecting both sexes.

If young men and women are to realise their plans, much will need to change. Young women expect equality with men. However, their plans to share domestic and paid work with their partners rely upon a sea-change in the patterns of men's participation in the private household. When they reflect on the young men they know, they pause. Some are already thinking about their tactics.

Young men's desires to share parenting with their partners will, in turn, rely upon very significant change in public workplace practices and cultures. Preferences for flexibility, for adaption over the life-cycle, and for equality are clear. The extensive negative spillover arising from unrealised preferences, which we have discussed in the previous chapters, has powerful effects upon children, parents and their households. The intentions of these young people provide a strong argument for change that allows their preferences – even as they change – to be realised.

For many, formal childcare will be critical to their work and care arrangements. Some of the predictable gaps between care preferences and existing provisions will require public policy solutions if they are to be fair, accessible and avoid disadvantaging women. If female preferences against exclusive maternal care dominate over husbands' hopes that women will do the job, and if both sexes' preferences for shared care are unmet because of workplace inflexibility, then demand for formal childcare may grow significantly. We turn to this in the next chapter.

CHAPTER 7

Kids as commodities?
Childcare in Australia

The effects of thinning private household capacity to care and inadequate public supports, with a market expanding to fill the gap, are nowhere better illustrated than in relation to care of children. The expansive market for childcare gives significant new momentum to the work/spend cycle. Keeping up with childcare costs accelerates participation in paid work and vice versa. There is now convincing international evidence about the importance of early life experiences to child development, emotional well-being and cognitive skills, which in turn shape life chances and social mobility. How children are cared for and educated in their infancy and preschool years, whether by parents or others, leaves a deep imprint and long-term social and economic costs (Heckman 2006; Press 2006). While development continues well into adolescence and beyond, and humans are capable of significant recovery and reorientation when things go wrong in the early years, a large body of literature tells us that the early years critically shape longer-term development (Press 2006). What is more, damage done early is expensive to - remediate later. Inequality is significantly shaped by early experience, with disadvantage often coming in complex, doubly and triply reinforcing packages where disadvantage at home is deepened by institutional and community deficiencies beyond home.

Many studies confirm this. Margaret McCain and J Fraser Mustard in Canada (1999, 2002), and the US Committee on Integrating the Science of Early Childhood Development (Shonkoff and Phillips 2000) provide extensive reviews of the current science of early childhood development in North America and its long-term implications for individual, social and economic outcomes. Research in many European countries also provides convincing evidence about these links.

The growing body of international research about markets, parental work, childcare and early childhood tells us that many things influence the development of young children, including the innate characteristics of the child, the nature of their care-givers, parents and home, and the early care and education they receive. Home and parenting are very significant in affecting outcomes for children: even where children spend a great deal of time in childcare, their parents remain the most influential people in their lives and development (Shonkoff and Phillips 2000, p 206). However, in terms of public policy, parenting and home are much harder to change than early childhood educa-tion and care. Interventions based around the latter are more effective ways of improving outcomes. So research suggests that this is where policy effort and interventions should be focused (Waldfogel 2004; Heckman 2006a).

Research about the developing brain, particularly the ways in which genes and the environment interact to affect the brain's maturation, has advanced quickly in recent years. This research tells us that genetic characteristics are less important, and early experience much more important, than was previously thought (McCain and J Fraser Mustard 1999, p 26). It is now evident that early care has 'profound' effects on early development and that genetic endowments are 'expressed' in the context of experience and environment, especially in relation to brain development (Shonkoff and Phillips 2000, p 219). The 'critical phase' for developing cognitive skills of thinking and knowing is in the Years 0-6 (McCain and J Fraser Mustard 1999, p 31; Esping-Anderson 2004). These skills are the foundation for further education and learning, and create a template for future success in learning, earning and social mobility.

These early care experiences have important implications for socio-economic and cognitive inequality. The quality of non-parental childcare and parenting are not unrelated: if all are poor or impoverished, disadvantaged children can be doubly or triply disadvantaged (Meyers, Rosenbaum, Ruhm and Waldfogel

2004; Esping Anderson 2004). This makes a system of quality early childhood education and care of vital social importance.

Kids as commodities

Our public discussion of children is saturated with the metaphor of the market. Public figures speak of children as 'assets' or our greatest 'resource', they talk of spending on children as an 'investment', and they talk of children themselves as vessels of 'human capital'. However, the reach of the market to children goes beyond the way we *think* about them, and the calculus of their 'cost'. It increasingly shapes the way we rear them. Growing participation in paid work means that parents, particularly mothers, increasingly parent around their jobs, creating a new market for childcare. As Eddy Groves, head of ABC Learning Centres, the largest publicly-listed childcare company, told investors in 2003: 'There are 4 million children under six years of age, and only 700,000 use private day care ... The [other] 3.3 million children represent an enormous opportunity for ABC Learning. We aim to continue to increase our standards in order to attract as many children as possible' (Horin 2003, p 39).

Thus children are a market to be 'milked', as *Business Review Weekly* put it (Kirby 2003), and from which large profits flow – an average profit of $600 per child in ABC Learning Centres in 2002 (Horin 2003, p 39). A small number of large childcare chains provide care to many thousands of children and make large profits. The Howard Government has vigorously fostered this market in the name of giving choice to parents and increasing women's labour market participation.

The shift in care amounts to what one set of researchers, referring to the USA, calls a 'dramatic, uncontrolled, natural experiment' where the care of infants and young children has been 'reapportioned away from time with parents to extensive hours in non-parental childcare settings' (Shonkoff and Phillips 2000, p 394). This 'experiment' has triggered explosive politicised debate about maternal employment, and the nature of proper mothering. Such debate has taken little account of the nature of pressures on private households and their capacities for care. It has all too little to say about fathering, about shared parental care and about community provision of quality childcare options through expanded public supports and quality, affordable care options. If our economy and our larger community are to rely increasingly on the paid work of mothers and women, how should we care for children? At present, the failure to either properly *ask* or *answer* this question loads up paid work, as well as care, onto mothers, and creates a large burden of maternal guilt. Mothers pay a price in terms of their own health and life-long earnings. Ad hoc arrangements mean that some children pay a price in terms of their well-being, health and welfare, and sometimes a lifetime of disadvantage. Society pays for the remediation of problems created early in life.

The care of our children is one of the fastest growing areas of commodification in Australia. As women enter paid work, households increasingly rely on purchased care for babies and children, and this trend is unlikely to abate. There are many positive effects arising from non-parental care, but recent research tells us that not all care is the same or benign.

Implicit in the future plans of young people in the previous chapter are plans for the care of children. In the first part of this chapter, I consider what some young people think of the child-care they have experienced, and how they plan to care in the future. The demand for childcare is likely to continue to increase, making good policy of great importance. In recent years Australia's childcare provision has expanded rapidly, especially through private provision. A critical question here is to what extent, and under what conditions, should the market, and especially large corporations, be part of it? In the second part of the chapter I consider how the market increasingly shapes the nature of care for children in Australia.

Care for children can be provided by parents, extended family or friends or, more formally, purchased from others – whether at a childcare centre, home-based family day care or by hiring a nanny. Care for children is generally either private familial care or commodified public care. Parental care can be facilitated by paid and unpaid leave from parental work, and commodified care can be facilitated by public support for childcare services or tax rebates or fee subsidies paid to those who buy care. Some significant subsidies of formal childcare are hidden and involuntary. For example, one study estimates that USA childcare workers contribute 20 per cent of the total costs of childcare through foregone wages, given their underpayment relative to other similarly skilled workers (Shonkoff and Phillips 2000, p 321).

However they are organised, care regimes for children have powerful effects on several social phenomena: first, on the labour force participation of parents, especially women, and thus their incomes both in the short term and over the life-cycle; and secondly, on human welfare, especially that of children. They also have powerful effects on social, demographic and economic outcomes like poverty, fertility and inequality (Bettio and Plantenga 2004). Good care regimes function as 'social joins' 'by ensuring complementarity between economic and demographic institutions and processes' in the words of Bettio and Plantenga (2004, p 107). In contrast, bad care dislocates economic, demographic and social outcomes that then fail to consolidate and reinforce each other. Unfortunately the invisibility of care – largely explained by its feminisation – conceals the quality of the 'social joins' it makes. Sometimes those least able to afford it pay the largest price, and the consequent inequalities and invisible consumption of care corrode social and economic life.

The Australian 'system' of care for children is very different from that prevailing in many other countries. Some countries have arrangements that are much worse than Australia's – poor in quality, scarce and expensive. In some countries, women – especially single mothers – are forced back to work and must find local cheap care where quality stumbles at the first hurdle. In these countries, childcare (and welfare) regimes function as engines of inequality, with rich households able to afford parental care or buy quality non-parental care, and poorer households dependent on cheaper care of variable and sometimes downright unsafe kinds.

In some other countries, arrangements for the care of children are better organised with paid leave to assist parents to care for infants, backed by guaranteed access to quality childcare for preschool children. This approach ensures real choice between parental care and formal commodified care by others. Where there is no option for non-parental care, or its quality is unacceptable or it is too costly, no real choice exists.

Childcare: What young people think and plan

How do young people view childcare, based on their experience? And what plans do they have for the future care of their own children? There is very little Australian evidence about the experience of childcare from the perspective of the child. Perhaps this is not surprising, given the ethical and methodological difficulties in collecting it. However, children's perspectives are important, both to parents who make decisions about care, and to policy makers who shape its provision.

Many of the 93 children in our focus groups had experienced non-parental care – often by extended family, friends and neighbours. About a third had experienced formal childcare like long day care in childcare centres, family day care, or out of school hours care. Given their ages (10-18 years old) and locations most of those with formal childcare experience have been to community-based rather than privately run childcare, since the latter was less available until the mid-1990s.

Of the 84 young people in our focus groups whose childcare experiences we know, 55 had no extensive experience of formal non-parental care. This included all who lived in the country town where no formal childcare options existed. These young people were cared for mostly by their mothers who were either at home or working during school hours. There was also less experience of formal childcare among young people in low socio-economic areas (as ABS data confirm for the larger population; see Flood 2004).

Twenty-nine children had experience of formal care. Just over half of these had been in centre-based care, a fifth in out-of-school-hours care, and a fifth in care like family day care (these proportions are close to the 1993 national breakdown).

Table 7.1. Childcare experiences and future plans of the young people in focus groups

	Number	Per cent of total
Assessment of care		
Of those who had experienced formal care		
Had positive views of this care	19	66
Ambivalent	2	7
Had negative views of this care	8	28
	29	101*
Future plans		
Would use formal care themselves	38	41
Would not use	48	52
Unknown	7	8
	93	101*
Of those who would use formal care		
Had experience of formal care themselves	21	55
Without experience of formal care themselves	17	45
	38	100

* Column adds to more than 100 because of rounding

Positive views of childcare and what makes good care

Most of the young people with experience of formal care viewed it positively and clearly articulated what they had liked, and what they thought their own children would gain from it. They had strong ideas about what makes good care. The majority of those who had experienced formal non-parental care themselves would use it, compared to less than half of all young people we spoke with. However, their plans to use formal care were often conditional: their use would depend on whether children liked it, whether it was good care, and on its cost.

Kelly, who had a positive experience of after-school care, said that she would use childcare 'but if they didn't like it, [I'd] have someone they could ring' (11, Struggle Primary). Nicole adopts a similar conditional approach:

> I'd probably see what it is like and if they like it, then they would go there. (Nicole, 12, Comfort Primary)

Although she had a negative experience of childcare, Jade was still considering it for her children, but not without being confident of the quality of care:

> I would probably really have to check it out, to be careful. I'd probably go there a few times. Make sure they didn't know that I was there but just to see how they interacted with other children to see if they were okay by themselves. And if they weren't, I probably wouldn't send them back there again ... making sure that the adults that were there and the other children were fair. (Jade, 16, Comfort High)

Where young people had experienced childcare, they identified positive effects of care on social skills and friendships:

> I think I would [use it] because they get to know kids their own age and what the others do and stuff like that. What they can expect going into kindy or school or high school or stuff like that and getting to know other kids as well. (Bob, 11, Comfort Primary)

> [I'd use a] Childcare centre, so they get used to what it is like to make friends. (Lea, 11, Strive Primary)

Relying on extended family

Just over half of the children in focus groups do not plan to use formal non-parental childcare themselves. Of these, almost half say they will rely upon the extended family, especially mothers and grandparents.

Young people without personal experience of childcare were reluctant to involve 'strangers'. Many – including younger and older children, and those from both higher- and lower-income areas – expressed concern about whom you could trust:

> I was considering it. But I don't know, 'cause I'd like my family to look after them instead. (Tanya, 16, Strive High)

> I use my family, I don't trust outside people because they can hit your kid or something can go wrong. (Vanessa, 16, Leafy High)

> Well, I got looked after by friends and relatives, and I don't really like the idea of putting kids with someone else. (Jenny, 11, Country Primary)

Some young people do not want to miss out on parenting time with their own children, even where they feel that the social outcomes of childcare as well as their own past experiences were positive:

> I mean, it would have been good for them to interact with other children and things like that but if you've got friends who are home with their kids, it would be better off your child spending time with them. I mean I went to after-school-hours care, and I liked it, but – I don't know – I just don't think it would be good. I've heard friends who put their kids in childcare [and] ... they've missed out on so much, and it just doesn't seem worth it. (Ann, 16, Comfort High)

Of course these comments arise from a small group of children. However, they suggest that *experience shapes childcare preferences*. The experience in this group of *actual childcare itself* is positively associated with a willingness to use it in future. Even where young people had a negative experience (such as a carer they didn't like), they were more likely to plan to use it than those who had no experience of childcare at all. Those without any experience were more likely to view childcare as unsafe or dangerous. Where experience existed, *and* it was positive, the preference in favour of formal childcare use was higher again. This is an interesting illustration of how preferences are constructed by experience, rather than autonomously 'given'.

What young people say about childcare they have experienced

Based on these conversations, young people have very clear memories about non-parental care. They can easily answer questions, and in many examples their faces and lively responses reflect positive memories. They can recount specific events or characteristics of carers and facilities in considerable detail. Their views about care differ for different forms of care, whether informal, centre-based or out-of-school-hours care.

Informal care

In the country and many low socio-economic areas, young people have more experience of informal care. Several described very positive experiences, their faces beaming:

> When I was little I was looked after by relatives or friends – I wouldn't let [my kids] go to strangers. (Jenny, 11, Country Primary)

> Interviewer: When you were looked after by a relative or a friend can you remember whether you liked it or not?

> I loved it … I was the little *princess*! (Jenny, 11, Country Primary)

Kelly describes her carer as a second mother who gave her memorable support, and Ellie loved her experience:

> She was my favourite adult in the world! She was really, really nice. We played games [and had] lots of fun … She is like a 'second mother'. If something bad happened in my family, I can talk to her. (Kelly, 11, Struggle Primary)

> I remember because the lady who looked after me had a daughter that was a couple of years older than me, and I got on really well with her as well. And I really loved it. (Ellie, 16, Leafy High)

Against these, Channel from a higher-income area spoke negatively of informal care:

> I can remember I used to be really scared of them because they threatened to chop off my thumb [when I sucked it] … they put it on a cutting board. (Channel, 16, Comfort High)

Long day care: A positive experience

In the higher socio-economic areas, with greater experience of formal childcare, many young people spoke positively of their experiences. They readily identified things that they enjoyed: varied toys and activities, space, movies, food and people:

> I used to like going there and playing with the stuff. Because at childcare they have different stuff to play with that you don't have at home, and different people. (Carrie, 11, Comfort Primary)

> It was good because they had a lot of play area. They watched movies, like kids' movies, Cinderella and stuff and they let you

have pretty good food … they did pretty good activities. (Rove, 12, Comfort Primary)

Like many others, Rove identified the positive social contacts he established in childcare which have persisted into school:

Well in childcare, I've had people from childcare who have gone through school with me. (Rove, 12, Comfort High)

Interviewer: It's been good to have those friendships all the way?

Yeah. (Rove, 12, Comfort High)

Older children also readily remembered positive aspects of their care experiences, including space, friendships and relationships with carers. Abraham, 16, from Comfort High remembers with pleasure the space to ride his bike and 'a really big sandpit all under cover', while Amanda remembers specific people and activities:

I went to the crèche and loved it – well what I can remember – only we were really little and I still know some of the people who I went there with and it was excellent, I loved it. (Amanda, 16, Comfort High)

Interviewer: What did you like about it? Can you remember?

I just remember the people who worked there, especially the chef guy who cooked all our food, he was really big, and I just remember him being like a bear kind of thing, that's just how I remember him. And all the ladies who worked there were so nice and I just remember doing activities. For Easter once it was really hot and we had a treasure hunt for the eggs and they melted and it was so much fun though and I just remember little things like that. It was really good. (Amanda, 16, Comfort High)

Out-of-school-hours care

Memories of out-of-school-hours care were less positive. Many young people found it boring, or the equipment outdated, or felt that they had outgrown formal care:

I hated it. Couldn't stand it. I was the kid who sat in the corner and got picked on. … I was in OSHC [out of school hours care]. I was the youngest there … and I sometimes snuck home cause there was a paddock and then I lived across the road from the paddock and I'd usually sneak home most of the time because I didn't like going there at all. I'd rather be home by myself than in after school care. The teachers were mean and it was boring. (Jade, 16, Comfort High)

I don't really like it and we go there often which is a problem. I suppose I've grown up a bit and I've grown out of some of the things they do there. (Karl, 11, Comfort Primary)

Age is a significant issue for those who think they have outgrown formal care, although social connection with other participants helps:

At first I didn't like it ... but then when I became friends with everyone there, it wasn't that bad, but then as I was getting older too in around year four, or five, in the holidays they would put me into those stupid school camps – not camps, just the school days where you go in – and I hated them. I ran away once. Went home and so they got angry at me, but yeah I didn't really like that. But the day care when I was young from like three to seven or so wasn't so bad. (Peter, 16, Leafy High)

I had to go three times a week, morning and night and it was crap because I was the oldest person there. (Mary, 17, Comfort High)

In contrast Kelly, Smithy and Mark had fond memories of out-of-school-hours care:

I did it for a while, fun, huge play area, and lots of activities – used to play games, lots and lots of friends, different areas for younger and older kids – where older kids could go and younger kids could not. (Kelly, 11, Struggle Primary)

I used to like that, heaps good fun, monkey bar and stuff and playing and trading toys with other kids. (Smithy, 17, Leafy High)

Young people in these focus groups are clear about what it is they liked and did not like about childcare. They are positive about childcare environments with good teachers or adults they liked, good play space and equipment, interesting, age appropriate activities, good food and positive relationships, whether with staff or other children. Where these were absent, the experience was negative. Young people stress the importance of quality care for their happiness and well-being. For those who think that they will use childcare in the future, the quality of that care – in all its various facets – is important. As we see in the next section, their concerns about quality are not misplaced.

Childcare: Residual rather than planned policy

National care regimes are evolutionary creatures. The powerful tendency in favour of private care solutions in many Western industrialised nations means that care has evolved in a haphazard, rather than planned, way. Care policy is 'a residual variable' rather than a thing that is deliberately planned. A recent survey of European care arrangements concludes that 'actual policy may be more the result of a complex interplay between established interests and party-political compromises than of explicit and well-focused considerations' (Bettio and Plantenga 2004, p 109).

Australia's regime of care for children certainly has a residual character. It is increasingly commodified with too little research on its outcomes. There are few signs of clear national goals, systematic collection of evidence to guide action, planning to realise objectives, or evaluation of progress towards them. Our system has grown like Topsy: while much Australian childcare is of high quality, demand is running ahead of supply, quality is variable and its increasing commercialisation fosters inequality.

While many other aspects of social and public life also have a 'residual' rather than a planned character, the character of our childcare 'system' increasingly affects both the public and private realms, with international evidence showing that uncontrolled evolution has potentially hazardous outcomes. The regime for care of infants and preschool children stands in strong contrast with that for Australian children of school age. The current growth in private school education is underpinned by the promise of a free place for each Australian child in a public school, regardless of where they may live and whether they use it. The failure to offer the same for younger children and babies is hard to justify, given the larger life-long ripples that flow from poor care in infancy and the early years.

Corporations are increasingly involved in childcare. This is not surprising, given its growth. In 2002/03, IBISWorld estimated that market turnover in childcare services in Australia was

$3.6 billion. Over 82,000 employees worked in the sector in 2004, with an additional 12,997 carers providing family day care, and a further 2,995 providing voluntary labour in these services (FaCS 2005a, p 17). Almost nine thousand organisations and enterprises offered some form of commodified care in 2004 (FaCS 2005a, p 7).

And there is rapid growth in various forms of informal care, including some that is free but unsafe, barely supervised and far from developmentally appropriate. At the other end of the spectrum, exclusive private care is purchased by some on the first rung of a commodified ladder that extends from exclusive private infant care through to private university. This has significant implications for inequality.

In August 2005, I was interviewed by a journalist who lamented her own childcare situation. Her two children attend an inner city childcare centre which, at that time, charged fees of $85 a day per child – of $425 per week and $22,000 a year. At the time this was equivalent to 43 per cent pf average ordinary full-time earnings before tax, so that two children in childcare would account for 86 per cent of an average full-time wage. The centre she used was not accredited so there was no access to any government rebate to defray costs, and indeed the incomes of most users meant that few were eligible for significant rebates. This centre was one of three centres privately run by its Sydney owners. In mid-2005, the centre had over 500 people on its two-year waiting list, and moving up it depended on personal recommendations by existing users. The journalist contrasted the superior care she now bought with the inferior care she had previously purchased at a centre run by a large chain: it was characterised by poor food and high staff turnover, with fees of $75 per day (bring your own nappies). This mother was able to work because of her partner's earnings which met the childcare costs of her labour market participation and – despite all her advantages – she experienced what she called 'a struggle to work'. She was keen to put her eight years of post-compulsory education to use and was committed to remaining in the labour market.

Large household incomes like hers can thus buy exclusive, if very expensive, care with high staffing ratios, very good food and a 'homelike' atmosphere. But what of those who cannot afford this cost? What does the growing marketisation of care of infants and very young children mean for children, society, parents and inequality?

Who cares in Australia?
Parents, the market and childcare

At present around 3.5 million children under 12 years old in Australia are potentially in need of some form of childcare. The employment rate of women with a child under four years old rose from 29 per cent in 1984 to 45 per cent in 2004, largely driving the increased demand for childcare (ABS Cat No 4202.0, 1984, 2004b). It is estimated that in June 2005, over 1.5 million children aged 0-12 years used some type of childcare (ABS Cat No 4402.0, 2005).

Informal care is the most common form of non-parental childcare in Australia but its use is falling while children's participation in formal care is increasing. The most common type of informal care is provided by grandparents, although their share fell a little between 1999 and 2005. In 2005, 23 per cent of Australian children aged 0-11 years used formal care, up from 17 per cent in 1999 (see Table 7.2). The rise in formal care has been especially strong among young children: in 2005, 35.2 per cent of children aged 0-4 years used some formal care (excluding pre-school), compared to 23.6 per cent in 1996 (ABS Cat No 4402.0, 2005). The proportion of those in informal care fell from 40.1 per cent in 1996 to 38.4 per cent in 2005.

Lone parents are the most likely to make use of childcare: 55.6 per cent did so in 2005, compared to 43.8 per cent of couples with children (ABS Cat No 4402.0, 2005).

The growth in children using centre-based long day childcare has continued apace, rising almost 10 per cent between 2002 and 2005. Participation in out-of-school-hours care is also increasing: 227,000 children used this care in 2005, an increase of 56,000 or 33 per cent on 2002 (ABS Cat No 4402.0, 2005, p 43).

Table 7.2. Per cent of children 0-11 years old in childcare in Australia, 1999, 2002, 2005 excluding preschool

Types of Care	1999	2002	2005
Per cent of Children Using Formal Care			
Before and After school care	5.0	5.5	7.3
Long day care	7.8	9.6	10.4
Family day care	2.8	3.1	3.4
Occasional care	1.5	1.2	1.6
Other formal Care	0.5	0.4	0.6
Children who used formal care	17.1	19.3	22.6
Per cent of Children Using Informal Care			
Grandparents	21.2	19.1	20.3
Brothers/sisters	2.4	2.3	1.6
Other relatives	7.1	6.7	7.2
Other person	9.4	7.3	6.4
Children who used informal care	37.2	32.9	33.4
Whether used any type of childcare			
Children who used formal and/or informal care	47.7	44.6	47.6
Children who used neither formal or informal care	52.3	55.4	52.4

Source: ABS Cat No 4402.0 June 2005, p 43.

Note: In surveys prior to 2005, the definition of 'formal care' included preschool. To enable comparisons over time, preschool has been excluded from 'formal care' in this table. Some children used more than one form of formal or informal care and some used both formal and informal care so the categories in this table are not mutually exclusive. The table reads as follows: of children aged 0-11 years in 2005, 7.3 per cent used before and after school care and 22.6 per cent used formal care, and so on.

Overall the number of children in formal childcare increased by 18 per cent between 2002 and 2005 and by 58 per cent since 1996. In contrast, the number of children using informal care fell by 7.8 per cent between 1996 and 2005 (ABS Cat No 4402.0, 2005, p 43).

Sixty per cent of children under five years old used childcare in 2005 in the survey reference week, excluding preschool.

In 2005, just over a third of babies less than one year old used childcare. Sixty-one per cent and 71 per cent of one and two-year-olds respectively used childcare and 70.6 per cent of three-year-olds used childcare, excluding preschool (ABS Cat No 4402.0, 2005, p 14). Many children experience multiple forms of care, especially as they get older, with around a third of those in some form of care using multiple forms, mostly a combination of formal and informal care (Qu and Wise 2004, p 2).

Only a small proportion of children are in care for very extended periods. The median hours in care for children 0-12 years old was 10 hours per week in 2005. Only 13 per cent of children were in care for more than 35 hours a week.

The availability of accessible, affordable, quality care has lagged behind rising demand in recent years, making childcare problematic for many parents. Analysis of HILDA survey data for 2002 shows that 29 per cent of parents with children under school age who had used or thought about using childcare had difficulties with childcare for a sick child, 27 per cent had difficulties in relation to the cost of care, and around a fifth had problems with getting their centre of choice, finding the hours they needed, finding the right person to care, getting quality care or finding a centre in the right location (Cassells et al 2005, p 7). In June 2005, parents needed but could not find formal care for 188,400 children (or 6 per cent) of children aged 0-12 years (ABS Cat No 4402.0, p 8). This is up from 174,500 in 2002.

The cost and accreditation of care

The Productivity Commission estimated that in 2003/04, total government expenditure on children's services was $2.4 billion, three-quarters of it from the Commonwealth (Press 2006, p 27).

However, compared to other OECD countries, Australia spends relatively little on early childhood services (OECD 2002, p 59).

The Commonwealth began funding childcare through non-profit centre-based long day care in 1972 with the election of the Whitlam Government. Means-tested fee relief for users of community-based centres was provided in Australia from 1984. In 1991 it was extended by the Labor Government to those who purchased care from private for-profit long day care centres. This fostered private care so that within a few years private providers of long day care outnumbered community-based centres. In 1997 operational subsidies to community-based services were removed and in 2001 private operators of out-of-school-hours care were given access to government funding (Wannan 2005, p 3).

In July 2000, fee relief was restructured by the Coalition Government and renamed the Child Care Benefit (CCB). It provides a means-tested payment (on a sliding scale in relation to income and type of care) to families that have children in approved or registered care. This shift of resources to purchasers, rather than to providers of services, was made in the name of choice. It has seen the private sector continue to pick up the growth in centre-based childcare.

In the 2004 election, the Howard Government announced a 30 per cent Child Care Tax Rebate (CCTR) which is capped at $4,000. It can be claimed from 2005/06 tax returns. The rebate is highly regressive, delivering larger benefits to higher-income earners.

The quality of care in Australia is managed through a National Childcare Accreditation Council which adopts a five-step process of initial registration through to accreditation. State governments also play an important role in licensing centres and setting and monitoring key indicators like staff/child ratios (which in themselves vary from State to State). Long day care centres are assessed against ten quality areas (including relationships with children, respect for children, partnerships with families, staff interactions, planning and evaluation, learning and development, protective care, health, safety and managing to support quality) and 35 principles (OECD 2002, p 110).

A key element of quality childcare is the ratio of staff to children. In a recent review, Press finds that more often than not, across Australia 'regulations and existing national standards fail to reflect the staff to child rations recommended by professional organisations as necessary for good quality centre-based care and education' (2006, p 37).

In 2003/04, the National Childcare Accreditation Council received 400 phone complaints and 50 written complaints in relation to centres (ABC 2004b) and the chairperson of the Council reported that nearly five per cent of operating centres do not pass accreditation inspections. Once every two-and-a-half years, centres are accredited by means of a self-assessment process, followed by one on-site inspection for which extensive notice is given. If a centre fails accreditation, it has 12 months to meet requirements, before parents are notified. This means that a childcare centre could have serious problems for three years 'before the watchdog alerts parents' (ABC 2004b). The absence of random inspections, lenient inspections and operator collection of validation surveys from staff and parents have been highlighted as significant problems with accreditation.

By 2002, only a small number of centres had been disqualified from accreditation. Rush reports that in New South Wales in 2005, the Department of Community Services 'found that 67 centres in Sydney breached their licence conditions but only one was successfully prosecuted' (Rush 2006a, p 9; Pryor 2006). As the OECD notes, the test for the Australian accreditation system lies in 'whether the standards can actually be properly enforced while there remains a waiting list for childcare places' and parents are 'desperate to get a place' (OECD 2002, p 110; Elliott interviewed for *Background Briefing*, ABC 2004b). Excess demand places a powerful downward pressure on care standards.

The cost of childcare accounts for a growing proportion of household incomes, as paid formal care substitutes for informal extended family and parental care. It also amounts to a significant government budget item, especially at the Commonwealth level. It is estimated that outlays on the Child Care Benefit will exceed $1.6 billion in 2005-6, while the Child Care Tax Rebate will cost around $915 million in its first four years of operation from 2005

(McIntosh 2005, p 1). State governments also make contributions to centres and services, especially to preschools. Nonetheless, Australia remains at the lower end of the OECD in terms of its overall expenditure on early childhood education and care.

Since July 2000, the Child Care Benefit (CCB) has been payable to offset the costs of care on a sliding scale relative to income (see Table 7.3). Families with a taxable income of $30,000 in 2005 received a weekly Child Care Benefit of $144, and they were able to claim a Child Tax Rebate of $16.80 a week, taking their total subsidy to $160.80 with 80 per cent of their childcare costs covered (if they had one child in long day care and the total fees were $200 a week, which is a low estimate (McIntosh 2005, p 2)).

Despite high levels of public subsidy, and very low wages, the cost of childcare has been rising rapidly in Australia. In 2002, 27 per cent of those who had used or thought about using childcare reported difficulties with its cost (Cassells et al 2005, p 14). Between 1990 and 2004 the cost of childcare rose by double the rate of inflation. While the real cost fell after the introduction of the Child Care Benefit in July 2000, steep subsequent rises have wiped out its effect, and in the 12 months to September 2004, the cost of childcare rose by over 10 per cent (Cassells et al 2005, p 14). Affordability of care has declined rapidly, generating lively debate about the tax treatment of childcare.

Cost issues increasingly affect access to childcare, with poorer Australian families more likely to report cost as the main reason their children do not get the childcare their parents want (Flood 2004, p 2).

Childcare workers subsidise childcare through their very low wages, relative to those paid to other workers with comparable levels of skill doing similar work. If childcare workers are exercising levels of skill and effort that are close to those of preschool teachers, they are currently subsidising childcare costs to the tune of at least 15 per cent. This is an involuntary but significant level of subsidy by a group of low-paid workers. Once again this increase in commodification contributes to a serious and widening labour market inequity, as higher-paid workers and the larger economy benefit from the labour of a poorly-paid, feminised service sector.

Table 7.3. Childcare benefit and tax rebate by income, 2005

Family adjusted taxable income	Child Care Benefit (per week)	Out of pocket amount	Child Care Tax Rebate (per week equivalent)	Combined CCB and CCTR	Per cent of costs covered*
	(CCB)		(CCTR)		
30,000	144.00	56.00	16.80	160.80	80.4
50,000	112.00	88.00	26.40	138.40	69.2
100,000	24.15	175.85	52.76	76.91	38.5

Source: McIntosh 2005, p 2. Assumes one child in long day care 50 hours a week, costing $200 per week. This is well below fee levels payable in many centres.

Demand outstrips supply

Long day care is the most common type of formal childcare in Australia. This care is centre-based, mostly for children under five, and is provided on a full-time or part-time basis. Alongside private companies, long day care centres are also run by community organisations (which until recently were the dominant providers) and other not-for-profit bodies and some employers.

At present, long day care accounts for around half of all formal childcare places for children under 12 years old in Australia, and most formal care for children under five (Table 7.4). It has been growing rapidly, especially in the form of private provision.

The demand for formal childcare runs well ahead of supply, with estimates of unmet demand in recent years ranging from 131,700 in 2002 (ABS Cat No 4402.0, 2002) to 188,400 in 2005 (ABS Cat No 4402.0, 2005, p 8). The ABS estimate a 2005 national shortfall of 64,400 places in before and after school care, 52,900 in long day care and 40,800 in occasional care (ABS Cat No 4402.0, 2005, p 31).

Table 7.4. Children in formal childcare by service type, 2004

	No of Children	Per cent of all formal care
Private long day care	269,330	36
Community long day care	113,690	15
(All long day care)	(383,020)	(51)
Family day care	89,300	12
In home care	3,240	<1
Outside school hours care	160,800	21
Vacation care	101,710	14
Other service types	14,700	1
TOTAL	752,750	100

Source: FaCS (2005a), *2004 Census of Child Care Services Summary Booklet*, p 13. Weighted data including estimates for non-responding services.

The Howard Government has increased the number of some kinds of childcare places in recent years by providing, for example, 40,000 new outside-school-hours childcare places and 4,000 family day care places in the 2004/05 budget (Commonwealth of Australia, 2004). However, these increases fall well short of demand and do not touch the issue of long day care, where the shortfall is very pronounced. This is having a measurable effect on factors like labour market participation, with growing evidence that the lack of childcare is inhibiting women's labour market activity.

Government policy and the growing reach of the market

Government policy has critically shaped market opportunities in childcare and underwritten the rapidly increasing profits of private companies (Brennan 1998). Childcare provision has changed dramatically with the 1991 extension of subsidies to private centres. The 1997 Howard Government decision to end operational and capital works subsidies for community-based centres, resulted in the closure of many community-managed centres and a decline in the affordability of childcare (Baxter 2004). Despite this, the total government contribution has increased dramatically. The expansion of private provision has seen a massive increase in expenditure. As Lynn Wannan, of the National Association of Community-Based Children's Services Australia, puts it, 'This escalation in expenditure was almost entirely due to uncontrolled commercial development as the growth of community-based services ground to a halt' (2005, p 5). She concludes that a market-based rather than planned system of provision has 'sent community-based services into decline, and increased government outlays, increased the cost to users while failing to match supply with demand', let alone match supply to other government objectives like women's labour market participation (2005, p 7).

Private providers now account for just over 70 per cent of all centre-based long day care places in Australia. Their share varies widely by State from 85.6 per cent in Queensland to around a third in Tasmania (see Table 7.5).

Table 7.5. Proportion of Commonwealth-supported long day care places provided privately, 2004, by State

	Per cent
Queensland	85.6
Western Australia	75.1
New South Wales	69.4
Victoria	66.9
South Australia	48.7
Northern Territory	38.7
ACT	38.0
Tasmania	32.8
AUSTRALIA	71.6

Source: Centrelink Administrative Data as at 27 September 2004. See Rush 2006a, p 3.

Within the short space of two decades, Australia's childcare system has taken a significant turn to the private market. And not the market of the neoclassical textbook, with many sellers, competitive pricing, perfect information and a ready local supply.

In terms of the dominant type of formal care for children, long day care, the market is dominated by one major commercial operator, ABC Learning Centres Limited, and supply is far from readily available. Another segment of private childcare is provided by independent owner-operated small businesses usually running a single centre (Rush 2006a, p 2).

The market for private long day care is underwritten by a very large taxpayer subsidy, through payments to parents who use formal centre-based care. In this sense, the market has a government guarantee and the industry a direct conduit to the public purse. It is no surprise that this direct line to secure on-going funding has made the sector a stock market favourite. Further, the childcare market is one in which supply is very uneven geographically, with very variable information about what is being sold, including the quality of the 'product'. This is far from a 'normal' market. Most importantly, this market sells a fragile service: safe, developmentally appropriate care of children. Mistakes in this market – most notably, poor quality care – can have significant life-long effects. While the profits of corporate childcare provision are privatised for shareholders, at least some of its public, potentially negative, effects for children are socialised through taxpayer-funded remediation later in life, and widening socio-economic and cognitive inequality.

Six specific features of childcare make it a problematic candidate for private provision. First, childcare is a complex 'soft product': its quality and output are difficult to measure, making it 'hard to monitor activities and performance', and a less than easy product to regulate. It is very difficult for the consumer to have perfect knowledge about the products in this market (Lundsgaard 2002). Secondly, there is considerable potential for 'creaming': that is, supplying more profitable services (like care for children three to four years old) while leaving more expensive services (like care of babies or children with special needs) to the public sector. Thirdly, the drive to deliver shareholder value has the potential to affect the quality of care – a feature of childcare that, as we have seen, is critical to long-term outcomes for children. The logic of the market (cost minimisation and profit maximisation) has particular implications for children's services. While centres might fear low utilisation rates if they develop a reputation for low-quality care, it is often difficult for parents to judge quality, with indicators hard to come by and difficult to 'read'. The direct childcare consumer – often a child under five years old – is different from the purchaser of care (a parent or care giver). The child cannot easily speak about experience, so that the feedback loop from consumer to provider is imperfect and indirect. Other issues also complicate parental choice. A number of studies suggest that parents tend to overestimate the quality of care relative to objective measures (Press and Woodrow 2005, p 282). This probably reflects several factors: 'parents' lack of knowledge about what to look for, imperfect information about what they are purchasing or an emotional need to view the childcare as better than it is' (Press and Woodrow 2005, p 282). In a market where supply is short, parental over-optimism is likely to be especially strong.

Fourthly, the uneven geographic availability of care options makes choice about care problematic. This contradicts one of the first principles of an efficient market: choice between accessible, multiple suppliers. Recent court battles to restrain the construction of new services in the vicinity of existing ones are testament to the particular 'lumpy' character of childcare places and the assertive efforts that existing providers make to protect their corner in very localised markets. This makes *real choice* a practical unreality for parents in many locations.

Fifthly, high levels of demand reduce choice in the childcare market. With over 100,000 parents in search of places beyond the number available, and little prospect of a reduction in demand, it is not surprising to find that choice is constrained in the shadow of serious undersupply. In this context, the market fails.

Finally, what happens to children and parents when investors find that their rate of return falls? If capital is relocated, many children, parents, households and workplaces will be affected in ways that are personally very significant, and not without economic costs. As Wannan observes:

> Private childcare providers' long-term investment is in real estate. Government fee subsidies have made this possible. But if returns on the capital investment fall, private operators may turn to other forms of investment. If the for-profit sector collapses, or sells off land and buildings, the children's services system will require enormous rebuilding. Will the government be forced to buy back facilities at hugely inflated prices? Will government be forced to keep raising the level of subsidy to keep private operators afloat? (2005, p 24).

These characteristics of childcare for children under five years old make it a far from ideal candidate for private provision. This is why so many countries adopt public childcare systems.

Some of the above general difficulties are already obvious in Australia. For example, there are signs that Australia's private providers are 'creaming' with a tendency to provide more places in cheaper forms of care. Sixteen per cent of children in private long day care centres in 2004 were under two years old, compared to 21 per cent in community centres (FaCS 2005b). Babies are more costly to care for given their higher staff ratios, with five children per carer for children under two, and ten to one for children four to five years old in most Australian States (OECD 2002, p 90).

Similarly, community-based centres have higher proportions of special needs children. Children with high needs include those with disabilities, those whose parents have a disability, Aboriginal or Torres Strait Islander children, children of culturally diverse backgrounds, or children at risk (FaCS 2005b). Each of these categories potentially requires higher-cost care and higher staff/child ratios. In 2004, 20 per cent of all children in community-based long day care had special needs, compared to 15 per cent in private centres. The gaps are wide in some States, especially the larger States: in New South Wales for example, 23 per cent of children in community-based centres were from culturally diverse backgrounds compared to 17 per cent in private centres, and 2 per cent were of Aboriginal or Torres Strait Islander background, compared to 1 per cent in private centres

(FaCS 2005b). Children with disabilities made up 2 per cent of children in community-based centres across Australia, compared to 1 per cent in private centres (FaCS 2005b). It also seems that provision of childcare services in remote (and thus more expensive) locations are more likely to be community-based than private: in 2001, 7.8 per cent of employees in community-based long day care centres in Queensland were from remote areas compared to only 1.2 per cent of employees of private long day care centres (Misko 2001, p 6).

In terms of cost saving and quality of care, there is 'an inexorable tension between obligations to shareholders and obligations to children' (Horin 2003, p 39), and this tension is evident to many observers, including business analysts, childcare experts and centre managers (ABC 2004a, 2004b). The logic of the market is such that it will drive key indicators like staffing ratios and skill levels (accounting for around 80 per cent of centre costs) down to mandatory minima, and encourage careful calculations around the likelihood of their effective enforcement. In such situations, the nature of regulation and the effectiveness of enforcement become critical.

A recent survey of Australian childcare workers confirms these concerns (Rush 2006). The 2006 study (which included 578 staff from a stratified random sample of childcare centres across Australia) found that childcare staff felt that the quality of care was 'generally quite high' across a range of issues, including adequate time for staff to relate to children individually, the responsiveness of the program to the individual needs of children, the quality of equipment and food (as well as its quantity), staff turnover and staff/child ratios. Community-based long day care centres and independent private centres (usually run by an owner-operator) were seen as offering similar levels of high quality care. However, persistent and significant negative differences were evident in corporate chains.

On all of the above criteria, corporate chains performed more poorly in the eyes of staff than community and independent private centres. On the key issue of time to develop relationships with children, around half of staff in these latter two kinds of centres said they always have time to do this, compared to only a quarter in corporate centres (Rush 2006a, p ix). This difference also extended to equipment, with around two-thirds of those in community-based centres indicating that the variety of activities and equipment in their centres was good – compared to a third in corporate chains. Similar wide gaps existed around the provision of nutritious food and enough food. Less that half of staff in corporate centres felt that their centre always provided nutritious food (46 per cent), compared to 74 per cent in community-based centres and 73 per cent in independent private centres (Rush 2006a, p 35). On the critical question of staff/child ratios, 40 per cent of staff in community-based centres said their standard ratios were above the legal minimum, compared to only 14 per cent of corporate centre staff (Rush 2006a, p 37).

Most tellingly, 21 per cent of staff in corporate centres said they would not send their own children to the centre they worked in (or one with comparable quality of care), compared to 4 per cent of those who worked in community-based centres, and 6 per cent of those in independent private centres (Rush 2006a, p 50). Rush concludes that 'there are good grounds for believing that the lower quality of care revealed [in corporate centres] is due to the very nature of the corporate enterprise', and its pursuit of a business orientation rather than 'humanist concerns' especially the warm, responsive, personalised care of children (Rush 2006a, p xi).

Corporate care: Super kiddie profits?

Business analysts suggest that the rate of profit in corporate childcare centres is 50 per cent (Kirby 2003, p 1). High levels of profit have been recorded by key companies like ABC Learning Centres in recent years. These profits are underwritten by government subsidies. Not surprisingly, Michael Gordon, then Chief Executive and major shareholder in Peppercorn Management, describes these as 'a very well targeted form of subsidy' (interviewed on *The 7.30 Report*, ABC 2004a). This level of subsidy is now potentially higher with the introduction of the Child Care Tax Rebate. Eddy Groves, CEO of ABC Learning Centres, hailed the rebate in the 2004 election as a 'remarkable' policy offer: 'the federal government in Australia has got it nailed. That 30 per cent rebate has definitely come out of the blue and that's remarkable' (2004b). Almost 60 per cent of ABC Learning's revenue was from government subsidies prior to this change (Horin 2003, p 39).

Rather than being reinvested in the industry, these profits are paid to shareholders. With low entry barriers, no controls on who can enter the industry and high returns, it is not surprising that analysts describe childcare services as an attractive investment target. As one Gold Coast proprietor told *Business Review Weekly*, 'the child-care business is the best business I've ever seen in my life. The Government pays subsidies, the parents pay you two weeks in advance and property prices keep going up' (Kirby 2003).

Unfortunately, it is children, parents and staff who pay a price for disrupted services when centres close as a result of corporate restructuring, as occurred in Child Care Centres Australia (CCCA) in Western Australia in 2004 (ABC 2004b). One board member of CCCA commented on her experience at this time highlighting the relentless competition between costs and quality of service:

> I found the hardest part was to constantly be reviewing the status of the children's services workforce within each childcare centre. Constantly reviewing the cost of the wages per week, constantly reviewing for profit not for the service provision ... In many cases it was a financial decision rather than the program which needed so badly to have extra hours for staff ... It was unsettling staff because they couldn't predict the hours of work that they were going to have. (Caroline Fewster, interviewed on *Background Briefing*, ABC 2004b, p 14)

Cost-cutting underpins profits

Cost-cutting is viewed as a predictable strategy in the industry, one that business analysts readily recognise. IBISWorld warned in March 2003: 'There are concerns that large for-profit operators will be more likely [than non-profit centres] to cut costs to an absolute minimum' (Kirby 2003) and some private centre owner-operators have expressed particular concerns about large chains: 'There are new people in this industry making profits in a new way. They just stick to the absolute minimum regulations and cut expenses to the bone. I get former staff from these big operators coming over all the time saying they won't work under such conditions' (quoted in Kirby 2003). Share analysts describe childcare centres as sharemarket 'darlings', whose recent performance is 'spectacular'. However, the implications of the push to lower costs and maximise returns for care quality are obvious to them:

> With economies of scale and generous government subsidies, the big chains look like sure-fire money-makers. However, some observers fear that the big chains' drive to maximise returns to shareholders might compromise the quality of services (Australian Business Intelligence, 11 October 2002).

Early childhood experts share these concerns, pointing to the market logic which ensures that private providers operate to meet basic licensing and quality assurance regulations, rather than offering 'top-of-the-range developmental and educational experiences, which research tells us are critical to outcomes for children's development and well-being' (Elliott 2004):

> The concern in any business is to maximise profit ... and the reality is, even the most elite private school is a non-profit organisation, where all fees and any other income raised by that group is ploughed back into the education of children. This is just not the case for childcare centres that are private for profit ... they have to give that money back to the shareholders. (Dr Alison Elliott, Research Director in Early Childhood Education, Australian Council for Education Research, interviewed for *Background Briefing* ABC 2004b)

Costs in the sector reflect at least five factors: staffing levels, qualifications, staff conditions, and the quality of facilities like buildings, food and toys.

Staffing levels

Staffing levels are the critical contributor to quality care. The proportion of budget allocated to staff is reported to be much lower in private centres (50 per cent of revenue) than in community-based centres (80 per cent of revenue) (ABC 2004a). Private centres have openly worked to lower required staffing requirements. For example, ABC Learning Centres took the Queensland Government to court in 2003 in an attempt to try to relax staff ratio requirements (ABCa 2004).

According to official reports, staffing levels per service are lower in private centres than in community services, with 14 staff per service in community services and 12 in private centres (FaCS 2003, p 18). This may reflect, at least in part, the higher share of infants (for whom staffing ratios are higher) in community-based services. Beyond staffing numbers, the level of workload is also relevant. In some private centres, care staff are asked to undertake regular cleaning duties as part of their workload (Groves, interviewed for *Background Briefing*, 3 October 2004; ABC 2004b). These concerns are substantiated by the 2005 survey of Australian childcare workers and its findings of poorer staffing levels and more intensive workloads in corporate centres compared to community-based centres (Rush 2006a).

Qualifications

Levels of qualification are lower in private centres. In 2004, in all States and in the ACT, the proportion of staff with qualifications as early childhood teachers was lower in private centres than in community-based centres. In Queensland, where private provision is highest, 28 per cent of staff in private centres in 2004 were undertaking training only (that is, had no other qualifications), compared to 19 per cent in community centres. A 2001 study found that a quarter of centre directors in Queensland's childcare centres (80 per cent of which were private at that time) did not have 'an approved or related qualification', while 28 per cent of group leaders and teachers did not have an approved or related qualification (Misko 2001, p 6). It is not surprising that training is lagging, given the difficulty of placing students in high quality environments: one early childhood educator recently estimated that in her State only one in ten centres was functioning at a high enough level of quality to place students with them (ABC 2004b).

Staffing conditions

Wages in the childcare sector are notoriously low, and this is accompanied by high levels of job insecurity and staff turnover. The OECD note that the high level of casual employment in Australian centres gives 'rise to concerns about staff turnover and therefore continuity for children' (OECD 2002, p 111). Average wages are lower in the private sector with high levels of job insecurity in some States.

The highly privatised Queensland service has a very high proportion of casual staff: 33 per cent of staff in private centres in Queensland in 2004 were casual compared to 28 per cent in community-based centres (FaCS 2005b, pp 41, 63). Casualisation is also high in South Australia in both private centres (43 per cent) and community-based centres (42 per cent). The national average of casualisation in private childcare centres is 25 per cent, and 24 per cent in community-based centres (FaCS 2005b, pp 41, 63). Analysis of the childcare workforce reveals that turnover in the Queensland industry is high (Misko 2001).

Working for love

Low wages for childcare workers are recognised as a serious problem contributing to high labour turnover and creating difficulties attracting and retaining skilled workers. In a 2001 survey of Queensland childcare workers, the majority said they would leave the industry if they could find a better-paid job, and almost half of respondents would not recommend the job to others because of its low pay and status.

The shortage of skilled staff is at a crisis level in many Australian locations, affecting both public and private services. This reflects low pay, a flat career structure with low returns for higher qualifications, low levels of community esteem and high job demands (including unpaid overtime and long hours of work in some services) (ACTU 2004; Misko 2001). This shortage has implications for quality of care. In some States shortages of skilled staff have led to the relaxation of the licensing provisions that underpin quality assurance: where there are not enough qualified staff available, centres are allowed to continue offering services even where they cannot meet licensing requirements.

Concerns about the quality of care in private centres, especially corporate centres, have been publicly raised in Australia (ABC 2004a; ABC 2004b; Rush 2006a) with commentary about standards of care and education, the quality of food and facilities, and pressures from private providers to reduce the level of staffing ratios (ABC 2004a; ABC 2004b; Kirby 2003; Horin 2003). These deserve further systemic study. They are cause for concern, and certainly provide an argument for further research.

The market unleashed

The story of the market's enthusiasm for commodified childcare and the transformation of childcare provision in Australia over the past decade is clear from the rise of ABC Learning Centres. The company is especially active in Queensland and Western Australia where private provision of centre-based care is especially high. The company is now turning its attention to international opportunities, especially the USA, and to other sectors like schools.

In 2001, ABC Learning Centres was the first for-profit childcare service to be listed on the Australian stock market. ABC Learning earned profits of over $50 million in 2004/05 (Rush 2006b, p vii). In the five years since the company floated on the stock exchange, its share price has increased by more than 300 per cent and in April 2006 it was capitalised at a value of $2.6 billion (Rush 2006b, p vii.). The company is said to be the second largest private childcare company in the world (AAP, 16 November 2005; Austin and Whiting, ABC Queensland Radio, 3 August 2005). It has aspirations to enter the larger school arena by supporting the creation of schools for profit, although these efforts have been hampered by the fact that public education funds for primary and secondary schools generally only flow to schools that are not-for-profit. As Anna Bligh, Queensland Education Minister put it, 'public subsidy should go to schools who are returning every cent of surplus, if there is any, back into that school' (Alberici, *The 7.30 Report*, 30 May 2005). Why are early childhood services, whose effects on child development are even more critical than schooling, treated differently?

ABC Learning now provides more than 20 per cent of all long day childcare in Australia (Rush 2006b, p vii). In mid-2006 the company owned over 800 centres, having taken over a succession of other providers and also managed a further 217 centres (Rush 2006b, p vii).

Significant figures in the Liberal and National Parties have had close associations with the private company, including Michael Kroger, Andrew Peacock and Sallyanne Atkinson. Controversially, Larry Anthony joined the ABC board as a non-Executive member only five months after losing his seat in federal parliament and ending his term as Minister for Childcare in the Howard Government (Jokovich 2004). Key issues in relation to the quality of childcare are child/staff ratios and other regulatory standards, like training of staff, and their enforcement. The growth in the powerful voice of politically well-connected, private for-profit organisations is likely to create downward pressure on both regulatory standards and the vigour of enforcement.

Markets and childcare in the future

Private familial childcare is likely to remain a strong preference in future households based on the perspectives of young people in our focus groups and parental attitudes in Australia. For many women, this includes their own mothers' help to care for their children. Some of these plans will founder on the shrinking capacity of private familism. Instead, 'market familism' will probably expand. The quality of childcare is very important to children who – when they in turn become parents – are determined to find quality care for their own children as a result of their own experiences in care. For them, this means good staff, facilities and food, and well-managed relationships with other children and staff. Some young people are already concerned about standards of care. In one focus group, young women expressed concern about falling standards:

[Whether I will use it] depends. Especially if [the quality of] childcare is going down which is what I have heard ... If the standard of childcare is lowering, so if it got any lower, I would probably rethink my decision. (Sarah, 16, Comfort High)

Many children we spoke with had experienced care when community-based childcare was the dominant form of centre-based care. It is reasonable to assume that these centres had a higher level of staffing and quality provision than generally prevails at present. There seems little to suggest that the quality of childcare provision in Australia has risen in recent years and there are indicators of the reverse with high levels of staff turnover, casualisation and inadequately trained staff. The accessibility and affordability of childcare, especially for children under two, is currently in decline in many parts of Australia.

Clearly, any presumption of parental choice is undermined by the absence of childcare, excessive costs or poor quality.

Current and projected trends in labour market participation and family shape (including extended family) suggest a thinning of 'private familism'. While some young people are eager for parental and grandparent care, many will be disappointed because their parents are far away, working or too old. They will turn to the market more than they expect, and they will be buying childcare in a marketised environment that has been transformed since the time of their own experience in childcare. In Australia, care of babies and very young children is a profitable service and the market is eager to gather these children into its thrall, and in some cases make great profits from them. Demand runs well ahead of supply, and information systems about quality of care – its key ingredient – are poorly developed and hard for parents to decipher. Insufficient and 'lumpy' supply inhibits real choice for parents. In this environment, quality may well be hard to judge and sometimes hard to find. What is more, in a market system, wealth can buy quality care, while middle- and lower-income families are more likely to struggle. Relying on the state to get the management of quality right may not work for the next generation of workers and carers in a childcare market that is highly politicised, where the stakes around required standards and their enforcement are high, and a

few large, political, well-connected corporations have real influence and can frustrate research.

The childcare market has flowered in the gaps around family
and public provision. It is oriented to the lowest mandatory
standards rather than high-quality care, and it cannot meet
demand. What is more, complex regulation by both State and
national authorities makes it hard for parents to be sure that
their children are in good care. As the young people in our study
say based on experience, and in total accord with a large body of
international research, it is the quality of relationships and
facilities that make good care.

The plans of these young people, and the rapid expansion of
the market in the provision of long day care in Australia, create
a strong argument for market intervention and for better public
provision. They are also a powerful argument for making both
the regulation of childcare and a national system of early
childhood education and care national priorities.

The rapid growth in the commodification of childcare is a
powerful stimulant to the market and to the work/spend cycle.
Women in particular need to organise and pay for childcare as a
first step to labour market entry. For many of them, the cost
of childcare eats up a significant proportion of their pay. Where
the quality of care is high and its hours are not excessive,
research suggests that children may benefit from childcare.
However, where quality is low, it can corrode the well-being of
children, causing long-term negative effects for children and
society. The use of formal childcare is likely to increase if young
people follow through on their work plans and turn to formal
childcare where their private families cannot provide it.

Alongside this probable high dependency on commodified
care, young people seem likely to be habituated to an early, fast-
paced cycle of consumption and paid work. It is this early
'training' in consumption and commodification that we turn to
in the next chapter.

CHAPTER 8

Runaway consumption, the work/spend cycle and youth

In the preceding chapters we have considered how changes in adult patterns of paid work and care affect young people, and how young people plan to organise these things in their own futures with the possible implication of greater demand for formal childcare. In this chapter we consider young people's own consumption. Their current patterns of paid work and consumption create an early-onset cycle of work-and-spend which presumes a high level of commodification of time and high levels of consumption in the race to construct the self. Young people are particular targets of advertisers and aggressive marketing – marketing that reaches into homes and schools – with important implications for their current and future patterns of work and care.

Current patterns of parental work affect children in ways that are obscured and privatised within the household and are externalities to the labour market. On top of this are young people's own patterns of work and consumption which seem likely to give further force to these factors in the future, rather than contradict or slow them.

This chapter falls into several sections. First, we consider young people's consumption, their views of competitive consumption and the kinds of products that matter to them, based on focus group discussions. Secondly, we consider the mechanisms by which young people say they get what they want. Finally, we consider the kind of work/spend treadmill in prospect and the opportunities it creates for a larger labour market attachment and – potentially – an expansive acquisitiveness. These may be good for measured economic growth, but may correlate poorly with the happiness of future generations.

Young people and consumption

Since at least the 1930s, advertisers in industrialised countries have been alert to the potential of marketing to children (Cook, 2000). There is no doubt that children are involved, one way or another, in the significant increase in consumption in industrialised countries like Australia. One US estimate suggests that children influenced about US$5 billion of their parents' purchases in the 1960s, but by 1984 that figure had increased to US$50 billion and by 1997 it reached $188 billion. Child marketing expert James McNeal estimates that by 2000 children under 12 years old influenced over US$500 billion of US consumption (Centre for a New American Dream 2003).

Many studies now suggest that young people's consumption is growing rapidly, that they increasingly influence household consumption and are the target of marketing especially through schools and social networks (Quant 2003; Fien and Skoien 2000). It also suggests that 'competitive consumption' (Lane 2000) is at work between children as they respond to peer pressure and use a variety of techniques to persuade parents to buy for them, including advertising and 'the nag factor' (Cook 2001, p 1).

Many corporations are acutely aware of the role that young people play in determining household consumption. In many cases, they deliberately target marketing at young household members, encouraging them to work on parental guilt and stimulate household commodification. This includes strategies for purchases that go well beyond those of immediate interest to children, like toys, computers and clothes, to purchases of cars, furniture, electronics, holidays and housing.

Juliet Schor has recently analysed the nature of the 'commercialized American child'. She finds evidence of aggressive marketing to children and young people, so that children now function as 'conduits from the consumer marketplace into the household, the link between advertisers and the family purse' (2004, p 11). As 'early adopters' of new products, they are a vital route to the parental purse. In this light, corporations have 'infiltrated the core activities and institutions of childhood, with virtually no resistance from governments and parents' (2004, p 13). These institutions include schools (with many examples of commercialisation through education), homes and – beyond them – family and childhood relationships, as well as leisure.

In Schor's view, increased television watching especially drives increasing commodification of childhood. In 1987, three to five year old children in the US spent an average of almost 14 hours a week watching television (with children in lower-income homes tending to spend more). This level is very close to that in Australia: in 2003, Australian three to four year old children watched on average 14.7 hours of television and videos a week (AIFS 2005). Children who watch more television make more requests for items like toys (Schor 2004, p 67) and of course they are exposed to high levels of advertising of junk food and many other products. Schor describes how many time-poor parents 'give in' on unhealthy food consumption, in particular, because of work pressures and the breadth of other important issues they must discipline children about.

In the US, the growing reach of materialism among children is powerful, with one study revealing that 'more than a third of all children aged nine to 14 would rather spend time buying things that doing almost anything else' and a similar proportion showing a strong preference for friends with 'special games or clothes'. More than half agreed that 'when you grow up, the more money you have the happier you will be' (Schor 2004, p 37). Corporations have actively encouraged the conflation of 'cool' with 'stuff' and the consolidation of a childhood and adolescent sense of self through possessions, so that 'living modestly means living like a loser' (Schor 2004, p 48).

Marketing experts in the US specifically work to mobilise 'emotional vulnerabilities to get the attention of young people. Kids are very sensitive to that' (Schor 2004, p 65). Corporations also deliberately encourage children to identify particular forms of consumption with independence from parents, so that 'cool' is associated 'with an anti-adult sensibility' (Schor 2004, p 48).

Schor analyses the implications of childhood consumption for children's well-being by means of surveys, finding robust indicators that 'high consumer involvement is a significant cause of depression, anxiety, low self-esteem and psychosomatic complaints'. She finds that children who are otherwise mentally healthy become worse off when they become more enmeshed in the culture of getting and spending (2004, p 167). She concludes:

> American children are deeply enmeshed in the culture of getting and spending, and they are getting more so. We find that the more enmeshed they are, the more they suffer for it. The more they buy into the commercial and materialist messages, the worse they feel about themselves, the more depressed they are, and the more they are beset by anxiety, headaches, stomach aches, and boredom. The bottom line of the culture they're being raised in is that it's a lot more pernicious than most adults have been willing to admit. (2004, p 173)

Her surveys among children are supported by a growing body of international evidence that finds that materialism is 'correlated with lower self-esteem' and 'higher rates of depression and anxiety' and is often associated with physical symptoms of ill-health among both adults and children (2004, p 174). The contemporary market thus has a lot to answer for in mobilising childhood vulnerabilities, harnessing them to consumption, creating needs (some of which are hazardous, for example, in relation to junk food), and thus drawing young people into a nag-war with parents, or into their own youthful work/spend cycle.

New childhood: 'I consume therefore I am'

Alissa Quant has also documented the strategies used by US marketers to build teenage consumption (2003). They are diverse and effectively penetrate households, schools and children's own networks. Cook argues that such marketing is part of the process of extending 'personhood to children'. He says that in order for the creation of '[young] personhood through consumption' to be untainted by the profane, it is necessary to naturalise consumption in ways that reaffirm 'the sacredness of childhood in the context of market relations by making self-expression appear as the inevitable, necessary completion of the commercial process' (Cook 2000, p 489). In other words, the creation of the self through shopping and consuming must be made to seem a good thing rather than a grubby thing if children are to be 'made' through it. Many young people increasingly construct their identities through what they buy and consume, a trend that marketers avidly encourage. 'I shop therefore I am' is an element of marketing to children, just as it is to adults. Young people see aspects of themselves confirmed and created through what they buy, a perception marketing manipulates by increasingly 'pitching' to them and their fragile, emergent identities (McNeal 1992; Seiter 1993; Acuff 1997; Cook 2000; Schor 2004).

How much money is enough?

Young people we spoke with in focus groups weighed up the costs and benefits of consuming by having 'a lot of money'. Many were cautious about money and its effects. One 15-year-old boy at Struggle High who sought more time with his parents rather than more money, observed that 'Money can tear things apart ... Money itself can become an evil presence. There are fights about money'. Young people from the country offered similar comments:

> I think it's important to have enough money, but not too much. It can wreck your family, and people who get too much get selfish, I reckon. (Robert, 17, Country High)

> Like Robert said. It wouldn't be good at all to have heaps of money. Cause then you always get what you want ... [You want] just enough money to be happy and enjoy what you are doing ... I wouldn't want to be rich. Money is just a tool. You need money to get things like food, clothes, a house. (Adam, 16, Country High)

> I agree with what Adam and Robert said. It's more important to have a good family environment, rather than money. Money is not everything in life. (Kevin, 17, Country High)

Like many of their peers living in financially comfortable households, they weighed up the value of money and did not consider that more of it, or a lot of it, was necessarily a good thing. A number of children in lower-income households shared these views. They were seeking relief from worry about bills for their parents and stable secure incomes rather than large sums of money for discretionary, non-essential spending.

Young people from across income, gender and age groups, however, identified a powerful culture of competitive consumption among young people, with negative consequences. Many participants felt that having too much money affects young people negatively. At Leafy High at Sydney, Aislan says that having a lot of money is not good for young people who 'just spend it all on useless junk':

> I think it is important for kids to have some amount of money to get out, have a social life and entertainment, otherwise you'd be cramped inside doing homework. Oh God, you'd be going mad! But not too much … and when you get to a certain age … you should start thinking of earning money. (Aislan, 16, Leafy High)

A group of 15-year-old boys in a lower-income area of Adelaide (described by their female peers as 'serious, political' boys) shared a critique of money and consumption. They deliberately carried 'a brick of a mobile phone', or 'abhorred' or 'deplored' them. They said they were not easily impressed by wealth. Rich people need to 'know how to deal with it'. In the words of Jack: 'You get the rich snobby people and you can get the rich nice people'. The difference is that nice rich people didn't waste their money and have everything. Jack is glad that 'I didn't have a lot of money at a young age' because:

> Well, at my age, moving on to 16, comes cars. Not for me, but people I know, they have access to drugs. Drugs come into it. Your life ends at the age of 20 if you've got drugs because you're rich. Getting a car, go buy the latest car … But having a lot of money at a young age, I think is a bad idea. (Jack, 15, Struggle High)

At the same school, 15-year-old girls also associate having money with drugs. Like many young people, they were critical of too much money on several grounds: young people wouldn't know how to handle it, it would lead to inauthentic relationships based on money, and they wouldn't know how to manage money later in life. Lower-income primary school children in Adelaide were scathing about children who have a lot of money:

> They are spoilt little brats. Think they own the world, think they can do what they like (Kelsey, 12, Struggle Primary).

At the same time they are well aware of what happens if you can't keep up with your peers in terms of possessions: 'you get called a geek, gay, dwerb or a lesbian' (Kelsey, 12, Struggle Primary). The association of 'coolness' with 'consumption' is well established: only losers go without.

Several primary school children in the country felt that it was unfair for some to have a lot of money. Young people with a lot of money are seen as spoiled and 'taking everything for granted' (Louise, 15, Struggle High):

> You might not be mature enough to handle the money ... As Jack said, you might go out and blow all you money on stuff you don't need. (Claus, 15, Struggle High)

At Strive High, Audrey has decided not to spoil her children because she wants them to value what they have: 'if it's not a necessity, they won't get it'. She points out that among her school peers 'A lot of people in our year who are working or getting money [for example Austudy] are becoming really tight. They don't want to pay anything cause they know it is their money, they won't give it. So I like the whole idea of working and getting your own money'. Her friend Melinda agrees: '[When I go into a shop] I'll look at that and think 'I want it, oohh, I'll have to work four hours to get it'. Audrey wants to save her money for 'important things', given that she has 'to work her butt off' to earn it in the first place.

Many felt that those with a lot of money would not learn how to save and would waste it. Thomas' family is collecting cans to save for a play-station: 'so far we've got $185 ... It will teach us how to save up, how to do it when we are older'. Jade, whose family has 'a lot of money', is careful not to take it for granted given how circumstances can change: 'I don't take money for granted, because maybe one day it may not be there'.

At Strive High, young people felt that there was a brittle link between money and friendships: 'People end up just liking you for your money and not for yourself ... And when you're out of money ... you get dumped':

> You buy people's respect. Buy your friends: 'Here I'll buy you this. You're my friend now'. I think it's a bad idea. It's not true friendship. (James, 15, Struggle High)

Claus was critical of the consumption mentality of young people: 'it's a motto for the human race: "let's go shopping"'. Several young people talked about the tenuous link between money and happiness. As Jacqueline says 'The downside is that money doesn't really equal happiness'. Things are more complicated:

> It's good [having money] but it's bad because when we were younger we had four of our bikes stolen and it's good because then you can pay off bills and you can give it to charity. The downside is that, the same as Coco said, both your parents would be working really hard to be rich and then you can never see your parents and you'd be sad. (Jacqueline, 11, Strive Primary)

Competitive consumption: Power through stuff

The children and young people we spoke with are aware of competitive consumption and consumption that is less about *need* and more about *want*, especially wants that arise out of competition to keep up with peers. When asked, 'Do you think girls and boys of your age try and keep up with each other with 'stuff?', many replied 'definitely!'. Competitive consumption was widely recognised by both 10-12 and 16-18 year olds.

Eleven-year-olds felt that their peers consumed competitively to belong and because they feared being teased:

> They don't want to be left out, and then everyone will be teasing them and saying like 'You're cheap' and stuff. (Lee, 11, Strive Primary)

They want to 'look cool' by being 'up with it'. According to Binh, some aim to impress by 'being different' but more commonly 11-year-olds speak of the pursuit of *sameness* as a road to popularity:

> I think everyone is trying to be like everyone else so they don't feel left out and people become popular if they buy new stuff, so they want to be popular too ... Because everyone will want to come over and play and stuff like that. (Emma, 11, Strive Primary)

197

In Adelaide, boys at Comfort Primary wanted the right clothes and toys, partly because they like to look good, and partly because 'it's cool', though they recognised that pleasure from consumption was often fleeting:

> Oh it just looks really good and then when you go out there and you start playing around with it after a few days or weeks or something it gets boring and you never play with it again. (Bob, 11, Comfort Primary)

However, Bob and his friends see a connection between stuff and power:

> You can go: 'This shirt cost $150'. (Bob, 11, Comfort Primary)

> And you can brag on about it and stuff. (Rove, 11, Comfort Primary)

> And rub it in their face, so other people will feel they need it as well. They feel that we're better ... That we've got power. (Bob, 11, Comfort Primary)

> That we've got power over them. (Rove, 11, Comfort Primary)

> Interviewer: And you feel that it makes you better?

> No, not really. (Bob, 11, Comfort High)

> Well, it probably does a bit, you know. (Rove, 11, Comfort High)

Despite their pursuit of power through expensive shirts, Rove and Bob are quick to deny that someone else with a better shirt has power over *them*. They find being on the receiving end of such bragging 'annoying', and try to convince the owner that his shirt is, in fact, 'hideous'. Competitive consumption is something they use to bolster themselves and their standing, but when others use it against them they say they try to ignore it or they undermine its currency. In either case, competitive consumption is endemic in their friendships and peer worlds.

Many adolescents in the focus groups defined themselves through their consumption: 'it's my identity', as one said. For example, young women at Struggle High thought it important to keep up with material goods like clothes, accessories, shoes, hair and makeup for 'image': 'So everyone thinks you're cool'. Girls at Strive High agreed: 'you want to be cool', 'to show off', 'to impress', 'to look better than everyone else. So there's competition [for sure]':

> Some people think it's a tragedy if you wear something that someone else has seen you wear before ... It's a competition. (Tanya, 16, Strive High)

Successful display brings popularity in their eyes.

Such patterns were obvious in both lower- and higher-income areas. Gary, at Leafy High, feels that 'a lot of what people think of you is based on what you wear'. At Comfort High in Adelaide, 'you are not good enough unless you have everything that everyone else has got. Mobile phones for example, and Billabong ... And I don't know who makes that rule. It just happens' (Amanda, 16, Comfort High). Her peers want to have 'nice things' to fit in.

Some distinguished 'belonging and identity construction' from the pure pleasure that having certain things gave them: 'I just do it cause I like it ... Not everyone does it just to be cool. It's just that they *like* it. You see this person, and think 'Oh that looks nice. I might get it'. That sort of thing'.

The race for fashionable brands is widely acknowledged. Several schools of thought are evident among young people: that brands are cool and help you join the in-crowd; or that they are a waste of money; or that they are signs of quality. 'Brands make better-looking stuff, so that's why I would buy it. Better quality ... Cause they look good' (Alana, 16, Struggle High).

Even those who said they don't participate in competitive consumption recognise the phenomenon among their peers, and define themselves *against* the 'cool' consumers. 'In' groups and 'out' groups are readily identified in many locations, based on consumption and look:

> You get the latest fashions. You find people with brand names. They're the ones who have got a big group of friends and then you get the ones who just don't worry about brands. They're the ones you usually find huddled together in a little corner ... It's the minority versus majority (Jack, 15, Struggle High).

Jack felt that this majority would have problems when they had to provide for themselves: 'When they find out that they've got to go out in the world and work, everything changes'. While these students readily critique the pursuit of social success through consumption, they thought that those who didn't keep up 'feel pretty bad'.

Others rejected the pursuit of 'coolness' and belonging through stuff: 'I don't have friends who are obsessed with material things' (Susie, 16, Comfort High). For some of Susie's peers, however, having the right stuff and keeping up was important because 'other girls are bitchy' and some are 'insecure, afraid of being left out'. The young men at Comfort High in Adelaide are aware of competitive pressure and feeling 'jealous' when they see people with things they want. Mark, 17, says: 'I get jealous of things that other people have but I don't publicise that' because he doesn't want to give others the satisfaction of feeling better than him. By having the right gear he felt: 'you get recognition'. At the same time, Geoff says, 'I find the nicest people are people who just don't care about things or objects'. He tries not to show off new things.

What products matter?

There are clear age and gender differences in the pursuit of identity through goods, although the mobile phone clearly crossed the gender boundary. Girls were more likely to mention competitive consumption in relation to clothes, jewellery, music and looks. Boys were more likely to pursue computer games and toys, while young men talked about cars and phones. For young men at Strive High, 'It's just *having* a car at the moment. But after a while you get a better car with spoiler, and a muffler, turbo'. While no one in their group had a really flash car 'as yet', they were aiming for them, for 'popularity'. 'You feel better for yourself. You're more of an individual', because you're mobile and independent of parents. At Leafy High, cars were not only desired, but many had them, including expensive cars 'to try to get the girls in'. While Aislan thinks this strategy is useless and it wouldn't work with her ('What's the thing with cars?'), others are more impressed:

I love cars! ... I have a friend who spent twenty grand doing up this car and then another friend of his went and bought a better car, so he had to sell his car and buy an even better one. (Ellie, 16, Leafy High)

Interviewer: And what do you think of that?

Oh, it's pretty stupid.

Interviewer: But did he get the girl?

Yeah, he did actually!

Many young people felt that adults were similarly competitive in their consumption.

I think adults are competitive, maybe not so obviously, but they can be. My aunt is, and my Mum is with clothes ... I think adults are actually sometimes more competitive than children, cause we are competitive but we don't have the money to actually buy it, but they do. (Audrey, 16, Strive High)

Young people in the country valued being brought up in a less consumption-oriented atmosphere, feeling that city kids could shop more often. However, most identified competitive consumption and clearly described 'in' and 'out' groups within their region built around possessions:

[You see] kids around here in Country Town that have a lot of money. They seem to be the ones that are too good for everybody else: Like, 'I've got everything, I've got all the brand names and the cool car and everything', and they seem to be really stuck up themselves and don't appreciate other people ... They are the cool people, and can't be seen with people who get clothes at a cheaper place, don't have the fashion stuff ... Being loaded is not a great thing because they don't appreciate anything, they have no values. (Judith, 18, Country High)

In the same group, Kate describes 'distinct' groups. Like Judith she has no time for wealthy people with values that she does not share.

The work-and-spend treadmill: Young people's critique

US studies reveal that many young people are well aware of the corrosive and unwinnable competition for stuff. A poll conducted by the Centre for a New American Dream in the US shows that of children aged nine to 14, 63 per cent were concerned that there is too much advertising that tries to get kids to buy things, three-quarters felt that it was 'too bad you have to buy certain things to be cool' and 81 per cent felt that 'lots of kids place way too much importance on buying things' (Schor 2004, p 22). In similar vein, many young people we spoke with clearly understood and criticised the pressures to consume to fit it.

A critique of the loss of quality of life as a result of the pursuit of material goods was evident in more wealthy areas among 16 to 18-year-olds, but there were few signs of it in lower-income areas where money was discussed in terms of meeting essential living expenses. A world of more discretionary expenditure in Sydney's northern suburbs drove a higher preference for parental time over money, and these young people were concerned about what lay ahead of them and the demands of being 'locked into' jobs. They wanted interesting jobs that would sweeten the years that work would take, and they hoped to avoid the long hours of their parents, and the sense of being trapped that they saw in some of their parents' patterns. They point to an unsatisfying, and insatiable, work/spend cycle:

> Everyone in their own little way wants to have more. It's the driving thing. You want more than you have. Everyone does, and so therefore you work and you get more, and you can never have enough. (Hannah, 16, Leafy High)

In Adelaide, at Comfort High, Mark, 17, is similarly critical of the competitive consumption treadmill, seeing its pleasures as fleeting and unsatisfying: you get the stuff and the brief happiness and 'then you just go back to where it was ... You get the great feeling for a little bit, and then you lose some of the good feeling'.

Young people at Leafy High see their futures narrowing in the pursuit of a secure financial life, and they are concerned about aspects of their parents' working lives. They want to travel before work because, as Vanessa puts it, 'seeing parents work, you just want to at least rest before you have to lock yourself into such an annoying life'. Later she continues, with general agreement from her peers:

> I think the quality of life is not increasing any more. It's decreasing because of work ... Like they might think they are increasing it because they're getting more money, and they're getting all these other things, but we're losing things that are much more important, that people don't realize. I just think it's really stupid. I don't usually think about it, but it's annoying ... Everybody has to have money now, because if you have money you have a higher status ... so that you feel like you're accepted with everybody ... and you feel more stable and all that. But I don't know. It's going the wrong way. We might be getting more things for ourselves but ... it's not positive at all, and it's scary to think what it's going to lead to. (Vanessa, 16, Leafy High)

Some discuss how their parents advise them to have their fun now because 'you're going to be working five days a week for the rest of your life'.

How kids get what they want

In rich countries, increasing incomes drive increasing consumption (Hamilton 2003). Children and young people in Australia are far from immune. Even in very poor households with welfare-dependent parents in poor health, children are keen to have the latest toys and games. These demands soak up incomes and, in some cases, dictate longer working hours for parents. Young people in all kinds of households want or have playstations and computer equipment; in many households a mobile phone for children is seen as important to family communication and social life. Young people strategise to get more of what they want.

Among participants in our focus groups, around three-quarters had a PlayStation or equivalent, 89 per cent had use of a computer in the home, and two-thirds had a mobile phone.

Among older students in senior high school, 85 per cent had a mobile phone. These levels of ownership are close to the national rates in 2004.

Beyond parental work, young people's *own* patterns of paid work finance their consumption of these kinds of items. The cycle of working and spending starts early. The proportion of Australian senior school students with jobs is increasing, although precise figures are not available. Robinson estimates that by the early 1990s one third of senior school students spent 'an average of nine hours per week in a part-time job' (2001, p ii). In the late 1990s, between 30 and 50 per cent of working-age school students held part-time jobs (Smith and Green, no date). This is more than twice the OECD average (Sweet 2001). Many young people are working and large numbers rely on their earnings as the chief means of acquiring stuff, especially inessential competitive consumption (brand name clothing, music, the latest mobile phones, cars). New generations of young people are making an early entry to work and consumption with a ready dividend for both retailers and labour markets.

In many cases, young people (like adults) perform a dual function in the changing product and service industries. On the one hand, they provide services (and receive low junior-rates of pay), while simultaneously fuelling sales of these services through their own consumption. Many love their jobs, mirroring the positive benefits they perceive their parents enjoy:

> I love it! I have friends there and we have fun. (Audrey, 16, Strive High)

> I love working. I like to show that I bought that for myself. I rely on myself for money. Plus the whole socialising thing, you make new friends and all. (Melinda, 16, Strive High)

They enjoy the social connection, sense of competence and independence that jobs and earnings bring. However, they are early entrants to a teenage work/spend cycle of their own at a time when their sense of self is nascent. This acclimatisation to 'self through consumption' creates fertile terrain for markets well into the future. These patterns are not without their critics, however, and most young people do not think that a lot of money is good for them, or necessarily for adults either.

Apart from their own earnings, young people also often simply ask their parents for the things they want. They may then back it up with the more pressured 'nag' or 'guilt' pitch. This tactic is recognised in other countries and actively encouraged by some corporations and marketers. In the US, Schor reports a study where 71 per cent of children kept asking for something that parents initially refused. She found that 'the average number of asks is eight, but over a quarter of kids ask more than ten times' (Schor 2004, p 62). In her study, around half felt they were successful in getting something they saw advertised that their parents didn't want them to have.

A large number of young people we spoke with felt that a straightforward 'ask' is the right approach to get what you want, often timed in relation to the family budget cycle: 'I ask my Mum' (Danielle, 11, Leafy High). Those in lower-income households often make deliberately modest requests and understand the household constraints; as one put it, she 'didn't ask' if she knew things were tight. Others were attuned to changes in financial circumstances. Todd (11, Comfort Primary) says that when his parents were together 'We'd get all the latest stuff. Now [they are separated] we have to be careful about what we buy. We don't want to waste all the money'. At Comfort High, Thanh, who lives with his hard-working single mother, restrains himself:

> It just depends on Mum's mood. I mean, if she's under heaps of pressure financially, I don't go near any money stuff. I just say I don't want it. (Thanh, 17, Comfort High)

Kate, 16, a farmer's daughter, is also very careful: 'I feel guilty taking money from my parents when they don't have it'. Spending her own earnings feels better.

Some 'asking' strategies go to the next level of nagging or mobilising parental guilt. A number of young people are open about 'the nag factor' both in lower- and higher-income areas:

> I wear him down slowly, and just nag. A gentle nag. (Jack, 15, Struggle High)

I would nag. I would scream and yell until she would yell. (Todd, 11, Comfort Primary)

I just bug away until I get it. (Nicole, 11, Comfort Primary)

Harry at Struggle Primary takes care not to overdo it: 'I don't torment her to get something. Because she pays a lot of bills, I don't want to torment her, otherwise I wouldn't get it anyway'.

As we saw in Chapter 6, a small number of young people mobilise parental guilt: a young man at Struggle High spoke of 'manipulating' his parents: 'I say "Gee dad, you haven't spent a lot of time with me lately, I'd really like it – if I put x amount of dollars towards it, would you come and get it?"' (James, 15, Struggle High).

Household-structure shaped some strategies. One young person felt that her father bought her things to balance what he spent on her step-brothers. Several observed that children from couple households are able to mobilise differences between their parents to get what they want and some reported doing so. Others observed that sole children have much more success getting stuff.

Several young people spoke of appreciating more the things they pay for themselves and valuing the independence that this brings. Some do not like to rely upon financially-strapped parents:

I usually save up for it ... I don't want to depend on my parents. I don't, because I've got my job. I don't feel like I should always be asking them for money. (Melinda, 16, Strive High)

Now that I work I don't ask them anymore. I have my own money, so I pay for everything ... I like to support myself. I like the independence I feel with having my own money, not having to rely on them any more. It feels really good. (Tanya, 16, Strive High)

Youthful commodified communication

Young people's consumption has been given considerable momentum by the increasing role of mobile phones in their social lives. For many young people, communication is increasingly commodified through the use of the mobile phone. This is not without its hazards: 'One of my mates clocked up a $387 phone bill for SMSing cause he was told it was costing ten cents a call. Well he did something like 50 a day'.

Those without a mobile phone are excluded from some forms of social organisation and activity. Keeping up with the latest mobile phone technology is important:

> It's like every time a new phone comes out it has something extra ... And you're going to want the newest ones, cause as if you wouldn't rather the phone with a colour screen and a camera rather than just a normal phone, do you know what I mean? (Ellie, 16, Leafy High)

Some see the competition to keep up as 'pointless', with useless new phone features they do not use. However, advertising about the latest thing stimulates demand, as many young people understand: 'I think they target young people because they like new things, want to try new things' (Melissa, 18, Leafy High).

Paid parental work also drives some forms of consumption as busy parents rely on quick market solutions. Children and young people see the obvious link between their parents' work and the food, clothes and things they have. Many referred to spending that is a direct result of parental work patterns, most obviously in relation to take-away food and eating out. This was often mentioned as increasing when a parent is tired, stressed or overworked:

> When I'm at my Dad's we go out more cause he can't be bothered cooking cause he's so stressed out. (Chloe, 16, Struggle High)

> We normally have tea at home unless Mum can't be bothered cooking and then we have stuff like pizza or something. (Louise, 15, Struggle High)

> We sometimes get hot chips or something like that after Mum's worked the whole day. (Alana, 16, Struggle High)

Conclusions: Modest expectations overrun by competitive consumption?

This analysis suggests that many young people share a well-developed critique of 'too much money and stuff'. While many enjoy getting and having things, they are critical of those with 'too much'. Such people are seen as greedy, spendthrift, socially inauthentic, irresponsible and poorly equipped for later life. However, young people live within a powerful force field of competitive consumption. They consistently name it and the items that matter, and clearly articulate the reasons for 'keeping up'; 'coolness', belonging, power and identity. This force field is alive in higher- and lower-income areas, among boys and girls, and among both primary and high school children. It seems less powerful in the country, but it is still a lively force in country towns and helps construct social success and 'in' and 'out' groups.

The cost of falling behind is seen as high: teasing, not fitting in, feeling bad and socially failing. There are those – a significant number – who define themselves against the prevailing fashions of clothing, phones or cars. They find identity by being different and by belonging to groups that are different, that are anti-market and anti-fashion. However, they are in the minority, and some of them are not above energetic consumption of particular items like computers.

This youthful competitive consumption drives paid work patterns in two obvious and significant ways: firstly, through pressure on parents to buy 'stuff' to keep up, and secondly through young people's own paid work to generate spending money. There is no doubt that working parents feel the pressure of this acquisitive race. The tactic of nagging is widely applied. Time-pressed working parents are perhaps least able to resist it.

Two further points are obvious. First, the mobile phone, now widespread among young people, drives consumption and is a critical means of social inclusion for young people. Most will acquire one as they approach senior high school and thus family budgets must meet a cost that previous generations did not face. Without it, they are excluded from some social opportunities and communication. However, providing it generates a whole new sizeable category of youthful communications spending. Secondly, many households make use of take-away food not only when parents are working but especially when parents are tired or stressed. Demanding jobs drive new levels of fast food consumption, stimulating demand in a market hungry for parental earnings.

Access to the right clothes, games, jewellery, movies, tele-communications and social events is widely viewed as an essential gateway to youthful social inclusion. While some take enjoyment and pleasure from their consumption, many talk about a competitive race for 'coolness-through-stuff' or describe a treadmill of endless desire: 'you get what you want, and then so do they, and you still don't feel good', to paraphrase Mark, 17, at Comfort High.

This sometimes sounds like a cruel and wasteful race. Many young people understand, resist, critique and mock it – but participate nevertheless. Some define themselves against brands and dominant trends, choosing unfashionable, daggy or old clothes. Others work hard to be in the mainstream, acquiring the cool things they hope will confer belonging, power and friends. Still others are perhaps affected by the negative outcomes that Schor documents for materialistic children in the US: depression, anxiety and low self-esteem.

Family work patterns and earnings are intrinsically asso-ciated with this race for material goods and partially motivated by it. Without parents' jobs, the 'stuff' is missing. It also stimulates young people's own increasing participation in paid work. Some young people are reluctant to ask their parents for money, conscious of household budget pressures or the precarious nature of parental earnings. They are also critical of 'kids who have too much', seeing them as spoiled, unappre-ciative of what they have and perhaps unable to manage when they are older. However, young people value being able to 'keep up' with the consumption of their peers; keeping up enables them to fit in, to 'have power through things' and to consolidate their identity.

Advertisers are keenly aware of this fertile psychological ground and they nurture it carefully, cultivating a sense of self through 'stuff'. They stimulate consumption and expenditure by associating 'success' with 'ownership'. Many young people are aware of the power of advertising but it takes a strong deter-mination to buck the trend. The children who reject competitive consumption and define themselves against it are in the minority.

CHAPTER 9

Children, work and a sustainable future

Work plays a powerful role in our lives for better and for worse. It is the basis of our living. It sustains us in physical, psychological and social ways and it feeds our children. Many Australians enjoy aspects of their jobs.

From the perspective of young people, both their own and their parents' work has good and bad sides. They see that it generates income, enjoyment, satisfaction and social connection, and it sustains the household. It also generates negative spill-over. It crowds out time with relaxed parents, as well as shared family time. These perceptions vary depending on socio-economic circumstances, with children in poorer households or in higher cost cities like Sydney more understanding about the time that parents give to work and less likely to look for more time over more money. However, many children in different settings look for more time, especially with attentive, calm, relaxed parents.

Some older children want 'hang around' time with that calm parent – not necessarily even in the same room, but in the household or at particular events. And in some cases, having one parent at home does not make up for a missing parent. In many such examples, children look for time with the parent who is most often absent – usually the father.

Others whose parents work long hours are – almost to a child in our conversations – aware of their parents' long hours and negative about their consequences for their parents, household relationships and for themselves. The perceived negative effects of long hours (which are worked by people in many occupations and industries in Australia) cross the socio-economic and urban/rural divides.

Where fathers work long hours, some children say they have given up on a real connection with their fathers – 'not much going on there'. Parental hope that this time can be made up and the relationship revived later may be misplaced where children are distant and give up. Others take action to stay close, joining Dad in his truck for example. Children certainly exercise agency. However, where parents are grumpy from long hours or other negative aspects of their jobs, children exercise agency by getting out of their way and withdrawing.

The negative effects of long hours perceived by children reinforce the results of other studies demonstrating that long or unsocial working hours are associated with measurable emotional and behavioural difficulties and stress for children (Strazdins et al. 2004). These effects sit alongside the international evidence about the impact of long hours – often in combination with work stress – on the mental and cardiovascular health of workers themselves (Spurgeon 2003).

Children who perceive that jobs upset parents, wear them out or compromise their health, worry about their parents. They can see when parents are unable to work in the ways that they want to – in terms of hours, occupation and location, for example, – and when this fit is poor they perceive more negative spillover.

For both parents and children, paid work is increasingly essential to highly commodified lives. Young people perceive a work/spend cycle. They observe that busy stressed parents are more likely to adopt quick food and care solutions that require money. And they observe parents sometimes dealing with guilt by buying things. Some are aware that these behaviours accelerate the work/spend cycle: the time-saving takeaway meal requires more money and thus more time into paid work, which only increases time pressures. The new pair of shoes to make up for an extra shift at work might help parents feel less guilty but many young people would rather have the parental time and see that the gift requires more earning. Young people are themselves increasingly drawn into a work/spend cycle where 'stuff' constructs social success and a sense of self, generating its own childhood and adolescent work/spend cycles.

The work/spend cycle is also aggressively fed by advertising. The market for both goods and services is voraciously enthusiastic about time poverty and self-construction by means of products and services. The sacred place of private familism has uninvited strangers at its table – big spending advertisers and wily marketers – using technologies that penetrate almost all homes for many hours a week. They keenly stimulate the appetites of both young and older Australians, fuelling and accelerating the work/spend cycle.

With changes in the employment base of Australia and the growth in service sector employment, workers in Australia are at one and the same time the essential labour that provides services and the essential consumer of such services. The busy working women who staff childcare services, cleaning and domestic services and the retail sector, are the same busy working women consumers. The demands of the labour market fuel their consumption. The young Australians who eat fast food are the same ones on the other side of the counter, providing the service.

In this world, care is increasingly commodified. As more and more people enter paid work, and for longer periods over the life cycle, there are fewer people to provide private household and neighbourhood care. The turn to the market fuels ever higher levels of labour market participation to meet the costs of that participation, and so it goes.

There are a variety of hazards implicit in thinning familial care and its commodification. In some cases parents take short cuts to find local solutions, using informal care and hoping that it is safe. While in many cases it is, in other cases young people are left in less than ideal situations and they do not gain access to early childhood education and development opportunities that research tells us are so important for all children.

Who cares?

As we have seen in the case of childcare, commodified services create their own problems. Care services are not like other kinds of markets. Those in care are not consumers, as in many cases the care is purchased by others for them. Quality is of critical importance and the market mechanism fails to guarantee it in many settings. Studies show that parents want to believe that the quality of care is good and that they overestimate quality relative to objective measures. What is more, measuring quality is hard for parents. It is hard enough for formal regulatory regulators who give lengthy early warning before their infrequent inspections, allow centres to work at less that regulated levels of staffing because of shortages of skilled workers, and set staffing levels that are minimal rather than ideal. Such regulation and enforcement is especially difficult in a situation of high unmet demand, as in Australia at present, when the emphasis is on supply not quality. The corporatisation of care in Australia – and its consequences for quality, cost and access – remains under-researched, not least because of the corporate sector's resistance to research (Press and Woodrow 2005).

Commentators like Anne Manne (2005) and Stephen Biddulph (2006) argue that parental care is better than formal childcare provision. While the Australian evidence about the effects of early institutional childcare is thin on the ground, the international evidence makes one thing starkly clear: poor quality childcare (whether parental or institutional) has negative consequences for babies and young children. This body of research also raises important questions about the effects of prolonged hours in early care, and formal childcare for very young babies in particular (Waldfogel 2004). The quality of care is critical to outcomes, with the essential ingredient being sensitive and responsive care – whether by mother or another.

On the other hand there is good evidence that good quality early childhood education and care can narrow cognitive and social inequalities, and benefit many children. In the future, most Australian children will spend some time in formal care before they enter school – as they do now. The absence of a national system of paid leave for working mothers contributes to this.

Unfortunately a fractured early childhood education and care 'system', with diverse state arrangements, various sources of regulation and funding, and inadequate supply results in sub-optimal care for many young people. Increasing corporatisation has been accompanied by ballooning costs (and profits), the demise of national planning and inadequate supply. Tax or subsidy relief for high costs may assist affordability (and boost profits) but it also increases demand. In a situation of inadequate supply, increased demand can only increase rationing and prices (and profits). This is neither fair nor adequate.

Glossy ads promise parents responsive quality care, but testing the rhetoric is difficult for the individual parent. Perfect information is very distant from market reality. Stability of service is of great importance to children, and high labour turn-over, high rates of casualisation and the possibility of market shifts in provision with changing economic scenarios give all too little value to long-term quality provision. Children with special needs do not fit in a funding scenario that makes them 'expensive' clients. And leaving the allocation of childcare places to the market does not necessarily result in the right care getting to the right places.

Sustaining reproduction and work

Higher labour market participation is in direct contradiction to higher rates of reproduction unless that participation is backed by other good sources of sustenance. While the Commonwealth Treasurer has exhorted Australian women to have more children – 'one for your husband, one for your wife and one for the country' – other government policies swim against this possibility, among them reduced rights for flexibility at work, the rising costs of health, education and childcare, and changes to support for sole parents that encourage labour market participation rather than facilitating maternal care. Countries that sustain high rates of labour market participation and high fertility rates do so through with quality public childcare, extensive paid leave for parents, and flexible workplace arrangements that suit working mothers.

Young people are well aware of some of the cost issues around reproduction. They plan to have jobs they enjoy, skills and education that they use and to have children as well. However, they pause when they consider the costs that this will mean. They are keen to establish financial, job and housing security before risking reproduction. Many young men's plans for both work and children are implicitly dependent upon a female partner who, they hope, will care. While a good proportion want to share care of their children with their female partners, and to share earning as well, they show an awareness that this might be difficult. They have observed their fathers. They will *lean* against the door of inflexibility and tradition but if they cannot get part-time work or parental leave then they assume their wives will step into the breech.

This is at odds with the youthful expectations of many young women. The majority of these want to share care, and they expect their partners to help. They are wary of the low levels of domestic contribution that they observe their male peers and brothers make, but they hope that they will find a 'good one' or that age, education, nagging, blackmail or threat of divorce will enlist masculine help when the time comes.

Many young women plan to look to their own mothers for help with care of children. They may well be frustrated by the rising rate of participation of older women in the workforce – a rate of participation which government policies are encouraging to meet the challenge of an aging labour force. Many grandmothers will be simply unavailable because they must or choose to give their time to a job: once again, the labour market eats into social care and reproduction.

Returning to the concepts in Chapter 2, there are three sources of sustenance that might underpin the choices of coming generations: 'private familism' (private household supports), 'market familism' (market products and services that sustain us) and 'public familism' (laws, institutions and public facilities and payments that sustain us).

For young women and men, the settings of these institutions that shape their labour market and care transitions remain critical to outcomes. A supportive regime of public sustenance that includes parental leave, integrated quality part-time work and quality accessible childcare, is of primary significance. Without supports that facilitate the combination of work and care and transitions between them, responsibility for children will jeopardise labour market status, and people will be forced to 'choose' between limited options. They may also experience high levels of private worry and family instability, care that creates risks for children, and growing gender and social inequality.

To come true, young people's plans rely on levels of institutional support that are currently missing in Australia. The support available for reproduction in the private family is thinned by the growing effort given out of households to the labour market. This thinning in a consequence of both more household hours going into paid work (and commuting) and also the increasingly greedy nature of that work. In the presence of such thinned private familism, family members will have to paddle harder or find other sources of support.

The market is ready to spring to their assistance – at a price. And that price includes increasing time and effort in paid work to pay the bills. The cure is the disease. It is likely to exact other hidden costs, where increasing labour market participation means thinner community fabric, weaker bonds of extended family and friendship, and less time for voluntary activity, neighbourliness and social citizenship.

And the market has more pernicious effects. As Juliet Schor (2004) has demonstrated in the US, marketing is increasingly predatory in relation to young people, creating the 'commercialised child'. It aggressively markets all kinds of products to children and young people, exposing them to unprecedented levels of highly persuasive and sophisticated advertising, including through all the usual means but increasingly also schools, sporting facilities and events, and product placements. This marketing has important effects on obesity, as well as children's general physical and mental health.

Beyond these, such marketing further embeds children into a powerful force field that reinforces competitive consumption and relies on both parental and child earnings. This aspect of the market increasingly affects private family life, where moderating parental norms about expenditure and consumption – where they exist – are frail antidotes to many hours of sophisticated television campaigns. Schor and other US commentators have joined Canadian researchers and child advocates in calling for restraint in advertising to children, and similar arguments apply in Australia. This aspect of marketing has important implications for the work patterns that it drives.

Finding familial sustenance through the market amplifies inequality and disadvantages the poor while advantaging the rich.

There are many social externalities of a world built increasingly around jobs without adequate public supports – indeed in a world of thinned public sustenance, where it costs private households more for health, education, and so on. In this world, work eats into our social and reproductive sustainability. Markets cannot supply the kinds of care that are good for children and other dependents without very careful and comprehensive regulation. In the absence of such regulation and enforcement they fail. They may generate high levels of corporate profit along the way (underwritten by public subsidy), but the costs of market failure are socialised in terms of family anguish, remedial help for children who are disadvantaged, or parents who cannot work for want of childcare.

Contrary to neo-liberal rhetoric, we already regulate many markets extensively. But in the case of fragile products with long-term effects like childcare, there are strong arguments for very significant, coherent and adequately enforced programs of regulation. These are currently inadequate in Australia. They need renovation. To work, they need to be matched with planned provision of care, adequate workforce planning and fair wages and conditions for those who work in the care sectors. These constitute powerful arguments in favour of public provision of care, or at least not-for-profit provision as exists in the schooling sector.

An expansion in public sustenance

Most young Australians expect to live in dual-earner households and have children. High levels of labour market participation are expected of them. Their success in doing this, in a situation of thinning private household support, depends on a greater household capacity to care or a sustained increase in public support. This can take a number of forms: contributions from employers, good labour law that supports the combination of work and family, more paid leave, support from community organisations and from public investments. Without these contributions, the labour market will eat into us. Participation in work will eat into our reproductive capacity and frustrate individual's preferences for having both a job and children.

This frustration will not be experienced evenly. High-income households will be able to find more help through the market. However, their solutions will in many cases rely on keeping the wages of those they rely on – for example, childcare and aged-care workers – low. Widening socio-economic inequality is the natural result of relying on the market and the commodification route as a solution to thinning sources of private and public familism. This is a poor road for many children: poverty of income will be overlaid with new cycles of cognitive and social disadvantage resulting from poor early care and education.

Other sources of inequality are also implicit in this road. The effects of thinning private household support will be visited more upon women than men – measured in overload and guilt. Women are likely to continue to curtail their family size and delay parenting while they search for that special partner who will share the burden, that special boss or workplace that can accommodate their worker/carer identity, or where they try to come to grips with the realities of being both a worker and a mother in an uncompromising labour market. Unless elements of this labour market change, their preferred choice of having a family is likely to either be disappointed or occur on terms that mean increasingly intensive motherhood work and care. They will either be paddling harder, or turn away from care on these terms. In some cases, this will not be for want of a partner who wants to share the burden: it will be for want of a labour market which allows these men to realise their desires to be active fathers.

The workforce and labour market supports that the choices and preferences of these young men and women rely on, include opportunities for leave from work, workplace flexibilities that are care-friendly, working hours that allow them to be parents and partners, affordable quality care options, and arrangements that facilitate a good fit between how they want to work and how they must. This fit will change over the life cycle and vary among households and individuals, but – as the voices of many young people through this book show – it is this good fit, and the high levels of parental satisfaction that flows from it, that really matters. It shapes the household microclimate. People's preferences vary, but public sources of support to underpin their varied choices are essential to their realisation.

Many countries invest in such public sources of support. They provide national systems of affordable, quality early childhood education and care services. Their labour law constrains very long hours of work and underpins employee requests to change their hours of work from full-time to part-time and back again. They provide extensive periods of leave for employees to care for their children and dependents, drawing on contributions from employees, employers and the community through community investment. They facilitate parental care for children in the early years, recognising that this is what most parents – especially mothers – want, but without surrendering their long-term earning capacity. They know that a secure early childhood and early education system is critical to a good social and economic future. They also know that an expanding labour supply, which increasingly relies on women, depends on such supports, as does social cohesion and family welfare.

In some cases the costs of a failure to thicken up forms of public sustenance like this are calculable and significant. Waldfogel (2004) has summarised some recent evidence. For example, the failure to provide paid parental leave results in higher depression among mothers, higher infant mortality, more babies with low birth weights, less breast-feeding and fewer preventative health care visits. The critical issue here is the provision of paid rather than unpaid leave, permitting parents of all income levels to care for their children at birth.

The international evidence about the components of good public sustenance that supports the welfare of children and contributes to social sustainability is convincing and compelling. Australian governments should be responding to it, in cooperation with employers, by adopting a system that supports the choices of parents, with positive implications for young people. The first step would be to introduce arrangements that give all parents an opportunity to take up to two years out of paid work with income support on the birth of child. These are the critical years for young children, and most parents prefer parental care. Not all parents will use such leave, but without its possibility, work undermines the welfare of parents, children and social sustainability.

Alongside this, Australian governments should develop a national system of quality, affordable early childhood education and development. This is a pressing national priority.

Finally, Australian labour law should be amended to increase the time autonomy of workers, especially those with care responsibilities. This autonomy should be within a framework that restricts long working hours that damage the health of workers, their social environment and their dependents. It should create new capacities for changes in working hours that are initiated by employees and provide more opportunities for part-time work that is integrated into the labour market (rather than peripheral to it). Such provisions will assist parents to work towards a better fit between working time and care preferences, so critical to outcomes for children.

In an environment where work matters more, and private household capacity is strained and thinned, more must be done to support and sustain those who work, if they and their children are not to suffer. And to suffer disproportionately if they are poor. If the values of fairness, equality and sustainability are to be more than rhetoric, a new public sustenance is essential in Australia. Such renewed public capacity is essential to future economic growth and social cohesion. It should put children first, value carers, share costs and benefits fairly, manage the market where it fails, facilitate a better fit between preferences and outcomes, and increase equality between women and men as well as between the rich and poor.

Appendix: Data Sources

This book relies on analysis of data from a variety of sources. It draws on a range of labour market and other data collected by the Australian Bureau of Statistics as well as some data available from the HILDA survey, the Australian Survey of Social Attitudes and the Longitudinal Survey of Australian Children.

The perspectives of young people, which are relied on through Chapters 3 to 8, were collected by the author, with the assistance of Jane Clarke, in late 2003.

We conducted 21 focus groups among 93 students in Australia in late 2003. These young people were in two age cohorts: one group were in Year 6 at primary schools (aged 10-12 years) and another in Year 11 in high schools (aged 16-18 years). These focus groups examined the perceptions of young people about parental work as well as their own plans for their work and household futures.

These perceptions, like the perceptions of adults, are not the same as reality or facts. However, perceptions of young people are relevant to their future actions, and to the actions and decisions of adults, as well as to policies that affect the world of young people and working and caring adults.

Table A.1 shows details of the focus group. The focus groups were selected from stratified sub-groups of schools in two Australian States. These schools fell evenly into high and low socio-economic groups, based on their score on the Index of Relative Socio-Economic Disadvantage (one of the five measures of disadvantage published by the Australian Bureau of Statistics). A score of 1000 on this index is the Australian average. We selected schools located in areas above the average and below the average.

Eight of the groups were conducted in Sydney and nine in Adelaide. Sydney has a population of over 4.2 million and is Australia's highest-cost city. Its housing is especially expensive. Adelaide is much smaller with a population of 1.1 million and a lower cost of living. Both cities are ethnically diverse.

A sub-group of schools, selected on socio-economic criteria, was approached to participate (following ethics approval by education departments and the University of Adelaide). Where schools agreed to participate, parents were invited to consent in writing to their child's participation. Before the commencement of audio-recording, young people consented in writing to the recording of their views. The participation of low-income schools and their students (through parental permission) was more difficult to secure.

Focus groups allow 'deep' analysis through the pursuit of complex issues within complex contexts, and they expose ambivalence and unanticipated factors more so than closed questionnaires or sometimes even interviews. They also allow an exchange of views among participants, which can reveal unexpected lines of thought and unanticipated views. Interviews do not always permit this kind of exchange and comparison of views, and they tend to rely more upon pre-prepared questions that are asked intensively, one on one. Young people – as young as ten years old – may have found being interviewed by an adult stranger intimidating, whereas discussion among a small group of peers was less likely to be off-putting, we hoped. More practically, focus groups can canvass the views of a large number of participants in a relatively short time.

The focus groups were recorded and transcribed, and detailed notes recorded the comments by participants individually, so that specific comments could be attributed to individuals and set in the context of their situations (including their family type and the occupation and work patterns of their household). Analysis then considered individual views in the context of the general level of household income, work and care patterns and geographic location, and we could analyse specific features like individuals' past experience of childcare, and its association with their views about the use of formal childcare in the future.

The focus groups were kept small in view of the age of participants: they included, on average, four participants. A group discussion might discourage honest individual statements and this might be expected to be stronger among young people who seek peer approval. To counter this, participants were specifically invited to say what they thought and not to be afraid to disagree, so that we could canvass the full diversity of views. Many offered contrasting views. Each young person was invited to comment on each issue as it arose, and individual opinions were canvassed while conversational exchange was also encouraged. Nonetheless, there were times when it seemed that some participants were performing for their peers, and we were conscious of this in the analysis.

Anyone who has worked with transcripts, especially focus group transcripts, knows that comments rarely emerge in whole sentences. Transcripts were therefore lightly edited to remove common 'fill' words used by young people. However, great care was taken to preserve meaning. Where there is intervening text that is extraneous to the point, or a probe question, it has been deleted and the edit indicated thus (…).

We call the two higher-income schools 'Leafy' (in Sydney), and 'Comfort' (in Adelaide). We call the two lower-income schools 'Struggle' (in Adelaide) and 'Strive' (in Sydney's west). This is not to imply that students were themselves 'struggling' or necessarily 'comfortable'. Instead, these labels are intended to help connect voices to relative socio-economic areas. Young people at Struggle Primary were unambiguously from poorer households and had a high level of geographic mobility. Incomes were more mixed at Struggle than at Strive High where one child spoke of his trust fund, and dual earner households included a manager and an engineer alongside truck drivers, nurses and the unemployed. However, in Sydney's west, 'Strive' accurately describes an area where households are financially stretched, and where, according to their children, parents hold strong aspirations for the educational success of their children and strive hard, as do their children, to achieve financial security and upward mobility. They are poorer, striving households.

No young person refused to have their views recorded. Of the 21 focus groups, four were conducted in rural community schools. We randomly selected the country town location, which was 200 km from a large city, with mixed income households, based mostly around rural and service industries.

Eight of the urban schools were in lower-income areas and nine in higher-income areas. Thirteen were conducted in South Australia and eight in New South Wales. Five of the focus groups mixed males and females while 16 were single sex (nine females, seven males). All the groups were age-specific, mostly Year 6 or Year 11. Two of the older focus groups were actually conducted among Year 10 students because of exam constraints for Year 11s in the school.

Focus groups ran for between 60 and 90 minutes except for two that were shorter because of a school excursion. A set of open-ended questions was used to stimulate discussion but commentary was liberally pursued in relation to the themes of the research. Participants chose or were allocated pseudonyms and the identity of schools and individual participants, along with any other identifying details, are concealed. In a few cases we have changed chosen pseudonyms because of repetition or to protect identities, or to clarify sex or ethnicity.

We set out with some concerns about the willingness of young people to talk about these issues with two adult researchers, particularly in front of their peers. We were also concerned about whether young men and boys would feel constrained in front of two female researchers. In fact, the participants were enthusiastic talkers, by and large. Most were eager to share their thoughts and feelings, as a lively set of tapes and over 700 pages of transcript attest. When we debriefed with students (some of whom were themselves studying social research methods) at the conclusion of some focus groups, both young women and men felt that they would have talked differently in front of participants of the other sex, so the decision to separate most groups by sex, especially among adolescents, was important. Young men did not feel that female interviewers had affected their views, but protective politeness may have been at work here.

Focus groups have strengths and weaknesses. They can be unrepresentative. We attempted to minimise this in three ways. First, by working through schools selected randomly within socio-economic groupings rather than, for example, a snowballing method working from a non-random group of individuals; secondly, by randomly choosing a rural location; and third, by including a sizeable number of people in relevant categories including sex, rural and urban locations, socio-economic status and age. We did not know anyone in any of the focus groups or schools personally.

The focus groups contained a good mix of family types. Australian households are now very diverse and many are complex. For example, one child described his situation: 'I've got two step-dads and a real dad. I don't know my real dad and my mum is separated from my first step-dad and now I've got a second-step-dad and he works'. An increasing number of young people live in blended households or have more than one household. Thirteen per cent of those in the study lived in blended families, double what ABS data suggests holds for the larger population, and a fifth lived in sole-parent households thus matching the figure for the population overall in 2001 (ABS Cat No 4102.0 2002, p 30). Seventy per cent of children living in couple households in the study lived in dual-earner households, while 28 per cent lived in traditional 'breadwinner' households with one earner, usually the father. These reflect current household and work population patterns whereby both parents work in almost two-thirds of couple families with children while a third rely on a single breadwinner (ABS Cat No 6203.0 2003). Eighty-one per cent of children lived in couple households (that is, with both original parents), close to the Australian average of 79 per cent (Sanson and Lewis 2001, p 5). Children from non-English speaking backgrounds were well represented in the group, while Aboriginal children probably were not (none were specifically identified).

The group under-represents males and children living in households with unemployed parents. Six per cent of participants were living in households with no working adult, compared to 18 per cent of all children in Australia in 1999 (Sanson and Lewis 2001, p 4). This probably reflects the fact that the invitation to participate mentioned paid work.

Forty-three of the participants (46 per cent) live in households where at least one parent works long or unsocial hours, based on the account of the child. This may be higher than for the overall population depending, as it does, on children's per-ceptions. However, in many cases children recount the working hours of their parents with persuasive precision, and most so-defined were working more than 45 hours a week (many do much more) or doing shift work. This proportion of households affected by long or unsocial hours may not be an overstatement for three reasons. First, 12 children in our study were living with self-employed parents who work notoriously long hours. Ten of these had at least one parent working long or unsocial hours. Secondly, in 2000 over a quarter of Australian employees worked more than 45 hours a week (up from 13 per cent in 1985) (Campbell 2002, p 94). Of the 93 participants, 57 lived in households with two parents (where each parent had at least a one-in-four chance of working long hours). Thirdly, these perceptions include both long and unsocial hours (for example, shiftwork or intensive prolonged stints away from home). The reach of long or unsocial hours is now widespread in the households of young Australians and these are well represented in this study.

Reliance on school administrators and teachers for com-munication about the project may have introduced a selection bias in favour of more articulate or 'good' students. It is hard to predict how such a selection bias might influence our findings; it may mean that more 'serious' anti-consumption views are included in the study than actually exist among 11- and 16-year-olds. Further, our methods relied on parental literacy and spare time to read about the project and give permission; this may have worked against the participation of children in low-literacy or time-poor households. Our method seems to have worked in favour of female participation. Alongside this, chil-dren of harried parents who are concerned about their children reporting negative work spillover effects (like the single mother who contacted us with this concern, discussed below), may be under-represented in the study. Overall, if a bias exists it seems more likely that our sample group under-represents, rather than over-represents, the negative effects of parental work on children.

Avoiding 'mother-blame' or parental blame:
A note on the research approach

During the collection of views among young people, one mother made contact when she received a request to participate. She asked whether the study would lead to blame of single mothers (like herself) if it found that their children were more negatively affected by parental work than others. She felt that context is important: she had neither sought to be a sole parent, nor to experience the ill-health that now prevents her from working in her professional occupation for the hours she wants.

She is right to be concerned. There is a very sizeable international and Australian literature that 'blames' children's characteristics – whether schizophrenia, emotional breakdown, homosexuality, rebelliousness, drug use, sexual activity or delinquency – on mothers' failures or characteristics, especially those of sole parents – who are mostly mothers (Garey and Arendell 2001; McDonnell 1998; Terry 1998; Thurer 1993). Prominent Australian public figures readily blame mothers and fathers for children's failures or mistakes. For example, not so long ago the Australian Governor General – then Governor of Western Australia – 'quoted approvingly a research study that claimed a "direct statistical link between single parenthood and virtually every type of major crime, including mugging, violence against strangers, car theft and burglary"' (Summers 2003 p 70). Both the Premier of South Australia and the Prime Minister have attributed youth delinquency in the poorer suburbs of Adelaide to parental inadequacy.

These criticisms often find fertile ground as many parents look to themselves when things go wrong for their children. However, parental preferences about health, hours and jobs do not determine labour market outcomes any more than children's preferences for certain Christmas presents can assure their delivery. No parent is omnipotent in relation to outcomes for their child, and families face diverse situations shaped by income and wealth, ethnicity and race, geography, family size, access to social, economic and human resources, relationship and marital outcomes and health. Each of these influences young people's situation and perspectives. While parental work choices certainly affect children's experience, they are far from the only determinant. In many cases, parents have only limited degrees of real freedom, especially in relation to labour market outcomes such as employment, hours, and earnings.

It is also very clear from our study that children do not – by and large – blame their parents for things they find hard about the work, care, money and time outcomes in their households; this is in accord with earlier Australian research (Lewis, Tudball and Hand 2001). Even in cases where a parent – usually the father – has left the child's life, children are much more likely to be *sad* and to wish for their return, than to *blame* – at least in conversation with us. The perspectives of young people are very alert to the *context* of their parent's lives (and they are surprisingly forgiving).

There are those who see such research as inevitably contributing to mother blame and feeding the epidemic of parental, especially maternal, guilt. A retreat from research on this basis, however, is a mistake. Parents, among others, need accurate information to inform their choices. Without relevant, reliable research they may act on assumptions that are wrong, overstated or that miss important information. This seems to be the case in relation to several issues discussed through this book.

Table A.1. Focus group details

Location	Number of groups	Number of participants	Per cent of total participants
Country Primary	2	5	
Country High	2	8	
Struggle Primary	2	7	
Struggle High	2	9	
Strive Primary	2	9	
Strive High	2	7	
Comfort Primary	2	9	
Comfort High	3	15	
Leafy Primary	2	12	
Leafy High	2	12	
Total	21	93	
Higher-income Areas	9	48	52
Lower-income Areas	8	32	34
Country	4	13	14
Female Only Groups	9		
Male Only Groups	7		
Mixed Sex Groups	5		
Females		57	61
Males		36	39
Family Type			
Two-parent, dual earner		53	57
Two-parent, single earner		20	22
Two-parent, no earner		2	2
Single-parent earner		13	14
Single-parent no earner		5	5
		93	100

Bibliography

ABC (2004a), 'Child Care Companies in the Spotlight', *The 7.30 Report*, 29 March 2004, Reporter: Emma Alberici, Sydney, Australian Broadcasting Commission.

ABC (2004b), 'Child-Care Profits', *Background Briefing*, Radio National, 3 October 2004, Sydney, Australian Broadcasting Commission.

ABC Learning Centres Limited (2005a), 'Media Statement', 25 February 2005, Brisbane.

ABC Learning Centres Limited (2005b), 'Presentation of Half Yearly Results', 25 February 2005, Brisbane.

ABC Queensland (see also Austin and Whiting 2005) (2005), 'Businessman Eddy Groves', Brisbane, Australian Broadcasting Commission.

ABS (1984, 2004), *Labour Force Status and Other Characteristics of Families, Australia, Cat No 6224.0*, Canberra, Australian Bureau of Statistics.

ABS (1995, 1997, 2003,), *Working Arrangements, Australia, Cat No 6342.0*, Canberra, Australian Bureau of Statistics.

ABS (2000), *Population Trends in Australia, Cat No 3222.0*, Canberra, Australian Bureau of Statistics.

ABS (2001, 2002, 2003, 2004, 2005), *Australian Social Trends, Cat No 4102.0*, Canberra, Australian Bureau of Statistics.

ABS (2003), *Labour Force, Australia, Cat No 6203.0.* Canberra, Australian Bureau of Statistics.

ABS (2004), *Divorce, Australia, Cat No 3307.0*, Canberra, Australian Bureau of Statistics.

ABS (2004, 2006), *Labour Force, Australia Cat No 6202.0.55.001, Spreadsheets, table 01, Labour Force Status by Sex, Trend*, Canberra, Australian Bureau of Statistics.

ABS (2004b), *Labour Force Status Australia: Electronic Delivery Annual, Cat No 6291.055.001*, Canberra, Australian Bureau of Statistics.

ABS (2004c), *Education and Work Australia, May 2004, Cat No 6227.0*, Canberra, Australian Bureau of Statistics.

ABS (2005), *Year Book, Cat No 1301.0*, Canberra, Australian Bureau of Statistics.

ABS (Various years), *Births, Australia, Cat No 3301.0*, Canberra, Australian Bureau of Statistics.

ABS (Various years), *Marriages and Divorces, Australia, Cat No 3310.0*, Canberra, Australian Bureau of Statistics.

ABS (2002, 2005), *Childcare, Australia, Cat No 4402.0*, Canberra, Australian Bureau of Statistics.

ACNielson (2004), 'ACNielsen Finds US Truly Is A Fast Food Nation', ACNielson, News Release, 21 December 2004, <http://us.acnielsen.com/news/20041221.shtml> (accessed 5/6/06).

ACTU (2004), *National Childcare Phone In*, Melbourne, ACTU.

Acuff, DS (1997*)*, *What Kids Buy and Why*, New York, Press Press.

AIFS (2005), *Growing up in Australia: The Longitudinal Study of Australian Children, 2004 Annual Report*, Melbourne, Australian Institute of Family Studies.

AIHC (2001), *Trends in the Affordability of Child Care Services*, Canberra, Australian Institute of Health and Welfare (AIHW).

Alberici, E (2005), 'Law Dampens ABC Learning Aspirations', *The 7.30 Report*, Australia.

Anderson, PM, Butcher KF, and Levin, P (2003), 'Maternal Employment and Overweight Children,' *Journal of Health Economics* 22: 477-504.

Arendt, H (1958), *The Human Condition*, Chicago, University of Chicago Press.

Austin, S and Whiting, F (2005), 'Businessman Eddy Groves', ABC Queensland Radio, 3 August 2005.

Australian Business Intelligence (2002), 'Building Blocks of an Empire', *Australian Business Intelligence*, 11 October 2002.

Barnett, RC, and Marshall, NL (1992), 'Worker and Mother Roles, Spillover Effects and Psychological Distress,' *Women & Health* 18(2): 9-40.

Baxter, J (2004), 'Increasing Employment of Partnered Mothers: Changes in Child Care use', Canberra, Conference Paper, 12th Biennial Conference, Australian Population Association, Canberra, 15-17 September.

Beck, U (2002), *The Brave New World of Work*, Oxford, Polity Press.

Bettio, F and Plantenga, J (2004), 'Comparing Care Regimes in Europe,' *Feminist Economics* 10(1): 85-113.

Bianchi, S (2000), 'Maternal Employment and Time with Children, Dramatic Change or Surprising Continuity?' *Demography* 37: 401-414.

Biddulph, S (2006), *Raising Babies, Should under 3s go to Nursery?* London, Harper Thorsons.

Bittman, M, Craig, L and Folbre, N (2003), 'Packaging Care, What Happens when Children Receive Nonparental Care', in M Bittman and N Folbre (eds) *Family Time, The Social Organisation of Care*, London, Routledge.

Bittman, M, and Pixley, J (1997), *The Double Life of the Family: Myth, Hope and Experience*, Sydney, Allen & Unwin.

Braddock, P (1998), 'Target Market: Your Children Under the Influence, Parents Feel Pressure Exerted by Boys and Girls Influenced by Advertisements,' *The Atlanta Journal*, 6 December 1998: 1.

Brennan, D (1998), *The Politics of Australian Child Care*, Cambridge, Cambridge University Press.

Brennan, D (1999), 'Childcare: Choice or Charade?', in L Hancock (ed) *Women, Public Policy and the State*, Melbourne, Macmillan.

Bryant, WK and Zick, CD (1996a), 'Are we Investing Less in the Next Generation? Historical Trends in the Time Spent Caring for Children,' *Journal of Family and Economic Issues* 17: 365-91.

Bryant, WK and Zick, CD (1996b), 'An Examination of Parent-Child Shared Time,' *Journal of Family and the Family* 58: 227-37.

Bunting, M (2004), *Willing Slaves: How the Overwork Culture Is Ruling Our Lives*, London, Harper Collins.

Campbell, I (2002), 'Extended Working Hours in Australia', *Labour & Industry* 13(1): 73-90.

Cassells, R, McNamara, J, Lloyd, R, Harding, A, (2005), 'Perceptions of Child Care Affordability and Availability in Australia: What the HILDA Survey Tells Us', paper presented at the Ninth Australian Institute of Family Studies Conference, Melbourne, 10 February 2005, NATSEM, Canberra.

Centre for New American Dream (2006), 'Thanks to Ads, Kids Won't Take No, No, No, No, No, No, No, No, No for an Answer', Tacoma, Centre for New American Dream, <www.newdream.org/kids/poll.php> (accessed 1 July 2006).

Commonwealth of Australia Commonwealth of Australia (2004), *2004-05 Budget – Overview, More Help for Families*, 11 May 2004, Canberra, Commonwealth of Australia.

Commonwealth of Australia Commonwealth of Australia (2005), *2005-06 Budget May 2004*, Canberra, Commonwealth of Australia.

Cook, DT (2001), 'Lunchbox Hegemony? Kids and the Marketplace: Then and Now', *Lip Magazine*, 20 August.

Cook, DT (2001), 'The 'Other Child' Study: Figuring Children as Consumers in Market Research, 1910s-1990s', *Sociological Quarterly*, 41: 487-508.

Cosgrove, D (2000), *Urban Congestion: The Implications for Greenhouse Gas Emissions*, Canberra, Bureau of Transport Economics, Information Sheet No 16, May.

De Botton, A (2004), *Status Anxiety*, Melbourne, Hamish Hamilton.

DEWR (2004), *Agreement Making in Australia Under the Workplace Relations Act, 2002 and 2003*, Canberra, Department of Employment and Workplace Relations and the Office of the Employment Advocate.

Dizard, JE and Gadlin, H (1990), *The Minimal Family*, Amherst, The University of Massachusetts Press.

Elliott, A (2004), *Perspective*, 29 April, 2004, Sydney, Australian Broadcasting Commission.

Esping-Anderson, G (1990), *The Three Worlds of Welfare Capitalism*, Cambridge, Polity Press.

Esping-Anderson, G (2004), 'Untying the Gordian Knot of Social Inheritance,' *Research in Social Stratification and Mobility* 21: 115-138.

Evans, A and Gray, E (2005), 'What Makes an Australian Family?' in S Wilson, G Meagher, R Gibson, D Denemark and M Western (eds) *Australian Social Attitudes, The First Report*, Sydney, UNSW Press.

FaCS (2003), Australian Government Report on the April 2003 Child Care Workforce Think Tank, Canberra, Family and Community Services.

FaCS (2005a), 2004 Australian Government Census of Child Care Services – Summary Booklet, Canberra, Family and Community Services.

FaCS (2005b), 2004 Australian Government Census of Child Care Services, Canberra, Family and Community Services.

Fien, J and Skoien, P (2000), *Towards Sustainable Consumption in Australia: Influences on Young Adults' Workshop Report*, UNEP/UNESCO Expert Workshop on Youth, Sustainable Consumption and Life Styles, UNESCO Headquarters, Paris, UNESCO.

Fisher, K (2002), *Fertility Pathways in Australia: Relationships, Opportunities, Work and Parenting*, Canberra, Commonwealth Department of Family and Community Services.

Flood, M (2004), *Lost Children, Condemning Children to Long-Term Disadvantage*, Canberra, The Australia Institute.

Flood, M and Barbato, C (2005), *Off to Work: Commuting in Australia*, Canberra, The Australia Institute.

Frank, R (1999), *Luxury Fever: Money and Happiness in an Era of Excess*, Princeton, Princeton University Press.

Froud, J, Johal, S, and Williams, K (2002), 'Heaven and Hell: The Macro Dynamics and Micro Experience of Inequality,' *Journal of Industrial Relations* 44(1): 62-87.

Galinsky, E (1999), *Ask the Children: What America's Children Really Think About Working Parents*, New York, William Morrow and Company.

Galinsky, E, and T, Arendell (2001), *Children, Work and Family, Some Thoughts on Mother Blame*, London, University of California Press.

Galinsky, E, Kim, S and Bond, J, (2001), *Feeling overworked: When Work Becomes Too Much*, New York, Families and Work Institute.

Garey, AI and Arendell T (2001), 'Children, Work and Family. Some Thoughts on Mother Blame', in R Hertz and N Marshall (eds) *Working Families: The Transformation of the American Home*, London, University of California Press.

Hamilton, C (2003), *Growth Fetish*, Sydney, Allen and Unwin.

Hamilton, C, and R, Denniss (2005), *Affluenza*, Sydney, Allen & Unwin.

Heckman, JJ (2006a), *Investing in Disadvantaged Young Children is an Economically Efficient Policy,* New York, Committee for Economic Development/The Pew Charitable Trusts/PNC Financial Services Group Forum on 'Building the Economic Case for Investments in Preschool' New York, 10 January 2006.

Heckman, JJ (2006b), 'Catch 'em Young', *Wall Street Journal (Eastern Edition),* New York, Dow Jones and Company Inc, 10 January 2006: page A.14.

Hirsch, F (1977), *The Social Limits to Growth*, London, Routledge.

Hochschild, A (1997), *The Time Bind, When Work Becomes Home and Home Becomes Work*, New York, Metropolitan Books.

Hochschild, A (2003), *The Commercialization of Intimate Life, Notes from Home and Work*, Berkeley, University of California Press.

Hofferth, S (2001), 'Women's Employment and Care of Children in the United States', in T Van der Lippe and LV Dijk (eds), *Women's Employment in Comparative Perspective*, New York, Aldine de Gruyter.

Horin, A (2003), 'When Making Money is Child's Play', *Sydney Morning Herald*, 4 October 2003, Sydney, p 39.

Jokovich, E (2004), 'Corporatisation of Childcare: New Issue of Rattler Out Now: Media Release', 21 April 2004, Sydney, *Rattler Magazine*.

Kendrick, C (nd), 'Money for Nothing: Is Our Guilt Causing Their Greed?' <www.fatherville.com/Articles> (accessed 5/7/05).

Key Note Publications (2003), *Marketing to Children: Market Assessment 2003*, London, Key Note Publications Pty Ltd, <www.marketresearch.com/product/display.asp?productid+886169&xs =r> (accessed 5/7/05).

Kirby, J (2003), 'Millions Milked,' *Business Review Weekly* 25 (17 November 2003).

Kuttner, R (1997), *Everything for Sale, The Virtues and Limits of Markets*, New York, Alfred A Knopf.

Lane, RE (2000), *The Loss of Happiness in Market Democracies*, New Haven, Yale University Press.

Lasch, C (1977), *Haven in a Heartless World*, New York, Basic Books.

Lee, S (2004), 'Working Hour Gaps: Trends and Issues', In *Working Time and Workers' Preferences in Industrialized Countries*, J, Messenger (ed) Abingdon, Routledge: 29-60.

Lewis, V, Tudball J and Hand, K (2001), 'Family and Work: The Family's Perspective,' *Family Matters* 59 (Winter, 2001).

Lundsgaard, J (2002), 'Competition and Efficiency in Publicly Funded Services,' *OECD Economic Studies* 35 (Summer): 79-129.

Manne, A (2005), *Motherhood: How Should We Care for Our Children?* Sydney, Allen & Unwin.

McCain, M and Fraser Mustard, J (1999), *Reversing the Real Brain Drain, The Early Years Study,* Toronto, The Founders Network of the Canadian Institute for Advance Research (CIAR).

McCain, M, and Fraser Mustard, J (2002), *The Early Years Study, Three Years On*, Toronto, The Founders Network of the Canadian Institute for Advance Research (CIAR).

McDonald, P (1998), 'Contemporary Fertility Patterns In Australia: First Data From the 1996 Census,' *People and Place* 6(1): 1-10.

McDonnell, J (1998), 'On Being the Bad Mother of an Autistic Child', in M Ladd-Taylor and L Umansky (eds) *"Bad" Mothers: The Politics of Twentieth Century America*. New York, New York University Press.

McIntosh, G (2005), 'The New Child Care Tax Rebate', Research Note, No 3, 2005-06, Canberra, Parliament of Australia, Parliamentary Library.

McKee, L, Mauthner, N and Galilee, J (2003), 'Children's Perspectives on Middle-Class Work-family Arrangements', in A Jensen and L McKee (eds) *Children and the Changing Family; Between Transformation and Negotiation*, London, RoutledgeFalmer.

McNeal, J (1992), *Children as Customers*, New York, Lexington Books.

Merlo, R and Rowland, D (2000), 'The Prevalence of Childlessness in Australia,' *People and Place* 8(2): 21-32.

Meyers, MK, Rosenbaum, D, Ruhm, C and Waldfogel, J (2004), 'Inequality in Early Childhood Education and Care: What Do We Know?' in KM Neckerman (ed) *Social Inequality*, New York, Russell Sage Foundation.

Misko, J (2001), *Training and Employment in the Queensland Child Care and Early Childhood Education Sector*, Adelaide, National Centre for Vocational Education Research.

Morehead, A, Steele, M, Alexander, M, Stephen, K, and Duffin, L (1997), *Changes at Work: the 1995 Australian Workplace Industrial Relations Survey*, Canberra, Addison-Wesley Longman.

Nasman, E (2003), 'Employed or Unemployed Parents: A Child Perspective', in A Jensen and L McKee (eds) *Children and the Changing Family; Between Transformation and Negotiation,* London, RoutledgeFalmer.

Nock, S and Kingston, P (1988), 'Time With Children: The Impact of Couples Work-Time Commitments,' *Social Forces* 67: 59-85.

OECD (2001), *Starting Strong: Early Childhood Education and Care*, Paris, OECD.

OECD (2002), *Babies and Bosses: Reconciling Work and Family Life in Australia, Denmark and the Netherlands (Volume 1)*, Paris, OECD.

OECD (2002a), *OECD Employment Outlook*, Geneva, OECD.

OECD (2003), *Babies and Bosses: Reconciling Work and Family Life in Austria, Ireland and Japan (Volume 2)*, Paris, OECD.

Plantenga, J (2002), 'Combining Work and Care in the Polder Model: An Assessment of the Dutch Part-time Strategy,' *Critical Social Policy* 22(1): 53-71.

Pleck, JH (1977), 'The Work/Family System,' *Social Problems* 24: 417-427.

Pocock, B (2003), *The Work/Life Collision, What Work is Doing to Australians and What to do About it*, Sydney, Federation Press.

Pocock, B, Prosser, R and Bridge, K (2004), *Only A Casual ... How Casual Work Affects Employees, Households and Communities in Australia*, Adelaide, Labour Studies, University of Adelaide,.

Pocock, B, van Wanrooy, B, Strazzari, S and Bridge, K (2001c), *Fifty Families: What Unreasonable Hours are Doing to Australians, Their Families and Their Communities*, Melbourne, ACTU.

Press, F (2006), *What about the Kids? Policy Directions for Improving the Experiences of Infants and Young Children in a Changing World*, Sydney, NSW Commission for Children and Young People, Queensland Commission for Children and Young People, and the National Investment for the Early Years (NIFTeY).

Press, F and Woodrow, C (2005), 'Commodification, Corporatisation and Children's Spaces,' *Australian Journal of Education* 49(3): 278-291.

Presser, HB (2000), 'Nonstandard Work Schedules and Marital Instability,' *Journal of Marriage and Family* 62(1): 93.

Preston, A and Burgess, J (2003), 'Women's Work in Australia: Trends, Issues and Prospects,' *Australian Journal of Labour Economics* 6(4): 497-518.

Pryor, L (2006), 'Child –care Horrors Kept From Parents', *Sydney Morning Herald*, 13 March.

Qu, L and Wise, S (2004), 'Multiple Child Care Arrangements in Australia,' *Family Matters* 69: 56-61.

Quant, A (2003), *Branded, The Buying and Selling of Teenagers*, London, Arrow.

Reed, R, Allen, M, Castleman, T and Coulthard, T (2003), " I Mean you Want to be There for Them': Young Australian Professionals Negotiating Careers in a Gendered World,' *Australian Journal of Labour Economics* 6(4): 519-536.

Robinson, L (2001), *Just a Phase in Life? School Students and Part-time Work*, Faculty of Education, Melbourne, The University of Melbourne.

Rush, E (2006a), *Childcare quality in Australia*, Canberra, The Australia Institute.

Rush, E (2006b), *ABC Learning Centres, A Case-study of Australia's Largest Child Care Corporation*, Canberra, The Australia Institute.

Sanson and Lewis (2001) 'Children and their family contexts", *Family Matters* 59 (Winter).

Saunders, P (2005), 'Reviewing Recent Trends in Wage Income Inequality in Australia', in J Isaac and RD Lansbury (eds), *Labour Market Deregulation, Rewriting the Rules*, Sydney, Federation Press.

Schor, J (1992), *The Overworked American: The Unexpected Decline of Leisure*, New York, Basic Books.

Schor, J (1998), *The Overspent American: Why We Want What We Don't Need*, New York, Basic Books.

Schor, J (2004), *Born to Buy, The Commercialized Child and the New Consumer Culture*, New York, Scribener.

Seiter, E (1993), *Sold Separately: Parents and Children in Consumer Culture*, New Brunswick, Rutgers University Press.

Shapiro Barrera, S (2004), *The New Wife*, New York, Nonetheless Press.

Shonkoff, J, and Phillips D (eds) (2000), *From Neurones to Neighbourhoods, The Science of Early Childhood Development*, Washington DC, National Academic Press.

Smith, A (1776 (5th edn)), *An Inquiry into the Nature and Causes of the Wealth of Nations*, London, Methuen and Co Ltd.

Smith, E, and Green, A (nd), *School Students Learning from their Paid and Unpaid Work, Preliminary Findings*, Adelaide, University of South Australia and Charles Sturt University.

Spurgeon, A (2003), *Working Time: Its Impact on Safety and Health*, Seoul, ILO and Korean Occupational Safety and Health Research Institute.

Standing, G (2002), *Beyond Paternalism: Basic Security as Equality*, New York, Verso.

Strazdins, L, Korda, R, Lira, L, Broom, D, and D'Souza, R (2004), 'Around the Clock: Parent Non-standard Work Times and Children's Well Being in a 24 hours Economy,' *Social Science and Medicine* 59: 1517-1527.

Sweet, R (2001), 'Understanding Youth Pathways: What Does the Research Tell Us?' Australian Council for Educational Research (ACER) Conference, Melbourne, 16 October.

Summers, A (2003), *The End of Equality*, Sydney, Random House.

Terry, J (1998), '"Momism" and the making of Treasonous Homosexuals', in M Ladd-Taylor and L Umansky (eds) *"Bad" Mothers: The Politics of Twentieth Century America*, New York, New York University Press.

The Mature Market (2005), 'When It Comes to Baby Boomer Women, Youth is the Marketing Watchword,' *The Mature Market*, 13 June 2005, <www.thematuremarket.com/SeniorStrategic/dossier.php? numtxt=4963&idrb=5> (accessed 5/7/05)

Thurer, S (1993), 'Changing Conceptions of the Good Mother in Psychoanalysis', *Psychoanalytic Review* 80: 519-540.

Waldfogel, J (2004), *Social Mobility, Life Chances, and the Early Years*, CASE Paper 88, London School of Economics, London, Center for Analysis of Social Exclusion.

Wannan, L (2005), 'The Changing Face of Child Care in Australia', Presentation for Canadian Tour, Corporate Child Care: The Australian Experience, Melbourne, October 2005.

Watson, I, Buchanan, J, Campbell, I and Briggs, C (2003), *Fragmented Futures, New Challenges in Working Life*, Sydney, Federation Press.

Weston, R and Qu, L (2001), 'Men's and Women's Reasons for Not Having Children,' *Family Matters* (Autumn 2001): 10-15.

Wilkinson, R (2005), *The Impact of Inequality*, New York, New Press.

Wilson, S, Meagher, G, Gibson, R, Denemark, D and Western, M (eds) (2005), *Australian Social Attitudes, The First Report*, Sydney, UNSW Press.

Young, L (2004), 'Portrait of the New Family,' *Marketing*, 15 March 2004, <www.marketingmag.ca/shared/print.jsp?content = 20040315_61585_ 61585> (accessed 5/7/05)

Zelizer, VA (1985), *Pricing the Priceless Child*, New York, Basic Books.

Zick, CD and Bryant, WK (1996), 'A New Look at Parent's Time Spent in Child Care: Primary and Secondary Time Use,' *Social Science Research* 25: 260-280.

Index

The Work/Life Collision

Barbara Pocock

Longer working hours, insecure jobs, child care, declining birth rates, parental leave, the 'mummy track', the success or failure of feminism – *The Work/Life Collision*, grounded in thorough quantitative and qualitative research, analyses how these factors affect each other, in particular the collision of work and care and its implications for how we live. ...

> *The stand out chapter in the book is Chapter 3 which considers the impact of the 'collisions and changes upon our community fabric'. ... The concluding chapter is simply magnificent. ... [The book] is an essential starting point for anyone researching the spheres of work, family and gender in Australia ... a landmark*
>
> Journal of Industrial Relations

> *The book is so graphic there are parts of it I could hardly bear to read but it is important to read it because it illustrates all the lifeless and painless socio-economic statistics we as policy planners see continuously rolling under our noses; it helps explain why those painless statistics actually represent a policy imperative.*
>
> Pru Goward

> *it should be a topic for discussion in staffrooms, at workplace union meetings, and on the agenda as an industrial and political issue.*
>
> Newsmonth

> *original and valuable ... It offers a new vision of the real experiences of Australian households ... This book is highly recommended and should be influential ...*
>
> Traffic

> *Pocock writes with persuasive clarity ...*
>
> Hobart Saturday Mercury

2003 · ISBN 186287 475 1 · paperback · 304 pp · $39.95